THE YOUNG
UNITED STATES

*Cast-iron insurance marker for
house wall*

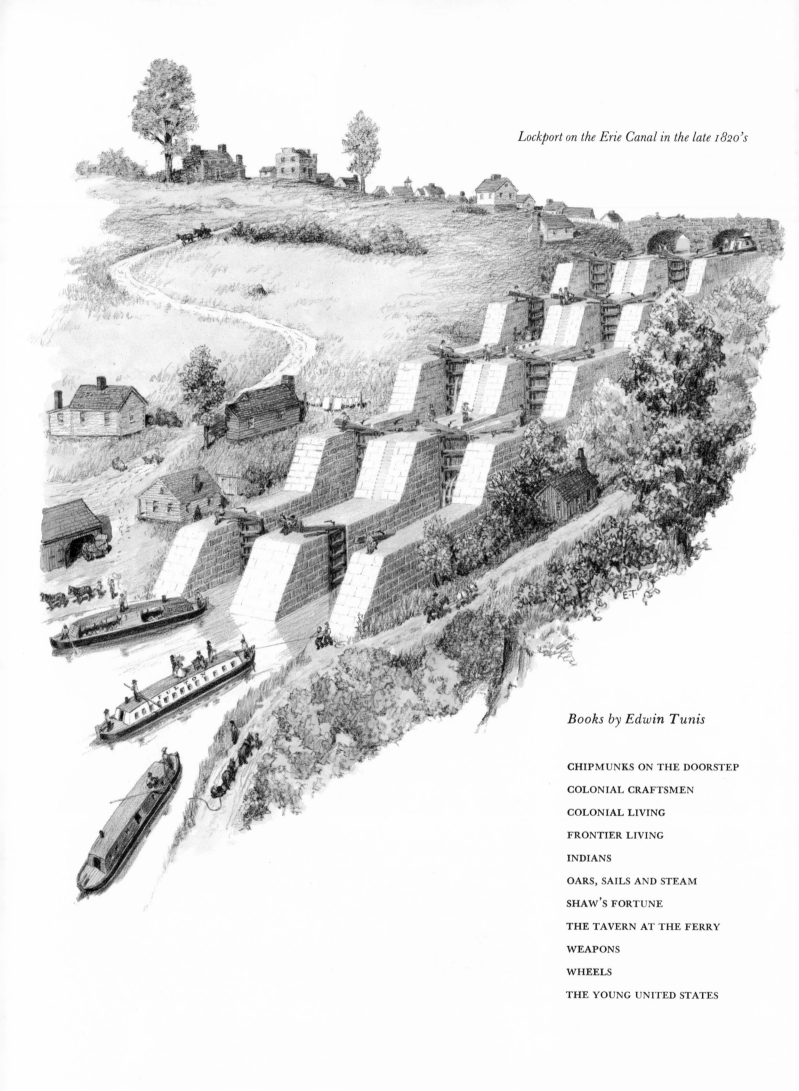

Lockport on the Erie Canal in the late 1820's

Books by Edwin Tunis

CHIPMUNKS ON THE DOORSTEP

COLONIAL CRAFTSMEN

COLONIAL LIVING

FRONTIER LIVING

INDIANS

OARS, SAILS AND STEAM

SHAW'S FORTUNE

THE TAVERN AT THE FERRY

WEAPONS

WHEELS

THE YOUNG UNITED STATES

THE YOUNG UNITED STATES

1783 to 1830

*A time of change and growth;
a time of learning democracy;
a time of new ways of living,
thinking, and doing*

Written and Illustrated by

EDWIN TUNIS

Thomas Y. Crowell Company
NEW YORK • ESTABLISHED 1834

Manufactured in the United States of America

L.C. Card 75-29613
ISBN 0-690-01065-6

Contents

Foreword		7
1.	The Yankees	11
2.	The League of States	13
3.	The Farmers	15
4.	The Villages	29
5.	The Inland Towns	37
6.	The Wilderness	43
7.	The Frontier	45
8.	City Life	49
9.	The Constitution	58
10.	Inventions and Factories	60
11.	Money and Some Foreign Affairs	72
12.	Turnpikes and Travel	75
13.	The Seafarers and the Countinghouse	81
14.	The Changing Americans	96
15.	New York City	113
16.	The Arts	123
17.	Schools and Colleges	129
18.	The Growth of the West	135
19.	"Old Hickory"	149
Index		151

Velocipede, or "Dandy Horse," about 1820

Foreword

THE FACTS of this account are as nearly accurate as
the author could make them but, in order to relate them
to life, a few imaginary people and places have been
introduced here and there. Specifically, the Whittle family
carries the weight of all the Piedmont farm families of
its time, as "Benson Town" represents all the small towns
above the fall line. Neither it nor "Standish" will be
found on a map. Standish is all tidewater villages.

On the other hand, the brothers Conner, and the people
connected with them, actually lived, and the events
described in Chapter 18 actually occurred. The facts there
are taken from *Sons of the Wilderness*, by Charles N.
Thompson, with the kind permission of the publishers,
the Indiana Historical Society.

My rendering of the Greek Revival cottage on page 99
is based upon a photograph in Talbot Hamlin's *Greek
Revival Architecture in America*, Dover Publications, Inc.,
New York, with the kind permission of the publisher.

I am grateful to the staffs of the Enoch Pratt Free Library,
in Baltimore, of the Cockeysville Branch of the Baltimore
County Library, and of the Maryland Historical Society.
Also, I thank the following individuals for aid given
where it was needed: Mrs. Helen K. Chittick, Lieutenant
Colonel Paul H. Downing, Mrs. George E. Hardy, Jr.,
Mrs. Alyce Meyers, Mr. Hugh Morrison, Mr. Harry J.
Patton, the Reverend Edwin A. Schell, and my wife,
Elizabeth.

E. T.

THE YOUNG UNITED STATES

1.

The Yankees

THE REVOLUTION was the first joint project of the American colonies. That the majority of the colonists agreed to fight England and did fight her is remarkable considering the physical barriers and the strong prejudices that divided them. Nature provided the distances, the rivers, the dense forests, and the Indians. Georgia and Massachusetts might as well have had an ocean between them because the land route was almost impassable. Isolation bred an intense local pride which led every colony to hate all the others; even those with common boundaries were forever quarreling—about the boundaries. And within each colony, section wrangled with section, town with town. Men differed strongly about religion. The Puritans of New England and the Anglicans to the south despised one another, and both despised the Roman Catholics, the Quakers, and the Jews. The colonies made as unlikely a team as would thirteen wild horses.

Still another division arose as discontent with English policies hardened. A majority favored independence as the only solution, but a large minority, the Loyalists, the "Tories," most of whom were just as opposed to taxation without representation as were the Patriots, could see active rebellion only as treason. They stuck to that opinion and had a very rough time.

Yet all of these people, so strongly sectional in their loyalties that they even resisted the opening of roads that would join them, had something in common that only a few of them realized: they were unconsciously thinking as Americans. The majority had been born here, and so had the fathers and grandfathers of many. They had put down new roots. They no longer belonged to the national tribes from which they were descended— English, Scotch-Irish, German, Dutch, French Huguenot, Swedish, and African (for, though most of them were slaves, there were also many free Negroes; Crispus Attucks, who was killed in the Boston "massacre," was a free Negro).

All of the colonies except two had been founded by Englishmen, and the exceptions, New York and Delaware, had been English for over a century. The British thought of their colonies not as extensions of England but as profitable possessions. They undertook to rule America, through governors and "proprietors," for the benefit of the Royal Exchequer. The Americans still spoke of England as "home," and maintained a fair imitation of England's rigid class system. Few of the English lords who owned huge grants of land in America ever visited them, and it seems that only one, Lord Fairfax in Virginia, ever lived in America for any length of time.

The American caste system, then, began, at its top, with what in England was the "upper-middle class," the landed gentry. In the colonies, some of the owners of large estates were descendants of younger sons of that class, but most of them merely had grandfathers who had acquired land. Groups of these joined forces with successful merchants and lawyers to run their colonies with benefit to themselves. Though many such men remained loyal, and many left the country when revolution threatened, it was from this class that most of the Revolutionary leaders came, the men who built the nation. The gates to the American upper class were locked, but not sealed as they were in England. Here the key was money, and sometimes the key to money was education; it was for Benjamin Franklin. With Thomas Jefferson it worked the other way; he got an education because his father made money.

Small farmers who owned their land belonged to the lower section of the middle class. Land gave them the right to vote, but they were men of little education and most of them were easily outtalked by the bigwigs. Classed with these yeoman farmers were "the better sort of mechanics," that is, prosperous skilled craftsmen such as silversmiths, cabinetmakers, printers, shipbuilders. In some colonies they, too, could vote if they owned a house and had some money, but their vote had no more effect on laws and taxes than did that of the farmers. The still lower class—tenant farmers, field hands, fishermen, laborers—hadn't even the pretense of a voice in the affairs of their colony. But by diligence they could accumulate a little money and thus move up the ladder a rung or two. Even in colonial times this could

happen in America, when it could happen nowhere else in the civilized world.

It was their unanimous resentment of the Stamp Act that first showed the colonists the value of union. Among the articles it taxed were all legal papers and all newspapers. This hit hard at lawyers and publishers—men who knew how to speak out and did so. The newspapers printed not only their own editorials but also the speeches of the lawyers. Most important, the newspapers traveled: Philadelphia read what Boston hotheads said; Charleston read Daniel Dulany's pamphlet from Maryland; New York read Patrick Henry's speech at Williamsburg, "If this be treason, make the most of it."

From then on, everybody heard about the riots in Boston and discussed them vehemently. And when, in 1772, its Town Meeting formed a Committee of Correspondence, similar committees crystallized all along the seacoast to correspond with it and with one another. Shortly the muskets went off at Lexington and the Second Continental Congress gathered, grim-faced, in Philadelphia.

In the vast excitement of rebellion few men noticed that a revolution was also occurring within America. Jefferson wrote in the Declaration of Independence that "all men are created equal." To most of the brave signers the phrase was mere oratory. John Adams called it "a glittering generality"; but to the lowly artisans in the towns, to the simple farmers of the countryside, to the taciturn frontiersmen in the western woods, it meant just what it said.

Yorktown to Boston—with a bride

2.
The League of States

THE ARTICLES OF CONFEDERATION

THE FIRST Continental Congress met in September 1774, resolved that Americans, though loyal to King George, would henceforth legislate for themselves, and then went home in October. The Second Congress convened on the tenth of the following May, with the shooting at Lexington and Concord still fresh in its ears. In August the King declared the colonies in rebellion. In January 1776, Tom Paine asserted in *Common Sense,* which everybody read or heard discussed, that Americans needed no king. In July the Congress declared the colonies independent states and prepared to fight.

Even before they phrased the Declaration, the members of Congress considered the form of a government. They argued about it for a year and a half, while at the same time running the war. The members had most of the same prejudices that had divided the colonies and that still divided the new states. With their recent troubles in mind, the majority feared any strong government, even if it were their own. This majority were farmers, and farmers wanted low taxes or, if it could be managed, none. The document they

finally agreed upon, in November 1777, was little more than a treaty between sovereign states, creating an organization not too unlike that of today's United Nations.

It had no executive. Congress, elected not by the people directly but by the state legislatures, was the whole central government. When it adjourned, it left behind a committee of thirteen, one member for each state. They could agree on little and could seldom act when they did agree. The Articles of Confederation gave Congress control of foreign affairs, of national defense, of Indian affairs, of the postal system, and of coinage. It could not regulate commerce, that is, impose any duties; the Americans thought they had had all they wanted of those. Congress could request money from the states (which reserved the right to refuse it), and it could borrow money from the public, but it had no power to impose direct taxes of any kind. This, too, was a sore spot on the Yankee hide.

Though Congress, in effect, governed under the Articles from the start, it took five years to get them ratified by the states. The smaller states, with no claims to the western wilderness, feared that the larger ones, which had such claims, would be able to support themselves by selling western land and so do away with state taxes entirely. Valuable taxpayers would then desert the small states. The wrangle was settled in 1781 when the big states agreed to turn their western lands over to Congress, with some reservations. Congress then had a hope of direct income; it was in the real estate business.

The launching of the United States was the greatest experiment in human affairs ever known. It wasn't the culmination of a carefully considered plan; it was improvised to meet circumstances as they happened. What is remarkable is not that the first try at a government had weaknesses but that it was good enough to work at all. Though the state legislatures went about their own affairs with small regard for the Congress, and often with no regard for the Articles they had ratified, yet from the first the people thought of the United States as one nation and took an increasing pride in being Americans.

Long before the treaty of peace was signed in 1783, all the states had adopted constitutions of their own. These were imperfect, but most of them paid more attention to the rights of men than had ever been done before, and most of them worked fairly well. Some states granted a vote to every white male, others required ownership of land, usually at least fifty acres. The ancient absurdity of jailing debtors who couldn't pay was kept, but limits were set to the term of imprisonment. The constitutions all provided what the national government lacked—a chief executive in the form of a governor, though his powers were strictly limited. He usually had no power of veto. The states set up their own currencies—some used "hard money," that is, gold and silver; some used paper money, which seldom was worth as much as the value printed on it.

Manufactures, begun during the war out of necessity, were often able to survive after it, in spite of a depression. They were aided by states other than their own, which, out of a new pride in American enterprise, allowed free trade across their borders for a while. The shipowning merchants of the large seaports were in trouble. Americans, used to British cutlery, pewter, pottery, and so on, still wanted those things. England was happy to oblige, but would not ship the goods in Yankee vessels. American merchants cried for duties on foreign imports but Congress was powerless to impose them.

Right at the start of the Revolutionary War, bands of men had set out across country to aid besieged Boston. They, and the many who marched later, found that people outside their home colony had neither horns nor tails. Quite a few soldiers married girls in "foreign" states and either stayed with them or took them home. This mixing went on after the war and broke down a lot of local prejudices. It didn't wipe them out entirely. (You may have noticed the weird driving of people from your neighbor state.)

Those Tories who left the country lived out discontented lives in England, Canada, or the West Indies; discontented because, regardless of their opinions, America was home. Their American property was confiscated. The United States lost heavily by their leaving. Most of them were educated people, and much grace and gentility left with them. Many Loyalists could not afford to leave. Of these, many lost their land, and some of the commissioners who seized it grew rich. Other Tories kept their property but had to pay triple taxes on it. Still others, who didn't speak their convictions too loudly—the "skittish," as John Adams called them—survived with nothing worse than harsh words and an occasional coat of tar and feathers. A gesture was made toward denying Tories the right of citizenship but it was shortly abandoned, and in a surprisingly short time after the war everybody forgot the whole thing.

The Whittle place

3.
The Farmers

THE FIRST official census, in 1790, counted a few less than four million Americans. Of these, more than three million lived on farms. These American farmers had accomplished and were accomplishing a population explosion, the *rate* of which far exceeded the one that worries the twentieth century. Rural people felt secure; they had enough food, and children meant help on the farm. Ten or twelve made hardly more than an average family. Rural New England was over-populated by 1783 and people there began to leave their stony farms for the West and for upper New York, which was newly open because the Iroquois Indians backed the wrong side in the war. Other New Englanders filtered into Maine, which was still part of Massachusetts and was largely wilderness.

Labor was scarce in this country as it had been from the first. The southern planters clung to their slaves because of this, even though many of them realized that slave labor cost more in the long run that hired labor. Some slaves worked on farms in the middle states; in New England, very few did. North of Baltimore a farm hand could

make the equivalent of a dollar a day and his board. This was from thirty to fifty cents more than he could earn in England. Land was cheap here. A German could buy a hundred acres in Pennsylvania for what a year's rent of less land had cost him at home. Many a Yankee hired man saved enough to buy his own farm while he was still young enough to work it.

Immigration resumed after the Revolution and continued at an increasing rate for almost a century and a half. Steerage accommodations seldom reached the point of common decency until after World War I; in the days of sail they were appalling. A sailing vessel took twelve weeks to cross. Its passengers had no privacy; in fact, they had scarcely room to move. Sanitary conditions were too dreadful to describe, and hundreds died at sea from typhus and smallpox. The fare was cheap. Ships carried profitable cargoes eastward, and passengers, carried westward at twenty dollars a head, yielded more money than would a load of stone ballast. Even so, many immigrants spent their last money for the passage and landed utterly destitute in the land of promise; but they could always get a job. Germans often indentured themselves—that is, rented out themselves and their children—for a term of four years. Though one French traveler described such a family as lazy and worthless, the Germans in general were the best farmers who came here and were far better than most native-born Americans.

But the settled Yankee farmers had prospered. During the Revolution they made a good thing of supplying the army with food at exorbitant prices. Though most of them were at least "sunshine patriots," many were not too particular as to which army they supplied. But then, the Rebels paid in paper money which dwindled in value by the week, while the British paid in hard cash, worth its weight as metal. The farmers hoarded the hard money, and used their bundles of Continental paper to pay off their debts at face value. This ruined many honest moneylenders. As the United States began, most farmers owned their land; most were financially independent at a simple level; and they were more nearly equal socially and financially than the people of any country in Europe. If the wealthy "aristocrats" recoiled in dismay from the idea of a literal equality of all citizens, the farmers could face it without

batting an eye; and the farmers of Confederation times had the votes.

These men made a living for their families, but even by the low standards of their times, most of them were bad farmers. They mined the land, doing little to maintain its fertility and doing nothing to keep its indispensable topsoil from washing into the streams. Hundreds exhausted their farms completely and moved west.

Early colonial farms lay along, or quite near, streams that at least in flood time were navigable, and in valleys where the soil was best, and where the surrounding hills broke the force of cold winds. In the East, such prime sites were soon taken, and by these Confederation times, fields had crept up the slopes, and farms had been cleared in more remote valleys where produce had to be hauled to the rivers in wagons. An industrious farm family could be nearly self-sufficient, but it could make a profit only by selling the excess of what it raised. Barter with the storekeeper in the local hamlet—two dozen eggs for half a pound of tea—wasn't enough. The buyers who would pay actual money for cured meat and grain lived downstream, on or near salt water.

Every river—the Charles, the Merrimac, the

Gundalow at a river landing

Connecticut, the Hudson, the Delaware, the Susquehanna, and many smaller streams—floated long narrow boats called gundalows (gondolas). Sturdy boatmen loaded these at tidewater towns with iron, salt, saltpeter (for curing meat), gunpowder, lead (for bullets), loaf sugar, tea, coffee, spices, crockery, pewterware, window glass. They poled and sailed the gundalows against the current, stopping at village landings to trade these wares for farm produce. Then they drifted back to the starting point and sold out. Sometimes a group of farmers cut logs and spiked them together as a long raft. They loaded their products on it and steered it down the river on the crest of a spring flood. At their destination they sold not only the cargo but the raft as well, for firewood. Much has been written about later traffic like this on the Ohio and the Mississippi. It was heavier on those rivers, but it only continued a long-established system.

THE WHITTLE PLACE

The farm of Silas Whittle lies in a fertile valley just east of the low mountains—actually big hills —that are the advance guard of the Appalachians. Measured by its boundaries, it is over two hundred acres, but only about sixty of them are cleared for farming. The rest stands forested with huge trees, as Silas's father found it in 1741. As a young man, Silas helped his father clear some of the fields, and Kurt, Silas's oldest son, has helped to clear the newest ones. Some big stumps still stand in these.

Kurt and his young wife, Susan, now live in the crude log cabin that his grandfather, Wethered Whittle, built and that Silas was born in. It is made of bark-covered logs. In this present year of 1785, new settlers are building cabins just like it in the Appalachian valleys, and westward into Kentucky. Silas and his wife, Bertha, with their seven younger children, and Bertha's mother, Wilhelmina Hansel, live in a larger house. Silas built it eighteen years ago, with the help of two neighbors. They used logs for its walls too, but they squared them, and notched them carefully at their ends so that they would lie close together, leaving only narrow cracks to be chinked.

THE FARM BUILDINGS

The Whittles' big barn is built of logs too. Logs make a warm building, and cost nothing but labor. Southern barns, for curing tobacco, and northern barns, for storing hay and straw, are built on ground as nearly level as possible. With large doors in opposite walls, a wagon can drive straight through one. The German settlers in central Pennsylvania and northern Maryland have developed a "bank" barn, built on a hillside. It serves not only for storage but as a stable also. A hay wagon has to be backed into the storage level from the uphill side. In the lower level there are stalls for horses and cows, enclosed by the high stone foundation, the south wall of which is entirely above ground. With the stored hay overhead acting as insulation, and the hill, in which the north wall is completely buried, acting as a

Post-and-rail construction, and the hole ax, used like a chisel by pounding its blunt end, to clear out the mortises

his neighbors build fences of rails which they split from logs twelve or fourteen feet long. Wethered Whittle built zigzag worm fences, and Silas has built some too. They can be put up quickly, but they use a lot of rails, and they waste a strip of land at least eight feet wide. Silas has put post-and-rail fences around his newest fields, and around the barnyard. These fences use less material, and go where they are going in a straight narrow line. Dan, the Whittles' second son, is nineteen and brawny. He splits rails, but Silas and Kurt shape the posts and cut oblong mortises in them with a special narrow-bladed ax. When the posts are planted, the flat-tapered ends of the rails lap over each other inside the mortises.

Fences are supposed to keep animals in pastures or out of crop fields. Usually they succeed, but horses, and cows too, can sometimes jump over fences if they have a strong motive, and small animals can get under, or through, rail fences. When the lure is likely to be great, Silas Whittle's animals, down to and including geese and turkeys, find themselves encumbered with wooden yokes designed to catch in fence rails.

The Whittles have five cows to provide milk,

windbreak, the body heat of a dozen or so animals can keep such a stable above freezing when the outside temperature flirts with zero. Farmers of English origin, like Silas Whittle, have copied the bank barns. New England and New York barns have always been framed with heavy timbers and sheathed with planks, as twentieth-century barns are. This isn't because of a shortage of logs; it is because their earliest settlers missed seeing the Swedish log buildings that the German settlers saw when they arrived in Pennsylvania.

All of Silas's farm buildings are log structures on stone foundations. Like the barn, they are not so carefully constructed as the house. The builders skinned the bark off with a spud and used a broadax to flatten two opposed sides of each log. Then they stacked them as a rectangular crib, with the round sides showing outside and inside. Where the logs lapped over one another at the corners, the builders notched them to lock them in place. They chinked the gaps between the logs with small stones and lime mortar.

FENCES AND LIVESTOCK

Though New England farmers build some wooden fences, they enclose most of their fields with dry walls, built of the glacial stones they endlessly clear from their land. The glacier stopped a hundred miles north of the Whittle farm, so Silas and

Yokes for livestock

butter, and cheese; two horses for errands and to take the family to church; and two span of oxen for plowing and heavy hauling. Oxen are slow but they are steady workers, and when well handled they are less likely than horses to get excited and lunge if the going gets hard. Oxen have the disadvantage of being unable to sweat, as horses can, hence they become overheated frequently in hot weather, and have to be "cooled out." On the plus side, a plowman behind a yoke of oxen has both hands free; he doesn't have to worry about reins. He controls his animals entirely by voice commands: "Haw" for left, "Gee" for right, "Whoa" for stop, "Come up" for get in there and work.

GRAIN

The bones of Yankees are made of Indian corn. In summer the people eat it green, but most of it they allow to ripen, and the hard grains become cornmeal and hominy. Even in South Carolina, where most of the land grows rice and indigo, the plantations raise enough corn to feed the livestock and the slaves; and the planters themselves eat it. The Whittle men cut corn with long knives and "shock up" the stalks to dry for some weeks before they are hauled to the barn, where the ears will be husked in cold weather. Husking is ripping the layered sheaths off the ears. As with many other things, the neighbors help, and make a party of it. A girl at a husking bee gets kissed every time her swain finds a red-kerneled ear. Bertha Whittle, helped by her mother and the older girls of the family, sets out an enormous supper when the work is done. Up until Christmas, one husking bee follows another, all around the neighborhood.

After the husking, the three "middle" children, Henry, fourteen, and the twins, Jenny and Sarah, who are twelve, have the chore of "shelling" part of the corn. They scrape the kernels off the cobs against the edge of a wooden pail, into which the kernels fall. A few cobs are saved to plug the necks of jugs; the rest go into the fire. Part of the shelled corn is stored in barrels, for feeding poultry; the rest is bagged in homemade "tow linen" sacks. Dan and Henry will load the sacks on the light wagon and take them six miles to Conrad Hoff-

19

man's mill. As he always does, Silas will caution them to watch the hoppers and make sure the meal they bring home is ground from their *own* corn. He will also warn Dan to watch Conrad measure his "toll," the one eighth of the meal the miller gets to pay for his grinding. In Silas's opinion, an honest miller has yet to be born.

Conrad's is a "custom mill"; all the grain it grinds belongs to his customers. In addition to corn, it grinds wheat, rye, and buckwheat into rather coarse gritty flour, all of it consumed in the neighborhood. "Merchant mills" buy grain, and sell flour to feed townsmen and to be shipped overseas. Most such mills are located as near to seaports as available waterpower will allow. They are large establishments, with three or four sets of grinding stones. Conrad's mill has but one pair of stones; the little stream that turns them couldn't handle more.

The mechanical reaper and the threshing machine powered by a horse are still fifty years in the future. When the Whittles' small grains ripen, their neighbors help to harvest them by hand. A line of men moves down the field. Each is armed with a cradle, and each cuts a strip the width of his swing. A cradle is basically a scythe, but a light wooden rack, standing above its blade, catches the straw as it falls, and allows the reaper to drop his sweep in a windrow behind him. The women and girls gather the cut stalks and bind them into sheaves with twists of straw.

Threshing is cold-weather work for the men on the place. They spread the sheaves of wheat or rye on the barn floor and knock the grain off the straw by beating it with wooden flails. Oats, barley, and buckwheat can be trodden out under the feet of horses or oxen. Horses are better for this job because they have bigger feet.

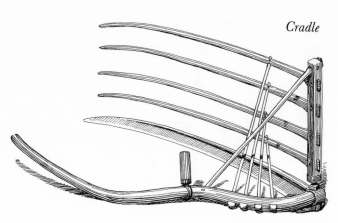

Cradle

Silas's wooden plow

IMPLEMENTS AND VEHICLES

Silas makes most of his simple farm implements himself, but he barters for some of them with neighbors who are especially good at certain work. In any case, the blacksmith in the village is likely to do part of the job. It takes a skilled man to make a cradle, strong, yet light and well balanced, with a perfectly curved snath, so that a reaper can swing it all day without overstraining. The blacksmith shapes and tempers the blade, and makes the latch that secures it to the snath. It takes skill to carve out a wooden grain shovel or a three-tined hay fork. Hay, cut with scythes, has to be raked into windrows by hand. Silas's rakes for this are six feet wide and are made entirely of wood. He has lately seen a horse-drawn "flop rake," also wood, and plans to make one.

The Whittle farm still uses plows with wooden shares. A few neighbors have cast-iron shares on their plows, but Silas has heard that the iron poisons the ground, so he won't have one on the place. He uses all-wood harrows too. They have oak frames set with tough hickory teeth driven through bored holes. The only implement on the place that can be called mechanical is a seeder, built like a wheelbarrow. A wooden spike fixed behind its wheel opens a small furrow into which seeds drop from a hopper. The mechanical part is a revolving regulator to control the rate at which the seed falls. A belt on the wheel hub drives it.

In early colonial days, a two-wheeled cart was more practical as a farm vehicle than a wagon because it could be readily maneuvered between trees and over rough land. But even the largest cart carried too small a load for long-distance hauling, or even for most general farm use. About 1750, the Pennsylvania Germans developed their

Wooden hay fork

Conestoga wagon to carry produce down to tidewater. It is high-wheeled and strong, and its body, with upturned ends and high flared sides, throws the weight of a load toward the center. Later this vehicle spread so far (all the way to Santa Fe), and was so widely used for hauling freight, that its fame has obscured that of all other country wagons. The Whittles still use the old wagon that brought Wethered and his family from New Jersey. It is much like an English farm wagon, with a box body and strongly coned wheels. Silas has added a "gallus" (gallows) to pile hay against.

When roads of a sort had been worn between farm and village, and between village and town, a lighter wagon became useful. Perhaps because its seat was cantilevered on two hickory "springs," when other wagons had no springs at all, it was known as a "pleasure wagon." This is the kind that Dan and Henry take to the mill. Henry drives three of his sisters to school in it; and on Sunday most of the family rides to church in it. Some farmers drive a one-horse chaise on local errands; usually they call it a "shay," or a "cheer." It has two wheels and a fixed top, and its body hangs on straps from a bar that joins the rear ends of two long hickory poles that serve as springs. The poles lie on either side of the body, and their front ends are bolted to the shafts. Rural men build all of these vehicles.

FRUIT AND VEGETABLES

Apples, pears, peaches, and plums grow in the Whittle orchard. Silas presses a lot of cider, and

Wethered's wagon

in due time distills some of it into applejack, which is apple brandy. He also makes peach brandy, and plum brandy, and rye whisky. Though no drunkards, Silas and Kurt drink liquor as a matter of course, and their womenfolk often have a little with water at meals. At every gathering of neighbors, a gallon jug stands handy to all. Whisky is money, too. The village storekeeper will take it as payment for anything he sells. Distilling grain into whisky makes the crop easy to transport; it reduces its bulk without reducing its value. So it is the principal money crop of the new farms in the western Pennsylvania mountains. (Later, when Alexander Hamilton undertakes to tax their product, the mountaineers will start the "Whisky Rebellion." President Washington will send out the militia in the fall of 1794; the trouble will evaporate, but the states will realize that the new government is running the country.)

Not all of the Whittle fruit goes into jugs. Bertha and her mother, and Nancy, Bertha's oldest daughter, and Susan, Kurt's wife, cut up a lot of it and spread it to dry in the sun. When rain threatens, all hands rush it under cover. Bertha also cooks fruit with sugar to make preserves and jelly, but of sterilization and vacuum packing, which we call canning, she knows nothing.

Some vegetables can be stored for use in winter, and any excess of them can be shipped to towns for sale. These the men raise in the fields. The root vegetables—turnips, beets, carrots, and potatoes—can be kept in pits, below frost level. So can cabbage, which isn't a root vegetable. They will all taste pretty earthy by midwinter. Pumpkins, winter squash, and onions keep fairly well indoors, where they are warm and dry.

Bertha raises the "garden sass." One of the men works up a patch of ground near the house, and she and the children plant it and hoe the weeds out of it. Some weeds are native, but the seeds of many came here from Europe, mixed in with hay and grain. Most of Bertha's vegetables are the kind that must be eaten fresh—peas, beans, cucumbers, summer squash, muskmelons (cantaloupes)—but she grows a row or two of salsify (oyster plant) and parsnips which will keep in the storage pits. Bertha grows no tomatoes. She knows about them, but her grandmother thought they were poisonous, and Bertha is taking no chances.

Most of the stored fruits and vegetables will be gone by late winter, and for six weeks the family will crave them. The need of their bodies in this period has mothered such strange inventions as vinegar pie. Before the frost entirely leaves the ground, Bertha and her brood will be out in the mud, hunting "greens." Sprouting weeds, like dandelions, wild mustard, lambs quarter, and pokeweed, will go into the pot to "thin the blood" of the family.

THE FARMHOUSE

Quite a few log houses, like the Whittles', still stand in our time, but most of them hide under a layer of clapboards, or of "colorful" asphalt shingles. Many other farmhouses also survive from this time—two-story houses of stone, of brick, or of stoutly framed clapboard. Nearly all of them are as plain as the log houses. Nearly all have simple pitched roofs. In New England, the rear face of a roof is often carried down to the

level of the first-floor ceiling to make what is called a "saltbox house." In the South, such a roof is a "catslide."

The inside arrangement of the Whittle house is much like that of small farmhouses everywhere—two rooms downstairs (three, if you count the "summer kitchen," in a shed at one end) and two upstairs. The larger downstairs room is the regular kitchen. It also serves the family as dining room and living room. The other downstairs room, which might have been the parlor and guest room in a smaller family, is used by Wilhelmina Hansel as a bedroom. It also shelters three spinning wheels and Bertha's loom, hence it is usually called the loom room.

A single large chimney, built of fieldstone, rises near the middle of the house. Its base is so wide that it leaves space only for a narrow passage at one side, and at the other side an equally narrow and very steep stair, with a door on its second step. The stair winds around the chimney and ends in the room over Wilhelmina's, occupied by the three girls and six-year-old Peter. Dora, who is two, sleeps in her parents' room, over the kitchen. In the winter Daniel and Henry climb a ladder to the attic where they sleep close to the warm chimney. In hot weather they sleep on the kitchen floor or on the little porch outside the kitchen.

The house has no bathroom, of course, though one of the Whittles' neighbors does have a fieldstone bathtub in a dark cubbyhole on his porch.

It has a drain hole, but it has to be filled with a pail. The Whittles make do with a pewter basin at the sink, and a washtub in the summer kitchen. Their kitchen sink is a luxury. It was chipped out of a solid block of stone. Water has to be brought to it from the well, but it can drain through a short lead pipe onto the ground outside.

The kitchen ceiling is coated with whitewash, applied directly to the supporting rafters and the underside of the floorboards of the room overhead. The walls are plastered, not too expertly, and coated with "bluewash." This is simply whitewash with a little indigo added. In the rest of the house, plain whitewash coats the inner face of the hewn logs. All of the doors and the window frames are painted a brownish red, achieved by mixing powdered clay with sour milk. The floors are made of bare boards, hardly two of them the same width, but some as wide as two feet. A little up-and-down sawmill, run by the same stream that grinds the corn, sawed them. The mill saws so slowly that the sawyer uses his spare time to make wooden bowls, scoops, and spoons of the kind called treenware. The floors are cold in winter, so Wilhelmina has woven small rag rugs for them.

The Whittles' windows are small because handmade glass is expensive, and because large windows let in too much cold air. The small ones let in plenty. There are no weatherstrips, though Bertha's homespun curtains help a little. The upper window sashes are all fixed in place. The

22

lower ones can be raised, but must be propped open with sticks since they have no counter-weights to hold them up. The Whittles have never seen a window screen; in summer, flies come and go as they will.

The family owns barely enough furniture for its needs. Furniture is seldom thought of as orna-mental, and the idea of deliberately matching any two pieces of it has never struck them. Silas sits in his grandfather's straight-backed armchair that traveled with Wethered from New Jersey. Wil-helmina is allotted the "Philadelphia chair," a hoop-back Windsor, painted green, the one com-fortable chair in the house. It came by wagon to Benson Town, seventeen miles from the farm, and Silas bought it for a cured ham and a gallon of whisky. Wilhelmina gets the best chair because she is considered, and considers herself, an old woman. She is toothless and somewhat stiff in the joints, but she is in fact not yet sixty. The rest of the family sits on homemade stools and painted ladder-back chairs. The chairs have rush bottoms and were all made in the neighborhood.

Sam Harnett, the joiner in the village, made the oiled black walnut table from which the Whit-tles eat their meals. He copied it from one he saw in Squire Buchanan's big house. Its two gatelegs swing out to support two drop leaves. With the leaves down, it can hug the wall and take up little space. Sam shaped its legs with a drawknife, and gave them pad feet, like the squire's table, but he didn't manage to get them all exactly alike.

Sam also produced the plain pine table on which the women prepare food. Its strong lower parts are painted red like the woodwork, but its top has been scrubbed almost white. He also built the corner cupboard and the dresser where Ber-tha stores her bowls and dishes. Some of the bowls are wood, some pewter, but the cups and plates are shiny brick-red pottery, shaped by Dietrich Weiser from clay he dug out of a bank not half a mile from the Whittles' land. The fam-ily's spoons are pewter; their knives and forks are iron with bone handles.

There is not a closet or even a wardrobe in the house. Some people do have wardrobes for their Sunday clothes, but the Whittles hang all their outer garments on pegs driven into the walls. Bedsteads are painted pine frames with ropes stretched across them to serve as springs. The mat-tresses are feather beds, big sacks stuffed with goose feathers plucked on the farm. Pillows are

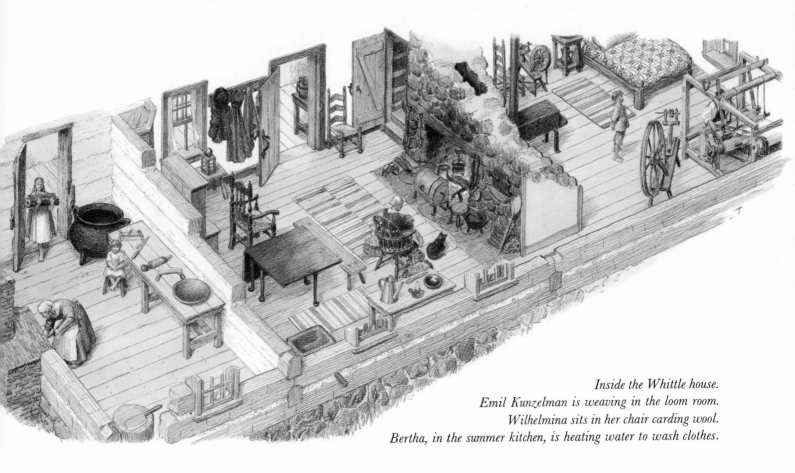

Inside the Whittle house.
Emil Kunzelman is weaving in the loom room.
Wilhelmina sits in her chair carding wool.
Bertha, in the summer kitchen, is heating water to wash clothes.

made the same way. The women weave linen sheets, and some woolen blankets too, but on cold nights everybody sleeps under a second feather bed. The women also make daytime covers for the beds from scraps of cloth pieced together to form patterns. Neighbors come to a quilting bee in the winter, and help with stitching the patchwork top to a plain linen backing. The purpose of the quilting is to hold the carded wool filling in place, but the lines of quilting stitches make patterns that are quite independent of the patterns of the patchwork.

Well before the Revolution, stoves began to be used for heating. They spread rapidly because they warmed more evenly than a fireplace could. Small country ironworks cast stove plates, so a farmer could often buy a stove right "at the Bank" of the foundry and haul it himself. The earliest were the "five-plate" variety, simply a long box on legs, open at one end. In houses with central chimneys, the box stood in the "stove room," corresponding to Wilhelmina's room in the Whittle house. The open end of the box passed through a hole made in the back wall of the kitchen fireplace. Wood went into the stove from the kitchen side and the smoke of the stove fire found its way out through the same open end, and up the kitchen chimney.

The Franklin, or Pennsylvania, stove, invented by Dr. Benjamin Franklin, was an improvement on the five-plate stove. It looked like an iron fireplace and burned like one, but it had its own flue and was fueled from the room it warmed. Its great advantage was that it circulated heat by means of a chamber, behind its fire, in which air was heated and vented into the room.

Silas Whittle bought a six-plate stove, though he had to go all the way to the foundry at Benson Town to get it. It is the same shape as the five-plate kind, but it has an iron door (the sixth plate) on its open end, and a smoke pipe rises from its top, at the back. When it needs fuel Wilhelmina can open its door and put wood in without going around to the kitchen. It burns better than a five-plate stove, because it has a draft. Its smoke pipe rises through a hole in the ceiling and enters the chimney, as high as possible, in the girls' room above. It can't be said to warm the upper room, but it takes a little of the edge off the chill.

FOOD

Stoves are not for cooking. Even when workable cookstoves appear in 1815, many a country housewife will try one—and go back to her big fireplace. Bertha has never heard of cooking in any way except on an open fire. She stirs her stew with a long spoon as it bubbles in an iron pot hanging from the crane. Her griddle for making buckwheat cakes hangs from the crane too, and she fries the sausage, to go with the cakes, in a long-handled iron skillet that stands high on three legs. The gridiron she broils meat on has four legs, and it, too, has a long handle. When she roasts meat, she turns it on a spit inside a "roasting kitchen." This is a sheet-iron box with one open side facing the fire. When Bertha bakes, which is often, she builds a hot fire in her oven. It is like a small fireplace, built breast-high in the wall, next to the big one, with a flue leading into the main chimney. She rakes the fire out when the oven's walls are hot, and dusts the ashes from its floor before she slides in her round loaves, with a flat wooden peel that looks like a long shovel. She shuts the oven door and leaves the bread to bake for hours.

At late-autumn hog-killing time, the summer kitchen is a busy place from long before dawn, when the men start the fire under the big outdoor scalding kettle, until far into the night, when the last ham has gone into the brine barrel for corning

Silas and Henry

and the last link of sausage has been stuffed with hand-chopped meat, and the place still has to be cleaned up. Hog killing makes an awful mess. Some farmers have special outbuildings, where they render lard and make scrapple and souse.

It is impossible to keep fresh meat except in very cold weather. When Silas kills, he always gives some of the meat to his neighbors, and they do the same in turn. In fact they arrange in advance that two farms will not kill in the same week. Beef and pork, thoroughly cured by salting and smoking, will keep for years and be good to eat, but both can become tiresome as a steady diet. A ham so cured is dark, hard, and smoky, quite different from the slightly salty pink pork that is called ham in our time.

Outside the cities, Americans of Silas Whittle's time are the best-fed people in the world. Wild game is one reason for it—this in spite of massive game drives organized by farmers in Wethered's time; all farmers hate wild animals because those that don't destroy crops kill pigs and sheep. The drives eliminated the woodland buffalo and most of the bears of the mountains, and greatly reduced the deer and the wolves, but small game and birds remain plentiful. Passenger pigeons and waterfowl are incredibly plentiful: the big pigeons actually darken the sky in migration, and break large tree limbs on which they crowd to roost at night. They fear men so little, or are so stupid, that a stick in the hand will get a dinner. In the fall, ducks, geese, and swans land on rivers and bays in flocks that cover the water over hundreds of acres. One blast of birdshot from a musket will feed a family. No one thinks of restraint; the supply seems unlimited. (But pothunters eventually wiped out the pigeons completely. Good sense appeared just in time to save the last of the waterfowl, and only constant vigilance preserves them today. Men who think of themselves as honest sportsmen don't hesitate to shoot more birds than the law allows, or to spread illegal bait around their shooting blinds.)

CLOTH

Silas Whittle grows not only food but also the raw materials for clothing. He and his helpers

beat the tough stalks of the flax he raises, to get the long linen fibers out of them. He can sell or trade the flaxseed to be pressed for linseed oil. His wife and daughters take over the fibers, clean them of impurities, and spin them into yarn. They spin linen on the "little wheel," at which they sit, turning its spindle with a foot treadle. In the spring, the men shear the winter fleece from the sheep. The women pick out burrs and sticks and matted "feltings," wash the wool, and card it—that is, fluff it into short lengths called "slivers." They spin it on the "big wheel," which has to be turned by hand, the spinner standing and retreating backward as her yarn lengthens.

All this is preparation for weaving. It is a rare farm that has no loom. Clear up to the 1830's more cloth will be woven in American homes than in American mills. Bertha Whittle's loom is about the size and general shape of a four-poster bed. Sam Harnett made it. It isn't elaborate; it can weave only "tabby," that is, plain over-and-under weaving such as is done with a needle on a darning egg. By alternating dyed yarn with white, Bertha can weave stripes or checks (which are crossed stripes), but no other patterns. Practically all country women weave in their spare time, but there isn't enough of that to let them make all the cloth a family needs, so they welcome the help of traveling professionals. Emil Kunzelman moves from farm to farm every year. He reaches the Whittles in the early fall, sleeps in the summer kitchen, and weaves on Bertha's loom (and gossips) until he has made enough woolen cloth for a year's supply. Emil takes "country pay" (salable farm products), usually surplus spun yarn.

VISITORS

Other itinerants visit the place. A traveling shoemaker, generally called a "cat whipper," repairs old shoes and makes new ones, using a farmer's leather and taking a side of it as payment. Silas sends him on, because there is a shoemaker in the village. The tailor who shows up makes Silas a new Sunday coat, and cuts down the old one to fit Dan. A tinker stops for a day. Watched with intense interest by the chil-

Bertha and the peddler

Whittle farm by 1785, but let's assume one has. Peddlers are an enterprising breed. The Patterson brothers made tinware in Connecticut, and started peddling it locally soon after 1738. Their business throve. Others took it up as the roads spread, and by 1800, a peddler could show a farm wife a large stock carried in a two-horse wagon. The few through roads of the 1780's are worse than rough, and once off them, the peddler must resort to packhorses. His main stock is tinware: basins, dippers, canisters, pie pans, candlesticks, betty lamps (which yield a smoky light from burning grease), and whale-oil lamps —a common source of light along the coast, but still novel in the back country. The peddler also carries "notions"—light articles that will appeal to a woman like Bertha, who is far from shops— needles, pins, scissors, horn combs, Germantown stockings, spices, printed calico. Like all the other itinerants, the peddler takes country pay, and usually manages to get more of it than the farmer wants to give him.

dren, he mends pots and kettles, and recasts three broken pewter spoons in a mold he carries with him. The new ones are not exactly the same shape they were before, but they are useful spoons again. He gladly takes a slab of salt pork for his work.

All year Bertha saves fat and wood ashes. The ashes she wets down in a wooden hopper, and then collects the lye that leaches from them and trickles out at the bottom. She can melt hard fat and make candles by repeatedly dipping soft-spun wicks into it, and cooling them between coatings. She can also mold candles, but her tin mold will make only a dozen at a time so she prefers to wait for John Witherspoon, the traveling chandler. His big pewter mold, which he brings along in a handcart, will cast fifty at a time. John will also boil soft fat and stir Bertha's lye into it, to make soft soap. He may even add salt to some of it to rid it of excess water, and thus make hard soap. None of these itinerants travels very far. They winter in centers not much more than twenty-five miles from the farthest farm they visit. They cover the same route every year, and become well acquainted with the people they work for.

It's uncertain that a peddler has reached the

CLOTHING

The peddler is welcomed for his wares, and also for his news. He is far-traveled and glib; he can talk politics with Silas, or describe the latest Philadelphia fashions to Bertha, Susan, and Nancy. The women modify their clothes only very gradually. Bertha's newest Sunday best is a good ten years behind the city styles. Silas's old coat, the one that the tailor cut down for Dan, was made sixteen years ago. It is wide-skirted, and it sports a long row of pewter buttons. His new coat, in which Silas says he feels like a rooster, has but six buttons, and its skirt is cut away in front from the waist down.

In the summertime, Silas works in wood-soled clogs, usually worn without stockings. His full linen canvas pants, which he calls slops, reach his calves, and his work frock (smock) reaches just below his hips. Wilhelmina plaited his wide-brimmed hat out of rye straw. In winter he changes to a double-thick cloth cap with a limp brim and a sides-and-back flap that can be turned down over his ears. He still wears his work frock, but he puts a vest and a hip-length coat under it. In very cold weather, he wraps a woolen scarf around his neck. His winter breeches are buckskin, tucked into cowhide boots, which he wears over knitted woolen stockings. He also has knitted mittens.

Bertha's work dresses are the same shape at any season, ankle-length and rather full. Her bodice is only moderately tight, with elbow sleeves. She wears a large apron; its blue checks are an inch square. In summer she wears linen, in winter, wool or linsey-woolsey (linen and wool mixed). There is always a petticoat under her dress, sometimes two or three, and there is a full-length shift under everything. She has never seen drawers.

Though her daughters go to church in dresses of linen or wool loomed on the farm, Bertha wears "boughten" cloth. In summer it is printed calico, in winter it is dark red "carsey" (kersey), a tightly woven, rather glossy, wool repp. Her Sunday skirts are fuller than those she wears every day, and her bodices are tighter. White linen ruffles show at the elbows of her church clothes, and the kerchief she pins over her shoulders is made of finer stuff than the one she wears at home. Around the farm Bertha's hair is nearly always covered with a simple clout but she wears a proper cap on Sunday. Even in summer she

wears her riding hood to church. It is actually a full-length cape, but it does have a hood attached to it. It isn't red by law, though it might as well be; there are few riding hoods of any other color. Bertha's shoes are definitely sturdy. In summer she prefers to go barefooted around home.

There is necessarily some conjecture in the descriptions of the Whittles' clothing. As described, they are probably better dressed than most of their neighbors. Country people appear, as incidents, in a few old prints too crude or too small to show much, and descriptions are equally rare and equally vague. With children's clothes the situation is worse. Both girls and boys wore "petticoats" until they were six years old. In the country version, these seem to have hung straight from shoulder to ankle, to have had round necks, and either short sleeves or no sleeves. When girls came out of petticoats, they started dressing like their mothers, though with their skirts a little shorter. Boys over six seem to have worn short smocks, and slops that were not quite as full as their fathers'. No doubt they had small buckskin breeches for cold weather. Their jackets, when they had to wear them, were most often waist-length "roundabouts."

Ready for church

*On the left of the road: the mill, the blacksmith's shop
and his house, the ordinary, the shoemaker's shop, the housewright,
the cooper, and the schoolhouse. On the right: the tannery,
the sawmill, the store, the potter, and the church.*

4.
The Villages

SOME FARMS lay within a short distance of sizable towns, but most centered on a settlement that their own existence had created. All of its householders were people who served farmers. Such a place usually grew up around a gristmill, where some enterprising soul had dammed a stream, with enough head to turn a waterwheel. Like the one mentioned earlier, the mill took toll of the grain it ground, and seldom had more than one pair of grinding stones.

Farmers waiting their turn (a subject of frequent dissension) could have a horse shod by the blacksmith, or have him make some new barn hinges, or merely discuss weather and taxes with him and with one another. The smith wisely set up his forge near the mill. Not far away, another waterwheel ran a sawmill, useful to the community but somewhat short on social attraction. Downstream at a considerable distance, and lacking any social attraction whatever, was a tannery. The tanner used the stream to wash his hides. The aroma of his vats and drying racks accounted for his isolation.

Scattered irregularly along the rutted wagon track stood some six or eight houses. One of them, near the road, might have some kind of sign in front of it, maybe nothing more than an old jug tied to a pole, to indicate that it was an "ordinary." It was something like a latter-day tourist home, except that it was also a tavern, and sold whisky and rum by the drink. The family had a

spare room or two in which travelers might sleep. They would eat whatever the family ate. Their horses would be stabled and fed. A shilling or so would pay the whole bill. Two or three of the houses had small buildings near them, where their owners plied trades. These had no need of signs; a stranger seeking service was a wild improbability.

The smallest of the buildings was the shoemaker's shop. The shoemaker probably made harness and saddles, too, and very often was also the tanner. He had to be in order to get leather for his work and to add to his income; he had strong competition from the traveling cat whipper. When a farmer killed a cow, a calf, or an old ox, he brought its hide to the tanner, who scratched the farmer's initials on it. After cleaning, dehairing, and soaking six months in a solution of tanbark, the hide became leather. The tanner got the hair, which a peddler would buy to resell for mixing with plaster. He also took half of the hide as payment for tanning. He could sell this, or, if he was also the shoemaker, he could use it for customers who owned no animals. As shoemaker, he hung the farmer's half in his shop, next to the wooden lasts shaped to the feet of the farmer's family. There was to be no mistake; Silas Whittle and his brood would wear shoes made of Silas Whittle's leather.

The shoemaker made dress shoes of calfskin, work shoes of cowhide. He cut the uppers by

The shoemaker

get a good coopered barrel. He and his boys split logs into rough staves and tried to accumulate enough of them to pay the cooper for "wet" barrels, with thick staves, to hold cider, whisky, brine for corning meat, and vinegar for pickling; and "dry" barrels, with thin staves, for grain, meal, or apples.

Even so small a place as this was likely to have a "pot house," though the potter might have to eke out his living with a second occupation, such as burning charcoal or operating a ferry. His pottery was the same "redware" that the Whittles used, made of common brick clay and glazed with lead. It didn't do to eat pickles that had stood overnight in a redware bowl; the lead glaze would make them poisonous. But most people knew the danger, and stored acid food in safe containers. Large potteries in towns made safe, and stronger, "stoneware," glazed with salt, but it required special clay, and long, hot firing that a country potter could seldom manage. Potters made plates, cups, saucers, large and small bowls, pitchers, bean pots, milk pans, and crocks of various shapes and sizes. A good potter could make a ring-shaped water canteen for a harvester to carry around his shoulder in the field. Most of these things he shaped on a "potter's wheel," a small revolving table which he kept spinning by "kicking" a larger wheel with one foot.

The local housewright had a big workshop with a storage shed built against it. He was a man who could turn a hand at almost anything in the way of woodwork, from hewing timbers to mak-

patterns, stretched them over the customer's last, and tacked them to it temporarily. Then he sewed the sole on with two "wax ends." These were stout linen threads, the ends of which he stiffened with wax so that they would pass easily through the holes he made with his sharp awl. Each hole carried two threads, so that a stitch would lie on the upper and one on the sole between each pair of holes.

In a large shed a cooper made barrels, kegs, washtubs, pails, and piggins. A piggin is a small pail with one stave left long to serve as a handle. Silas needed piggins but nobody now can think of a use for one. We need few barrels, but the farmer needed many. He could hollow out a thick log as a makeshift barrel, called a "gum," but no farmer would use one of these if he could

The sawmill

ing window sashes. He was a joiner, too; he could make a chest, a table, a chair, or a coffin. He worked with other materials as well as with wood. He was a stonemason and a bricklayer. He could plaster a wall on laths he split himself. He could glaze windows, making his own putty with chalk and linseed oil. He could paint whatever needed painting, grinding the colors himself.

Almost all of these men did some part-time farming on land near the village. Sometimes it was a retired farmer who kept the store, sometimes one of the craftsmen ran it as a sideline, working behind the counter himself only when trade was brisk, on Saturdays, and leaving the job to his wife on weekdays. The store was a clearinghouse for the whole countryside. It might be an official post office, but even if it wasn't, a letter for anyone in the district would be held

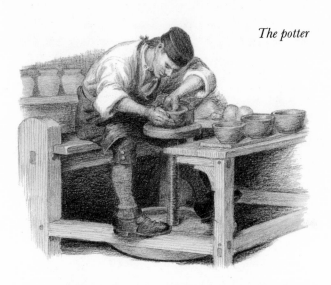

The potter

there. If a farmer had an animal to sell, he told the storekeeper, who passed the word along. The storekeeper served as the local "newspaper," too. He knew who had a new baby, which young people were "keeping company," who was sick, and who was dead. He sold people the things they couldn't raise or make for themselves. Some of these things were necessities: salt, nails, gunpowder, lead shot. The blacksmith could make nails, and many farmers made them in their kitchens at night, but the handmade nails now coming from Europe were cheaper than the homemade ones. Simple though they were, the other articles in the store must be classed as luxuries, things the farmer's family could live without, but not so well: tea, coffee, tobacco, sugar, 31

molasses, pepper, cinnamon, nutmegs, cloves, cheap felt hats, printed calico, drugs (mostly English patent medicines). The store also offered school supplies: battledores, (wooden paddles with the alphabet, printed on paper, pasted onto one side), primers, spellers, readers, arithmetics, writing books, slates and slate pencils. There were a few other books too: Bibles, hymnbooks, and almanacs. A farmer planted crops according to the phases of the moon, and he needed an almanac to find out when they occurred.

Piggin

One book the storekeeper had was not for sale, but it was invaluable to him and to the community. It was a "ready reckoner" which gave the values of all coins in terms of pounds, shillings, and pence, or in terms of the Spanish milled dollar. This silver dollar had been for years the most familiar coin in America. Eventually our national coinage was based upon it. Following the new French decimal system, we divided our dollar into tenths, but the Spanish divided theirs into eights. The coin that represented this division was the *real*, or "piece of eight." It circulated in America, but was generally called a "bit." Since two made a fourth of a dollar, the United States twenty-five-cent piece was obviously "two bits." All kinds of other coins circulated: English, Spanish, Portuguese, Dutch, French, and various issues by individual states of the Union. All of the silver and gold ones were worth their weight as metal, but their values varied in relation to one another; the ready reckoner sorted them out. Paper money varied in value, too, from its face value to nearly nothing. Farmers liked it. There was a lot of it, and after all, it had lifted the mortgage. Small change had always been scarce and it was still. To try to supply change, some paper money appeared in very small denominations. People often reduced its value further by cutting it into pieces; half of a shilling note was worth sixpence.

RELIGION

Somewhere in the little settlement stood the church, almost always a Protestant church. Southern Maryland had some country churches which were Roman Catholic; elsewhere, only a few large towns had them. On Sunday, everybody

Up to 1776, every colony except Rhode Island and Pennsylvania had an established church, that is, a church supported by taxes. In New England it was the Congregational Church (Puritan), and elsewhere it was the Church of England (Anglican). Except for the Congregationalists—who had originated in New England—and the Lutherans and Presbyterians—who had set up their own American synods—the Revolution cut the churches off from their overseas headquarters, and organizational chaos resulted.

The Anglicans had long tried to get an American bishop, but had never succeeded. So they had no head to rally around, and worse, most of their clergy was Loyalist and had left the country. In 1783, small groups of them sent representatives to Annapolis to organize the Protestant Episcopal Church. The word "episcopal" means governed by bishops. Tradition demands the actual presence of three bishops to consecrate a new one. It took until 1787 to get three properly accredited American bishops who could perpetuate the succession. The Roman Catholics, too, had no American leader, and resisted the efforts of Canadian prelates to take charge of them. Finally, Father John Carroll took the bit in his teeth and petitioned the Pope. Father Carroll was first made an apostolic delegate, and in 1808 he became the first American archbishop. Only a beginning had been made at establishing the Methodist Church in the colonies. After the War, Francis Asbury and Thomas Coke cast off English control, to the dismay of John Wesley who had appointed them as his American "superintendents." The Baptists, who had been subject to general contempt before the Revolution, gained respectability by their conspicuous and active patriotism. They further distinguished themselves by admitting Negro slaves to membership in 1779.

Though scattered individuals preceded them to North America, the first group of Jews came to New Amsterdam in 1654; four years later, a second party arrived at Newport, Rhode Island. All of these were the descendants of refugees from the Spanish Inquisition. They came from Dutch colonies which had failed in South America. Even in Rhode Island, where Roger Williams had established a tradition of real toleration, these people felt compelled at first to worship in secret. But by the middle of the eighteenth century, they had

went to church; even if some didn't actually attend the service, but stood around under the trees and discussed matters that were not spiritual. Even the devout did a lot of churchyard gossiping before and after service. Weekly churchgoing was a social occasion; only weddings and funerals were better.

The churches had a bad time in the 1780's. There were lots of them, and lots of people went to them. But they went because it was customary, and because it gave them a chance to see each other. Clergymen complained of the lack of enthusiasm, particularly among young people. Back in the 1740's there had been an evangelical ferment, known as the Great Awakening, sparked chiefly by a fiery young preacher named George Whitefield, but most of those his stentorian voice had awakened now slept again. Much of the apathy was due to the spread of a new religious idea known as deism. It followed the teachings of Jesus but denied his divinity. The Unitarian Church is an outgrowth of it. Benjamin Franklin, Thomas Jefferson, John Adams, and George Washington were all deists. So was Tom Paine, whose book *The Age of Reason* spread deism's ideas far and wide and caused its author's name to be coupled, in orthodox profanity, with that of Beelzebub himself.

organized open congregations. The first of these, Shearith Israel, still functions in New York. In Newport, Touro Synagogue, one of the loveliest of American buildings, is now a National Monument.

In the eleven other colonies, the more dispersed Jews were mistreated, or barely tolerated, and had no civil rights whatever. This denial of citizenship persisted into the nineteenth century in many states, in fact, the last state to enfranchise the Jews didn't do so until 1868. Yet, inconsistently, almost everywhere individual Jews attained positions of dignity and public respect. Moses Hays was a leading citizen of Boston, beloved and admired; in Newport, the same was true of the merchant Aaron Lopez. But Lopez had to move to Massachusetts temporarily in order to attain citizenship. Philadelphia's Haym Salomon reduced himself to poverty by lending *all* of his large fortune to support the Revolution. The nation has never repaid a cent of it.

"ISMS"

The theories of philosophers filter down to the rest of us and affect our lives, though we may not have read the philosophers' books, or even heard of them. The eighteenth century is tagged as "The Age of Reason" because most of its notable men believed in the system called rationalism. Put crudely, they assumed that they could deduce the truth about anything by reasoning from the known facts about it. They preferred to do this

without impressions gathered by their senses, hence their facts were sometimes incomplete. They mistrusted intuition and emotion. For example: the inventor of the power loom proceeded rationally, without ever having watched a man weave. His loom wove, but he assumed that the work used much more effort than it actually did. He made the springs that threw his shuttle so stiff that a Hercules could barely turn the crank that restored their tension.

Rationalist and Romanticist

The rationalists liked everything impersonal and also in order. Both preferences made them admire the formalized art, architecture, and writing of the Greeks and Romans. They considered no man educated who could not read Latin; students at Harvard had to speak it. The rationalists talked much of "Nature," and wrote volumes explaining Nature's failure to follow the neat formulas they had worked out for her. All of the deists were rationalists.

Toward the end of the eighteenth century, some French and German scholars became interested in old writings in the medieval Romance languages. These were a blend of Latin with the northern Germanic tongues. Romance literature dealt with the mysterious and the supernatural, with emphasis on religion, honor, chivalry, and the idealization of women. Above all,

romantic writing stressed individual people. Its writers rather floridly expressed their own thoughts and feelings. To strong rationalists, this was merely barbarous, but interest in the new ideas spread in spite of them. Romanticism reached the United States even before 1800. From the 1820's on, it affected writing, painting, architecture, manners, and even clothes. Ultimately, it produced a rank sentimentality expressed by pressed flowers, and brooches with the hair of the dead in them.

SCHOOL

There was also a school in the village run by its schoolmaster for profit. Sometimes he was also the minister of the church, but often he was a less learned man. In the 1780's, public education was much discussed, but no one outside New England had done anything about it. The schoolmaster's fees were modest, so most children went to school at least long enough to learn to read, write, and "do sums." School closed at harvest time, when even young children had chores to do on the farms. Those who lived no more than three miles away walked to school; from beyond that distance, they either rode a nag or formed a "car pool" in a farm wagon driven by the oldest boy. The school, as well as the church, provided a long shed to shelter horses.

All of the pupils sat together in one room on backless wooden benches. While the master (it was nearly always a man) dealt with one grade, the others studied their lessons, and since they studied aloud, the school was audible at some distance. Men who began their educations this way have defended the vocalizing, saying that it forced concentration and strengthened the voice.

The poet John Trumbull wrote of a schoolmaster of this time:

> He tries with ease and unconcern,
> To teach, what ne'er himself could learn.

Whatever his abilities, he was the autocrat of his own realm. The dunce cap, the birch rod, and worse, are not fictions. It is recorded that a whipping post stood outside at least one school. The boys bowed to the master when they entered the

34

room, and the girls dropped him a curtsy. All were expected to rise and repeat the genuflections to any adult who came in.

There was no blackboard. The children did their sums and practiced their writing on their small slates. In some frontier schools, slates could not be had, so the children spread sand on boards and wrote in it with their fingertips. They copied the pious maxims in their writing books, to achieve a "clear, running hand." Many school-books had been passed on from the childhood of parents and had been first printed long before that. Noah Webster's "Blue-backed Speller," actually titled *The American Spelling Book*, appeared in 1783 and penetrated even to so remote a spot as our village. It was loaded with edifying precepts, many of which preached its author's political opinions. Clearly these were not the best of schools, but men of notable achievement began their educations in them.

It may be said of such small centers as the one we have discussed that all were alike but all different. In the middle states they all served the same purpose, but doing so did not standardize them. New England villages were larger because there farmers lived in a village and went out from it to work their land. The deep South had few villages; even a county seat might be smaller than our little hamlet, with only a church and an ordinary, and perhaps a blacksmith, to keep the courthouse company. This was because the big plantations were villages in themselves and small planters could get simple services from them. Except in the large towns, a craftsman had to take wages from a plantation in order to live in the South.

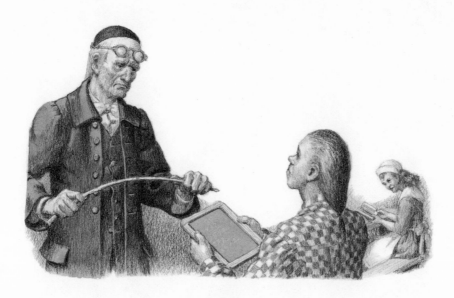

Retribution

The Court Square at Benson Town

The High Street

5.
The Inland Towns

THE EARLIEST inland towns grew "wild," or were planted, on rivers which were navigable at least by small sailing vessels. Very shortly, frontier settlements took hold farther upstream, just below the first falls, where only gundalows could reach them. By the middle of the eighteenth century towns sprang up in the Appalachian foothills where there was no navigable water. Lancaster, Pennsylvania, Frederick, Maryland, Winchester, Virginia, are such towns. Some were self-starting because of need, but men who owned large tracts of land started many of them deliberately, to help sell real estate.

ROADS

No town could survive in isolation. If there was no river, there had to be a road to the coast. The roads developed according to a fixed pattern: at first mere paths, often following an Indian trail and only wide enough for packhorse trains. The trails followed stream valleys when they could, taking the easiest but by no means the shortest way. In time the settlers widened the path into a "road" for carts and wagons by cutting the un-

derbrush and the saplings along its sides. The trees still stood and the road snaked its way around them. Then the smaller trees were cut. Their stumps stayed in the roadbed along with surface roots and rocks. The tree trunks, laid crosswise, served to pave the soggy spots in the valleys, making "corduroy roads." Shallow streams could be forded and the road would turn aside a mile or more to reach a good ford. If a flood made a ford too deep to cross, travelers simply waited until the water went down.

Bridges crossed deep streams that were not too wide. Two or three large logs with corduroy laid on them made the simplest bridge, better if stiffened by king-post trusses at its sides. The king posts stood in the middle of the bridge, with timbers slanting from their tops to both ends of the structure. Two such truss bridges, meeting on a stone pier in midstream, crossed a wider creek. Frequently the same spate that delayed the travelers at the ford carried away the creek bridge.

If the road met a river, even one no more than a hundred feet wide, traffic crossed on a flatboat ferry poled by a ferryman. Crossing was quite a performance. Later, on larger rivers, flatboats became long enough to accept a wagon and four horses; the early ones made two trips, one for the wagon, another for the horses. If the horses crossed before the wagon, they could haul it off the boat, but loading it without them on the embarkation side presented problems.

Such highways as these were known as "through-land roads." Here and there they were connected with one another by horse trails which, since they served little traffic, often were not widened for years. One through-land road, called the Great Philadelphia Wagon Road, ran all the way from South Carolina to Lancaster, Pennsylvania; another, nearer the coast, known as the Great Eastern Road, connected Williamsburg, Virginia, with Philadelphia, after a fashion.

LOCAL VARIATIONS

In New England, towns spread outward from their central squares, or commons. Nearly all of the buildings were wooden, including the white Congregational church at one end of the open square. The colors of houses varied pleasantly: some white, some yellow, some gray, some dark red, and some old ones unpainted as they had always been. In many a northern town the stocks still stood near the church, but they weren't getting the use they had had earlier, when too strong language, or even a too handsome coat, could seat a man on the edge of a narrow rail, with his wrists and ankles locked into holes in planks, and with a note on his chest describing his shortcomings.

South of Connecticut, all the way to Georgia, the frame houses were interspersed with brick ones and, north of the Patapsco River, with some stone ones, also. No one designed any of these houses; they were simply "put up" by local builders who unconsciously followed the patterns of the sturdy style that architects call Georgian, but that most of us call Colonial. Entrance doors stood in the middle of the front walls, and windows on one side of them exactly repeated those on the other. The crossbars that held the glass in those windows were twice as broad as they usually are now.

Towns in the middle states tended to grow lengthwise along both sides of the main road which, within the town, became the High Street, now changed to Main Street. If the place had been deliberately planned, the High Street was likely to be straight; if it had merely accumulated, the windings of the road persisted, and in many a town they still persist. Again, if the town had been laid out, that is, surveyed and divided into lots before it was settled, its cross streets would probably be straight and placed at regular intervals; but if the town just happened, its cross streets did, too. Houses crept outward along country cart tracks which joined the High Street at any point, and at any angle convenient to the farmers whose vehicles had made them.

Most of the houses in these towns would be no more than a story-and-a-half high, a few, the homes of the well-to-do, would be a full three stories high, with servants' rooms in the attic. The large houses usually had ample grounds and almost as many outbuildings as a farmhouse. Stables, washhouses, smokehouses, and woodsheds were an essential part of town living. The next-door neighbor of a large house might be a shop or a laborer's cottage. Social position was

Ferry

The courtyard of the inn

rigid, and everybody understood it, but, except in the largest cities, it didn't produce exclusive residential districts.

"BENSON TOWN"

It is a sunny afternoon in October of 1784. The Court Square of Benson Town is busy, as it alway is on Saturdays. This is the center of the town's life, but is not its geographical center, as it was intended to be. For their own reasons, more people have settled west of the center than east of it. The square provides a place to hitch horses while the lawyers are wrangling in the brick courthouse facing the middle of its north side. The High Street crosses the square from east to west. Two other streets end here: the Sunderland Road comes in at the east end of the south side, by the inn; the Three-notch Trail wanders in at the northwest corner. The road leads to a small village about six miles away; the trail, originally marked by three blazes on the trees, is now actually a road, though it serves only the farms along it, and goes nowhere in particular.

The inn on the square is a good one, where travelers make an effort to break their journeys. Its sign, on a post out front, shows the crudely painted bust of a man wearing a cocked hat. The hat was added some years ago when what had

been "The King George Inn" became "The General Washington Inn." The two-story frame building is L-shaped, its wing facing the Sunderland Road. A narrow porch fronts the square along the full length of the main building. Two doors enter from the porch; one, in the middle, serves guests; the other, near the east end, admits patrons to the bar. There are also back entrances which open on a large court that is partly surrounded by the building. The "carriage trade" entrance is opposite the front door. A door to the ell is for the use of wagoners, who park their big freighters in the court and stall their horses in the stable that walls its south side. The wagoners eat in a large room in the ell and sleep, in their own blankets, on its floor.

Across the square from the inn, in front of the courthouse, on this Saturday afternoon half a dozen farm wagons are drawn up in an irregular line. Their owners stand at their tail gates selling vegetables, fruit, smoked meat, and some fresh pork to the townspeople. The horses that brought the wagons here are tied to hitching rails under the trees. Other horses, some in the shafts of passenger vehicles are tethered to rails and posts around the square. A scattering of people amble through the square and along the narrow brick walks that most of the householders have put down. Here and there two or three men have stopped to talk, and women are gossiping in little knots. A chaise has stopped to water its horse at the trough by the town pump, in one corner of the square. The driver and his wife are beaming down at the plump woman who stands by one wheel, talking up at them animatedly.

Outside the bar door of The General Washington three young men sit on a bench holding pewter ale pots in their hands, and a fourth lounges against a post, facing them. This man wears a linen hunting shirt, and fringed leather leggings cover his long legs. He may be a hunter from the western woods; more likely, he is a town boy who likes to dress as a hunter. The men on the ends of the bench are conventionally dressed in breeches and white shirts. One has on a hip-length homespun vest, dyed brown with walnut hulls. The man in the middle is talking, and now and then making a slight gesture with his tankard. His short black gaiters are torn. His patched and threadbare coat is dark blue with red facings, held back by the few brass buttons he hasn't lost. The fringed green tab on his right shoulder marks him as a corporal. He has come home; the war is over.

A thudding of heavy feet and an occasional bellow sound from the High Street to the west, and the vanguard of a hundred cattle pours into the square. In no time the place is full of steers and dust. The animals scatter as they reach the open space, and their drovers need the help of bystanders to get them into the road to the east. The beasts are half wild; they grew up browsing in the woods. They are headed now for a farm east of the town, where they will eat grass to cover

The post rider

their ribs a little, before they move on to furnish Sunday dinners in an eastern city.

The dust has not settled when a harsh blast on a tin horn startles the square, and a man on an ambling nag appears from the road the cattle have taken. His saddlebags are bulging. He is the post rider bringing mail and newspapers to the post office in the printshop at the northwest corner of the square, by the Three-notch Trail. Presently the rider will cross to the inn bar where he knows somebody will buy him a pint of ale for the sake of hearing the news (and rumors) without waiting a week for the newspaper.

Except for its farm-market aspect, the square is by no means a shopping center. The printshop exists by the work it gets from the court and from the four lawyers who have offices in the square. They buy blank forms for deeds, mortgages, and notes. The printer, a newcomer in Benson Town, tries to make ends meet by selling books, stationery, window glass, and dry colors, and by occasionally rebinding old books, which he doesn't do very well. He also buys rags, and ships them east to the paper mills. Sometimes he looks across the road at the jail and glumly considers the possibility of being put into it for debt. He has no family or friends who would bail him out.

Elijah Thompson, always called Old Man Thompson, lives alone in a small cottage at the corner of east High Street and sells tobacco in its front room. Two hundred pounds of raw leaf is brought to him by wagon twice a year. He sweetens it with molasses and twists it into "thread" for pipe smoking. He hammers some of it into holes in a log to make "plug" for chewing, and grinds the rest, the stems and poorer leaves, into snuff. Elijah was once a journeyman glover, and he still makes good gloves, but his neighbors don't buy enough of them to support him.

Just as the post rider leaves the printer's (and leaves his mail unguarded in his saddlebags), a gate in the picket fence by the pump clicks shut, and Major Jonathan Benson swings the noble bulge of his vest in the direction of the inn. The Major was an ensign of militia with Braddock. Time, courtesy, and respect have improved his rank. The Major's father founded Benson Town. Just now he plans to hear what the post rider has to say. As he directs his dignified steps toward the bar, not so much aided as enhanced by his walking stick, a tall, spare man approaches him

40

with a dignity at least equal to the Major's. This is Judge Murray. The necks of both men stiffen. They glare for an instant into each other's eyes, and though they have known one another from boyhood, they pass on with no further sign of recognition. They are Declared Enemies. The Judge rendered a decision against the Major, and they haven't spoken to each other since. They cherish their enmity as carefully as other men might a friendship.

As the Major reaches the inn he encounters an elderly lady, followed by a servant carrying a large market basket. There is an instant melting of the gentleman's manner. A warm smile, marred a little by two missing teeth, lights his face. He plants his stick firmly with his left hand, extends his right leg slightly, and bows, sweeping off his cocked hat with a full-arm gesture. The lady replies with just a hint of a curtsy. Perhaps it is ungracious to record that her smile reveals rather worse dental havoc than his. With satisfactory answers to inquiries as to one another's health and that of relatives, the Major proceeds to the bar, and the lady to the baker's shop in the High Street.

TRADE

Benson Town has shops scattered all through it, which doesn't put them far apart. Nearly all are in, or next to, the houses of their proprietors. All of the previously mentioned crafts are practiced here with some differences. For instance, Jared Lick, the blacksmith, sticks to ironwork, and leaves wagon building to Amos Whiting, who is a full-time wheelwright. Amos's shop is on the Sunderland Road next to the inn yard, a location which gets him a lot of repair work. By way of a sign he has an old cart wheel hung on a long wooden bracket above his door.

Along the High Street west of the square, quite a few signs hang from brackets, or stand at the tops of poles set in the ground. Many show only a symbol, like Amos's wheel or the coppersmith's kettle, but some are lettered with the proprietor's name and business: MARK DAGGETT, TAYLOR AND HATTER, arranged above and below a very stiff representation of an empty coat. Mark isn't actually a hatter, but he sells hats that he buys from Philadelphia. Some shops show nothing more

than a notice, written in large letters on a sheet of paper and pasted behind a windowpane: JOHN COMPTON, WEAVER, HIGHEST PRICES PAID FOR SPUN YARN. Mr. Compton can get all the business he can handle, but he has trouble finding raw material. His loom is more complex than Bertha Whittle's. By arranging it to let some of the wefts skip over several warps instead of being restricted to alternate ones, he can weave "overshot" patterns. He would be surprised if he knew that some of his beautiful coverlets, with named patterns like "Whig Rose" and "Star of Bethlehem," will be cherished in museums.

Its people haven't thought of Benson Town as a frontier settlement for thirty years, but its High Street is, and will be down to our own time, part of the pathway to the West. The most frequent travelers on it are families, with all they own loaded on a wagon or a cart, headed for new land and a new life. Lone young men, riding, or walking with backpacks, also pass westward. Some are going ahead to make a start for a bride they intend to return for, but who often waits in vain. Most are discharged Revolutionary soldiers bent on claiming the land beyond the mountains that was awarded to them instead of pay for their service. Some, of all of these, pass through in the other direction, dispirited, overcome by hardships beyond their strength.

Visitors, too, come east to Benson Town from clearings in the mountain valleys. They guide trains of packhorses clanging along the street "with the bells on." Most of the horses carry two bushels of "black salt," distributed in two splint panniers. Black salt is potash which the mountaineers leach from their vast supply of wood ashes. It is black because much ash remains in it. Some of the trains bring kegs of rye whisky and peach brandy that are the essences of mountain crops. Others carry bundles of pelts.

There are Benson Town dealers who will buy all of these things and pay for them with goods for the frontiersmen to take home with them: salt, in kegs of such size that two, weighing some eighty pounds apiece, make a load for one of the small horses. The kegs keep the salt dry, and will return in time to Benson Town filled with liquor. So will the gunpowder kegs. Even gunflints travel in kegs.

Jared Lick sells iron bars, cut to length and bent to a U-shape to hang over a horse's back. Mountain smiths will make knives, axes, even guns from the bars. There is a gunsmith near Benson Town who makes and sells fine flintlock rifles, most of which go west, but his best seller is the flintlock itself, sold without the gun. The mountain gunsmiths know how to make the locks and often do so, shaping the parts with files and making springs from old saw blades, but it is tedious work and they prefer to buy locks from experts.

All of the stuff the mountaineers bring to town is salable on the seaboard, and this gives rise to another business, the contract wagoner. He started with one wagon and six horses, which he drove himself. Now he owns a dozen wagons and a drove of horses, and he stays home to dicker with customers, and to regret the good old days. There's Matt Randall, too, of whom it is said that he would skin a louse for its hide and tallow. Matt buys horses and sells them—workhorses to the farmers, packhorses to the frontiersmen, carriage horses to the "gentry."

Major Benson owns the Duck Creek Iron Furnace, a couple of miles out of town. It makes pig iron from surface ore, with charcoal and limestone. Aside from it, there is little industry here; but there are signs of change. The tannery is growing and specializes now in deerskins which sell well in Philadelphia for making buckskin breeches. The brickyard is thriving. Duck Creek has enough water and enough fall to turn a dozen waterwheels, so the miller dreams of a merchant mill, with three sets of grinding stones; and, Compton, the weaver, thinks longingly of a fulling mill which will properly finish woolens. Buck Sunderland, who buys and ships a lot of black salt, thinks of how much more money he could make if he had an oven to "scorch" it white, so that he could sell it as usable potash; come to think of it, he could even refine it into pearl ash. It would take a little money. . . .

"Howdy, Major," says Buck, as he steps into The General Washington bar, "I got a little idee I'd like to talk to you about."

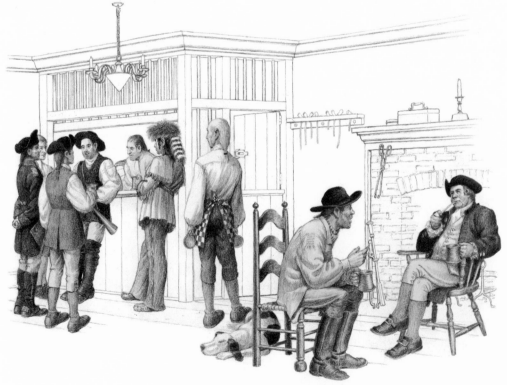

6.
The Wilderness

WESTERN LAND

WHEN it added up all the western claims that the states ceded to it, Congress had a noble sweep of land north of the Ohio River. The Northwest Territory had more area than all of the middle and southern states together. At least Congress had it on paper. Some Delaware and Shawnee Indians, who were actually on it, thought it was theirs, but they were tragically wrong.

When Virginia surrendered her western claims, which imperially covered the whole territory regardless of conflicting interests, she demanded that the land eventually become states equal in every way to the original thirteen. So, in 1784 and 1785, Congress divided it (on paper) into seven subterritories, and (still on paper) divided the territories into townships six miles square, further dividing each township into thirty-six "sections," each a mile square. The sections were for sale at a dollar an acre. Any man could buy as much as he wanted, but not less, at first, than one 640-acre section.

Here was a glittering opportunity for speculators. Two generals, Rufus Putnam and Benjamin Tupper, formed the Ohio Company in Boston. They sent the Reverend Manasseh Cutler to New York, where he made a deal with Congressman William Duer to buy more than four times as much land as the Ohio Company wanted, and to turn the surplus over to Duer and his associates,

43

mostly congressmen. The dollar-an-acre price was payable in paper money, with one third off for bad land; in hard cash this came to less than nine cents an acre. The Ohio Company got a million and a half acres, the Scioto Company, as Duer's group was known, got five million. Both tracts were later made smaller because the buyers couldn't pay.

This fancy deal needed a special act of Congress, known as the Land Ordinance of 1787. In spite of its sordid origins, its ultimate results were good. The ordinance applied only to the Northwest Territory, over which it strengthened Congress's control, but for 150 years, it set the pattern for settling and governing all new territory and for grooming it for statehood. Congress would appoint a governor, a secretary, and three judges. When five thousand free adult males had moved in, they could elect an assembly, though the governor could veto its acts. As soon as the area had sixty thousand people, they could write themselves a constitution and apply for admission to the Union.

Just beyond the western boundary of Pennsylvania, surveyors laid out the first townships in Ohio. An auction, held in New York, fell flat because most of those who would like to buy were already in Ohio as squatters and they had neither the inclination nor the means for a round trip to the East. They simply sat where they were, and defied Congress to move them.

Cabin in a "hacking"

Arks on the Ohio

7.

The Frontier

ROANOKE ISLAND was the first frontier, in 1585. And of course Jamestown, Plymouth, New Amsterdam, and Salem were all frontiers in their time, but we commonly use the term for the western edge of the migration into the interior. That began in Pennsylvania with the Palatine Germans and the Scotch-Irish, soon after 1710. By 1720 Germans were farming near the Susquehanna River. The Scotch-Irish were there, too, clearing out the game.

The Germans wanted land of their own, and most of them preferred to stay in one place and carve it methodically out of the wilderness. They paid the Indians for their land, and displayed crude metal silhouettes of Indians on their neat cabins to show that they had done so. The Scotch-Irish liked hunting better than farming, so they lived by it, and raised just enough corn to round out their diet. They built slapdash cabins in the woods. When neighbors began to "crowd" them, and game grew scarcer, they moved on westward. They knew the French held the land beyond the Appalachian Mountains, so when they came to them, they turned south into the valleys of Virginia and North Carolina.

As time passed, the original vanguard were joined by some of the children of the German settlers and by young English emigrants from the coastal colonies. Daniel Boone's father brought

45

his family all the way from eastern Pennsylvania to the North Carolina hills in one long trek. Daniel opened the path to Kentucky and many followed him. That was in 1775, and the British soon stirred up the Indians to make bad trouble for the Kentucky settlers, but many stood fast, and more came in.

The whole story of the advancing frontier is fascinating and complex. Complex because things happened in many places at once, but the basic things were similar everywhere. A family traveled slowly westward along a blazed trail, carrying a little corn, and hunting as they went. Sometimes they branched off the trail and stopped to settle; sometimes they followed it to its end. Only a few hardy souls went so far as to have no neighbors.

These pioneers looked for flat land in a valley. They tried to judge its quality by the kind of trees that grew on it. The first need was shelter. The husband threw together a "half-faced camp." It was a lean-to, built against a bank. It had log ends and a bark roof, but its downhill side was open to wind and weather. Before snow fell, the neighbors would gather, and make a party out of raising a cabin for the new people. Meanwhile, the settler cut small trees to accumulate a stock of logs for it. Large trees—and many were huge— he "deadened" by girdling their bark with his ax. This let sun into the dark forest, and the man and

his wife planted a corn patch in the "hacking," between the dead trunks.

The log cabin was small, perhaps ten feet by sixteen. Its builders piled the logs as a crib, with their bark on and with their ends projecting beyond the walls. Where they crossed at the corners, axmen notched them, top and bottom, to make them lie close together. The women chinked the cracks with clay mixed with moss. The roof was either bark, which leaked badly, or clapboards, split from logs, which merely leaked. Even the fireplace and chimney were logs, daubed thickly with clay to make them resist fire. A man cut the doorway with a saw after the walls were up. Elegant cabins, with stone fireplaces, also had floors of split logs, flat side up, but most people made do with packed earth.

A one-legged bedstead, built into a corner, held a mattress of skins thrown over dry leaves. Bearskins, with the fur on, made warm blankets, but George Washington, who tried them often, said they harbored fleas. A rough table of split logs clung to one wall. The man of the house made "block cheers" for seats by sawing a log into short sections and standing them on end. His wife did her cooking in the fireplace with a couple of iron pots hung from a green pole that was fixed across the chimney.

These were rough people; they had to be. Few of them could read; all of them were intensely superstitious. If many of them were heroes, just as many were scoundrels. When they caught a thief, his neighbors tied him to a tree and beat him, but they never exiled him; any man who could shoot was needed. Every pioneer owned an ax, a knife, and a long flintlock rifle. Without those three things, life in the wilderness was not possible. The rifles shot a lot straighter and farther than the muskets of the easterners, and the "leatherstockings" became almost incredibly good marksmen with them. They could also throw their knives with deadly accuracy. A frontier boy practiced knife throwing almost from the time he could stand alone. When he was thirteen he got a light rifle, and was considered a man.

With wild game plentiful and such marksmen to hunt it, there was an abundance of meat, but bread was often scarce. It was cornbread, of course. The little hackings didn't yield too much, and often animals, or Indians, destroyed the whole crop. Whatever was harvested had to be ground into meal by hand before it could be

46

eaten. This situation improved as life became more organized. Sugar maples yielded sap that could be boiled into "sweetenin'." Pigs and cows foraged in the woods. Fields were enlarged, and little "tub" mills were set up in swift streams to grind corn.

By that time some cabins had spinning wheels and looms, but at first, cloth of any kind was scarce. The packtrains that the settlers sent east every year to such centers as Benson Town brought back a little linen and linsey-woolsey. The people much preferred these materials when they could get them; when they couldn't, they had to use leather, or go bare. Probably it wasn't as good as the leather of the Indians, but the settlers made moccasins and hip-high leggings of it, and also hunting shirts—if they had to. A wet leather shirt was miserably uncomfortable.

Except in midwinter, there was always the threat of an Indian attack. A man who grew up on the frontier wrote that the children there couldn't imagine a life without fear of Indians. A cabin seldom had windows, but however crude it might be, its strong door could be barred at night; and it was never opened in the morning until someone had scanned the clearing from a crack under the eaves.

When a real attack threatened, the whole settlement moved into the community fort. It was an enclosure about 150 feet square, surrounded by a stockade of tall posts placed side by side. It occupied the crest of a knoll which had been cleared of every tree and bush that an enemy could hide behind. Sometimes the settlers had to stay in the fort for weeks, living in the huts built against the inside of the stockade. An unusually large fort might have a two-story log blockhouse at one corner. Defenders could shoot from its loopholes, and a last-ditch defense could be made from its upper level, with the ladder pulled up. In a small fort, firing was from the roofs of the huts and through cracks between the stockade posts. Of course such a fort could not have withstood an organized military attack for more than a few minutes, but it gained strength from the nature of Indian warfare, which depended on stealth and surprise, and used mass attack only as a desperate measure. The hilltop location of the fort made defense easier, but at a cost. Springs seldom occur on heights. Somebody had to go out the gate and down the hill for water. He went at night, of course, but quite often he didn't come back.

At the end of the Seven Years War, in 1763, France withdrew from the Ohio country, and settlers began at once to cross the Appalachians, filling up the valleys as they went. The king of England had forbidden this, but he was far away. In this push there were many American militiamen, who had been this way with General Braddock and had seen things they liked. A small village grew up around Fort Pitt, on the tongue of land between the Allegheny and Monongahela rivers, which join there to become the Ohio. That

great river made an easy route westward, but the Indians on its banks made the trip almost suicidal. Nevertheless, hardy souls built wooden "arks" of heavy timbers, almost floating forts, and drifted down the river in them, with their families and all their worldly goods. The arks tried to travel in squadrons so that they could protect each other, but it was hard to keep them together; they drifted at the mercy of the current, and the river had its own ideas.

In 1788, Rufus Putnam and his group of New Englanders floated down as far as the mouth of the Muskingum. They were the vanguard of the Ohio Company settlers. The General opened a land office, and the rest of them built, first a fort, and then a New England village in the wilderness, complete with Congregational church. They called it Marietta. Arthur St. Clair, the first gov-

ernor of the vast Northwest Territory, came to Marietta that same year. He had been the president of the Congress that granted all that land. Quite a few people had, by this time, slipped across the Allegheny at Pittsburgh, and squatted in the Ohio country, ahead of the government surveyors.

In August of 1794, the Indians, wrongly assuming that the British would help them, abandoned their natural tactics and fought a pitched battle with the troops of "Mad" Anthony Wayne at Fallen Timbers. They lost; and with the loss confidence dwindled. At Fort Greenville, the following June, they agreed to give the southern part of Ohio to the United States. From then on, settlers could drift down the river on any kind of raft that would float them. Their chief danger was from white pirates.

The land office of the Ohio Company at Marietta

8.
City Life

UNTIL after 1810, Philadelphia was the largest city in the United States, and by far the handsomest. It was as large as any provincial city in England. Thomas Jefferson thought it finer than London or Paris; but those cities, like Boston and New York, still kept their medieval look. Their streets ran in all directions and their houses crowded each other irregularly. Mr. Jefferson admired symmetry, and Philadelphia houses sat neatly along the straight streets, which crossed at right angles as William Penn had decreed.

By the mid-1780's, most of those streets were paved, full width, with cobblestones, though some of the lesser ones still made do with a narrow strip of paving down the middle. Nearly all had sidewalks, some of brick, but most of six-foot-square flagstones. The law made householders build and maintain the sidewalks, and also the gutters. In Boston and New York, gutters ran down the middles of the streets, which sloped toward them from the curbs. Philadelphia's streets were high in the middle. Gutters everywhere carried sewage that smelled to heaven, but that was familiar; not even Jefferson noticed it. Philadelphia paid street cleaners, and travelers marveled at its cleanliness, ignoring the gutters. They did complain, as they did with all American towns, of the animals that ran loose—pigs and poultry at all times, and an occasional cow or stray horse. Dogs ran in dangerous packs. In Charleston, goats joined the melee.

Except for that city, which, needing less, had an enormous supply, all of the seaports had fuel trouble. Nearby wood had long since been cut, and as the source moved farther away, the price rose drastically. Boston depended on precarious shipments from Maine. Newporters found a little coal, and mined it, but it didn't help much. New Yorkers could buy English coal cheaper than local wood. Wood for Philadelphia came down the Delaware, except when the river was frozen, which of course was when the Philadelphians most wanted it.

THE QUAKER CITY

Let's take a closer look at Philadelphia. Stop a moment here at the corner of Seventh Street and Filbert. You are not far from the edge of town. From where you stand, steppingstones cross both streets from curb to curb. They are eighteen inches square and are set in a line about eight inches apart. Each stone stands a couple of inches above the cobbles. Water can flow between them, but only a deluge will cover them. It is a fault of

cobblestone paving that wheels depress it in wet weather, and notable puddles result.

Both of these streets are pleasantly shaded with well-grown linden trees. This is a decent residential area, with a few scattered shops, one or two of which have awnings stretched over the sidewalk. As in Benson Town, most shops are wherever the shopkeeper lives. A majority of the houses are red brick with white trim, but some are wood, painted in pleasant colors. Halfway up the block, on the north side of Filbert Street, you can see an old log house. Its shingle roof is the only one in sight; all the other roofs are tile or slate. Most of the houses have narrow walkways between them, some arched over to make tunnels, and all closed off by gates or doors. Quite a few houses sit right against one another. The front walls are all the same distance from the curb. Nobody has a front yard, but everybody has a small square porch, with two benches facing each other on either side of the front door. Alongside the porch, steps leading to the cellar are covered by a sloping door which sports a huge padlock.

A few houses are only one story high, but most have two stories and an attic lighted by dormer windows. Most of them have their kitchens in small connected buildings at the rear. You'll notice an oddity about these houses: almost all have a narrow strip of roof above the first-floor windows; on the corner houses, it runs along both walls. It is called a pent, and it is peculiar to this part of the country.

Except for half a dozen children on Seventh Street, who are playing some game that requires a lot of running and squealing, this neighborhood is quiet. Grass grows between the cobbles in the streets. A woman, wearing a big apron and a calico cap, is sweeping her porch and exchanging comments with an old man, two houses down, who has brought his pipe out to a bench. At the far end of the block, a Negro man carries armloads of firewood from a cart down into an open cellarway. The housewife watches him from her front door, holding her stomach with her folded arms.

There are some other things worth notice about these streets: set in the sidewalks along the gutters are rows of white posts, and among them, here and there, stand tall wooden pumps with long iron handles. The posts keep vehicles off the walkways. There are more than eight hundred of the pumps in the town; six of them can be seen from here. The houses have their own pumps in their backyards or in their cellars. Those you see are public pumps; anyone may get water from them, but their real purpose is supplying water to fight fire.

Diagonally across the street from us stands a high post topped with an iron gooseneck from which hangs a square glass-sided lantern. There is another like it in the middle of the block, and still another at the next corner. These are Philadelphia's famous street lamps, the first public ones in America. They burn whale oil. Except when the moon shines, lamplighters light them every night. This city is better lighted than London. It has need of light, but so has London. Men who have to "walk abroad" at night prefer to do it in groups, and to carry pistols or sword canes for defense. The city pays watchmen to patrol the streets all night. They carry lanterns and large wooden rattles. They call the hours, "Three

o'clock, and a-l-l's well." They watch for fires, and rattle everybody awake if they find one. They also endeavor to keep the peace (several have been killed trying), but they are not policemen.

FIRES

Fire is the chief menace to all American towns. Boston had had eight "great fires" before 1743. In 1740, fire destroyed nearly all the old buildings in Charleston. Fire is the reason for the slate roofs in Philadelphia. Chimney sweeps keep busy because the law requires that all chimneys in use be swept every six weeks to keep them from catching fire. The city maintains several fire companies, but many more are paid by insurance associations. Each association provides the houses of its members with cast-iron markers to attach to their walls. Regrettably, if an arriving fire company finds the wrong marker on a burning house, it is likely to stand by and watch the fun. Worse, the idle firemen may taunt the rival company fighting the fire into a pitched battle, while the building burns to the ground.

The members of a company pull its fire engine to a blaze at a dead run. When they reach the fire, they unfold the engine's pump handles, which have long extensions, to let as many as twenty men work in unison. A bucket brigade, which includes all the neighbors, forms a line to the nearest street pump. There, shifts man the pump handles to fill leather buckets for the brigade to pass from hand to hand and empty into the reservoir of the fire engine. The engine's pump forces this water through a leather hose to

51

a nozzle held by a fire fighter. It sounds absurdly complex and slow, but the hose stream does reach the blaze more effectively than water thrown from a bucket can do it.

HIGH STREET

If we move south on Seventh, a short block will bring us to High Street (Market Street) and to a very different scene. The same posts, pumps, and lampposts keep vehicles off the sidewalks. Men are leading the horses of drays and carts. It is a municipal rule, designed to keep them from driving too fast. There are fines for this, but they do little to slow down the young men who clatter by in chaises and sulkies, or the men on horseback, who travel at the same fast trot. The sidewalks are not crowded but there are many people on them. Most of the women carry baskets for their purchases, over which many spread a napkin. Paper is too valuable to be used for wrapping; even bread and meat are sold unwrapped. In Philadelphia all the housewives, including the wealthiest, do the family marketing personally, on foot. Here comes a wheelbarrow, taking up most of the walkway. It is loaded with leather, and is pushed by an apprentice wearing an apron of the same material. Across the street, a sedan chair blocks the sidewalk, as its two Indian bearers put it down to allow the lady in it to enter a bookshop. That's what it must be; there is a book painted on the swinging sign over its door. A big country wagon is forcing its way across High Street, so we can cross at the same time. If you glance to your left, you can see the roof and arches of the Jersey Market, standing in the street some distance away. The printshop of Franklin and Hall is down there, too. Its senior partner has been retired for some years now, but he still lives nearby in a court opposite Carpenter's Hall.

INDEPENDENCE SQUARE

Look to your left again at Chestnut Street. You can see, quite near by, a massive group of buildings that looms above the houses and shops. But don't go down Chestnut to look at them; continue to Walnut, so that you will see them first from their better side. This is State House Row, the largest and handsomest civic center in America. Its dominating central building is the Old State House, already beginning to be called Independence Hall (see page 58). The Declaration was signed here, and here, shortly, a new constitution will be hammered out, and some of the signers will help. Seen from Independence Square, the building is a little disappointing. Where is its lovely white steeple? It had to be taken down in 1781; it wasn't very well built, originally. It was so shaky, in fact, that the Liberty Bell could never be hung in it. The bell hangs now, uncracked, in the stumpy brick tower. The steeple will be put back, but not until 1828.

That enormous stone "grandfather clock," standing against the end of the main building, has a mate at the other end. Both will come down when the new steeple, with four clock faces, is built. Just now, a single clockwork in the middle of the attic runs both clocks by means of long shafts.

A block away, to your right as you face the State House, you can see the gables and cupola of Carpenters' Hall. It is the headquarters of the Carpenters' Company, and in 1774 it was the meeting place of the first Continental Congress. That new building under construction just to the left of Independence Hall will be the County Court House. The United States Congress will meet in it for ten years, from 1790 until it moves to the District of Columbia, so it will be known, of course, as Congress Hall. In it, too, George Washington will be inaugurated for his second term as President, and so will John Adams, his successor.

COMMERCE

Members of the Society of Friends founded Philadelphia, and for years it was run by them, with decency and sobriety. Even when the town's great growth—and the floods of immigrants, whom they encouraged—had made the Quakers a minority, their influence was still great. Some of them became wealthy merchants, and a few of those who did forsook the old simplicity for pomps and vanities, and joined the Anglican Church. Those pomps and vanities made great headway in Philadelphia during the gay nine months of British occupation in 1777–78. Though most of the girls who danced with the English officers were from Tory families, and almost none were Quakers, the whole town took on a more tolerant attitude and kept it. The times had something to do with it. The same thing was happening in Boston.

Philadelphia's growth was due to its importance as a seaport. This is remarkable because its wharves and warehouses stood along a riverbank, a hundred miles from the sea. The drawback was overcome by the great productivity of the area for which the city was the outlet, and by the enterprise of her merchants, who made the most of what they had. Wharves ran for two miles along the waterfront, and reached far into the river, though none so far as the twelve hundred feet of Boston's famous Long Wharf. The town corporation built most of them, but some were privately owned. Instead of wooden platforms supported by piling, rubble and earth were dumped behind wooden bulkheads to create "made land." The masses of ice, brought down by the river in spring, would have carried away anything less substantial. Warehouses stood on most wharves because of the scarcity of space ashore.

This area ashore was far from William Penn's dream of "a greene country towne which may never be burnt." (Penn had seen the Great Fire of London.) Instead of the houses surrounded by gardens that he had envisioned, warehouses crowded run-down dwellings where sailors boarded, and grogshops of dubious reputation throve. Water Street ran along the river, and the traffic on it was dense and noisy. Rubber tires didn't exist, and iron ones, four inches wide on the

large vehicles, made a deafening racket rolling over the cobbles. Carts, drays, and huge six-horse wagons from the back country, moving both ways on a narrow street, created traffic jams which had to be untangled by shouts and imprecations. There was nothing and nobody to control them.

In the midst of all this turmoil and squalor stood a few decent, if not quiet, inns. They served travelers waiting for ships to sail. The wait could be three weeks or more. A ship sailed when it had accumulated a cargo, when the tide was right, and when a "conjurer" decided that the stars favored the voyage. Hardheaded merchants paid these humbugs for horoscopes. The center of Philadelphia's business world was William Bradford's London Coffee House, at High Street and Second. Here the merchants gathered at noon to learn the prices of goods, the probable sailing dates of ships, and the latest news of politics. Sitting around the big coffee urn on the first floor, they traded goods or borrowed and loaned money among themselves. Bradford posted all public notices in the coffee room, and provided newspapers from all American cities and from some English cities. He also offered a hall on the second floor for meetings and functions. On post days, the place was crowded with men waiting to hear the latest dispatches.

Most of these men were not content merely to buy cheap and sell dear. They sent agents into the Pennsylvania, New Jersey, and Maryland hinterlands to barter goods at country stores for local products. Quite often they loaned promising men money, to help them to start stores or to set up small manufactories. Lancaster was their western base, and they made it for a while the largest inland town in the nation. It was they who persuaded the city fathers (they *were* the city fathers) to set up sheds on the south bank of the Schuylkill to keep wagon cargoes dry while the drivers waited their turn for Gray's ferry.

The merchants owned many of the ships whose masts and spars forested the bank of the Delaware. In them they shipped wheat, flour, iron, flaxseed, furs, and lumber to England; beef and beer to Boston (which found Philadelphia porter as good as English); flour, bread, butter, and pork to Charleston, where little food was raised.

Merchants

*The two women on the right are wealthy
and one of them is a Quaker.*

CITY CLOTHES

Philadelphia merchants of the 1780's wore clothes not too different, at first glance, from those of Revolutionary times. Strict Quakers, and many other men, showed no change whatever. They still clung to wigs, perhaps because a wig was preferable to a bald pate. Younger men now wore their own hair, tied in a queue with a narrow ribbon, and they seldom powdered it anymore, unless they were going to a ball. In John Copley's 1782 portrait, John Adams still wears a full-skirted velvet coat with low-slung pocket flaps, just like his grandfather's. But the Adams vest is shorter than the one he wore to the Continental Congress. His juniors now wore much shorter vests, and had the skirts of their "shadbelly" coats cut back sharply in front.

Staid Quaker wives made a point of being about fifty years out of fashion. Their bodices were laced, and their long overskirts, open in front, covered most of a plain but handsome petticoat worn over hoops. The famous Quaker bonnet was still twenty years in the future. Quaker ladies usually wore cloaks on the street (all ladies did), and either a hood or a broad-brimmed beaver hat, tied on with silk cords under the chin.

Queen Marie Antoinette influenced American ladies to suffer a thing called a "head." It was

largely stuffing, with the hair, eked out by some false curls and ribbons, drawn up over it and stuck into place with flour paste. The whole thing was powdered white. The American version didn't tower as high as the Queen's, but high enough to be an uncomfortable nuisance. So elaborate and costly a structure had to be left in place, undisturbed and unwashed, for several weeks. As a covering for the "head," perhaps most worn when it was time to see the hairdresser, a lady could put on a huge ruffled hood. It was called a "Queen's nightcap," though nobody slept in one. It seems to have been favored by mature women. Martha Washington had her portrait painted in one.

Along with this headgear went a dress known as a polonaise. It tended to be quite straight in front, but was extended, sometimes extremely, over a bustle in the back. Like the Quaker lady's, it had an overskirt, but this one was either cut away at the sides, or bunched there into two large panniers. Either way it exposed a large

The Queen's nightcap, and the "head"

area of quilted petticoat. The polonaise featured wide, stiffly pleated bands and ruffles of "taffety." The "heads" soon grew lower and wider, in fact were often replaced by bushy white wigs, on which the ladies perched hugh picture hats, à la Gainsborough. A good many women covered the very low neck of the polonaise with a large white fichu, which grew still larger, and became known as a "bouffant."

Women so elaborately turned out appeared in the streets only in carriages, or sedan chairs, and walked only far enough to cross a sidewalk. They

Philadelphia streets; comfortably prosperous craftsmen in brown or blue wool suits, without wigs, powder, or ruffles, wearing felt hats, simple linen neckcloths, and gray woolen stockings. Their employees, in similar coats of cheaper linsey or corduroy, with flannel for Sundays, usually wore buckskin breeches and wool hats. Their cowhide shoes were fastened, it is said, with leather buckles. No buckle of this material seems to have survived.

LOCAL ENTERPRISES

There were plenty of these artisans. Most of them worked in small shops which tended to cluster together, by trades. In addition to the standard trades, Philadelphia supported highly skilled specialists who needed many well-to-do patrons to survive. The wealthy merchants wanted handsome carriages, fine furniture, elegant silverware, and they could bespeak these in the city along with many other things.

The town's extensive commerce gave Philadelphia artisans a chance to sell in distant ports. So, in addition to the fine work of small shops, enterprises which needed the work of many hands did a booming business. Wissahickon Creek provided pulp water and power for several paper mills. Large tanneries served the leather-breeches makers, whose product was the earliest ready-

did their marketing in plainer outfits. Simpler women, who did all of their errands on foot, couldn't afford to follow French fashions and made no attempt to do so. No towering "heads" on these, and no wigs; they gathered their hair up simply, and covered it with a linen clout, or a close cap. A kerchief covered their shoulders, above an unstiffened bodice. (Grand ladies wore whalebone stays.) The long shift, which a goodwife wore as her basic undergarment, showed only its elbow-length sleeves. Her petticoat missed the ground by six inches or so. She wore neither hoops nor bustle, but she gathered up her overskirt to make panniers of it at the sides. Stout leather shoes, fastened by buckles or latchets, completed a costume which had changed little for years, but which was nearing its end.

The Revolution had put new ideas of equality into people's heads, but it had not wiped out class distinctions. You could still tell a man's social position by a glance at his clothes. Benjamin Franklin, Philadelphia's most prominent citizen, was the exception. In spite of wealth and fame, he still wore the homespun clothes of an artisan. This plainness has led many to assume that he was a Quaker, but he was not, and never had been. Though a deist, he was a member of the Episcopal church.

You would see many dressed like him on

Craftsmen: journeyman, master, and apprentice

made clothing in this country and was in demand in every state. The woolen stockings knitted on foot-powered machines in Germantown were also in demand. Fabric printers and wallpaper printers kept busy; large printshops, like Franklin's, issued newspapers and printed books, and they also sold stationery; a busy cutlery made knives, scissors, and swords.

Mathew Carey published books in Philadelphia. Most were reprints of English works, but he also issued the weird tales of Charles Brockden Brown, this country's first professional novelist. Among the most popular of Carey's books were the biographies of national heroes by Mason Locke Weems, better known as Parson Weems. He was, in fact, an Anglican clergyman, but one with unorthodox ideas which had left him without a church. The parson had a merry eye. His books had enormous vitality and color too, though they concentrated on being good yarns and hang the precise facts. He invented the cherry-tree fable for his biography of Washington. He also dealt with William Penn and Benjamin Franklin, and wrote a small masterpiece about "the Swamp Fox," Francis Marion. Weems had a wife in Bel Air, Maryland, with whom he lived contentedly in the rare moments that he was at home. He drove his battered wagon from New Jersey to Georgia, peddling Carey's books. Redfaced and hearty, he played his fiddle at country weddings, drank wine in mansions, and never missed a horse race. Wherever he was, he sold

Parson Weems

books. He sold his own or Brockden Brown's; he sold John Milton's, and even Tom Paine's *The Age of Reason,* which most clergymen wouldn't touch with tongs.

THINKERS

The mark of Benjamin Franklin was everywhere on Philadelphia. He concerned himself with such practical matters as designing its streetlights, reforming its night watch, starting a fire company, founding an insurance association, and also serving in municipal offices. He promoted the establishment of the Pennsylvania Hospital, the Philadelphia Academy (a high school), and the College of Philadelphia, which later became the University of Pennsylvania. At the suggestion of the great botanist John Bartram, Franklin successfully founded the American Philosophical Society, which spread its influence through the whole country and had a notable group of local members, most of them scientists. Science was then considered a branch of philosophy. Bartram was the first to describe many American plants and he assisted the Swedish botanist Linnaeus in classifying them. David Rittenhouse, astronomer, accurately measured the planets. Thomas Hopkinson, the Society's first president, assisted Franklin's electrical experiments. Thomas Godfrey, a mathematician, invented the double-reflecting quadrant for the use of mariners. His son Thomas, though not a member, wrote the first American play, *The Prince of Parthia,* which was produced at the Philadelphia Theatre in 1767.

Dr. Benjamin Rush belonged to the Society. In addition to signing the Declaration of Independence, he became famous for his courageous efforts to treat the victims of the great yellow-fever epidemic in 1793. Dr. Rush was a serious researcher and an enlightened man, though many of his medical theories now seem preposterous. He thought yellow fever was caused by coffee that had spoiled on the wharves. Joseph Priestley, the discoverer of oxygen, came to Pennsylvania in 1794, after long persecution in England because of his Unitarian ideas.

Ordinary Americans, outside of the learned world, began technical experimentation. In 1784,

56

The Philadelphia stage wagon

Peter Carnes made a hot-air balloon, a copy of one that had succeeded in France. He tethered it to a Baltimore hilltop, sent a boy up in it, and got him down again safely. Three years later, John Fitch demonstrated his first steamboat.

TRAVEL

As the result of an order of Congress, delegates from twelve of the thirteen states began arriving in Philadelphia for a convention early in May 1787. Most of them traveled on horseback. General Washington came in his private chariot, with six horses, as did a few other wealthy men. Some delegates endured miserable journeys in the public stage wagons. Two big horses normally pulled a stage wagon; in bad weather it took four. The nine or twelve passengers sat three abreast on blackless seats which were nothing softer than transverse boards. A canopy top and roll-down curtains protected them from rain. The sturdy

undercarriage of the wagon included nothing whatever to serve as a spring.

Established lines of these wagons advertised their schedules in the newspapers. Two from New York started on the New Jersey shore of the Hudson, and took a day and a half to reach Philadelphia. In good weather, they crossed the Delaware on flatboat ferries and brought their passengers directly to an inn. Few of the convention delegates stayed at an inn longer than the time it took to find lodgings in private houses. Inns were expensive, and even the best of them were noisy. Some of the lines from the South stopped at Newcastle, Delaware, and sent their passengers on to Philadelphia by boat. These passengers had come by boat from Annapolis or Baltimore, and caught the stage at Frenchtown, on the Elk River. Stage schedules paid scant attention to the convenience of travelers. The one for Lancaster left Philadelphia at three-thirty in the morning, and stopped at an inn for breakfast at nine.

Independence Square in 1789

9.
The Constitution

IT WAS intended that the Philadelphia convention should strengthen the Articles of Confederation, chiefly to give Congress the power to regulate trade. But Alexander Hamilton, James Madison, George Washington, and a few others had bolder ideas. They wanted a strong national government. One of the Articles provided that amendments to any of them must be approved by *all* the state legislatures. Most of these legislatures had expressly limited their delegates to amending the Articles. They may have smelled the same rat that Patrick Henry "smelt" when he refused to be a delegate. Two other notables were absent: John Adams and Thomas Jefferson were in France. But the fifty-five active delegates included most of the best minds in America. To mention but a few: along with Hamilton and Madison, there were Benjamin Franklin, Edmund Randolph, George Wythe, Gouverneur Morris, James Wilson, John Rutledge, Elbridge Gerry, William Peterson, John Dickinson, Roger Sherman, with George Washington presiding.

Over the protests of a minority (at least one of whom walked out), these men threw the Articles and their provision for unanimity out the window. Nine states, they said, would be enough to put their "amendments" into effect. It's as well that

they debated in secret. No official minutes were kept and Madison's private notes weren't published until fifty years later. A discreet member went along with old Dr. Franklin to his convivial evenings, to shush him when wine made him a little confidential.

These men have been accused of shaping a constitution that would protect their personal fortunes. It's true that most of them had large financial interests, and owned Continental bonds that Congress had neither power nor money to redeem; it's probably true, too, that most of them tried to place restraints on democracy because they considered it dangerous and unrestrained— perhaps it is; it's even true that they weighed carefully what, to put it bluntly, they could get away with. But on the whole, they were honest men and wise. They produced the best plan for government the world has seen. With a few modifications, including some unsuccessful ones, it has worked for nearly two hundred years, under conditions they couldn't possibly have foreseen. It serves today as a model for the governments of new nations whose very names would have mystified the delegates.

All through a hot summer they wrangled and compromised. The agricultural states, with fewer

58

people than the commercial states, protested that if representation in Congress was based solely on population, they would be always on the losing side. So the population basis was kept for the lower house, but each state got equal representation in the Senate. By far the majority of the delegates favored abolishing slavery. Even so early, they were embarrassed by slavery's contradiction of the great phrase "all men are created equal." Virginia and North Carolina were willing to end the importation of slaves at once, but South Carolina couldn't run her rice plantations without them, and her delegates said a blunt "No!" Again they compromised: Congress could tax imported slaves up to ten dollars a head, but it could not forbid their importation before 1808. Also, weirdly, in counting for representation, a slave would equal three fifths of a man. But notice that Congress could *tax*.

The convention did one thing according to its instructions; it sent its final version of the new Constitution to Congress, but with the recommendation that it be ratified in each state by specially elected conventions—not by the state legislatures, which had had heavy majorities of farmers who wanted no part of the Constitution's strong central government. Both Congress and the legislatures meekly, and rather astonishingly, accepted this. The Constitution itself declared that it would be effective when ratified by nine states.

The arguments in Independence Hall were as nothing compared to the national uproar that followed. At once, everybody was either for or against, a Federalist or an anti-Federalist. Led by Delaware, four states ratified the Constitution as soon as their conventions met. A majority of Pennsylvania's convention favored ratification;

the rest of the delegates, since their votes couldn't win, blocked the vote by walking out and thus preventing a quorum. A Federalist mob seized them bodily and dragged them back. New Hampshire, the ninth state, ratified on June 21, 1788. The fight was won, but the two largest states held out. Virginia quickly accepted the inevitable with reservations, but in New York, with two thirds of the delegates anti-Federalist, the struggle looked hopeless. Alexander Hamilton's newspaper published eighty-five articles, now called *The Federalist,* which he and James Madison and John Jay wrote. They explained and defended the Constitution, and made an impression which has lasted far beyond their time. How much the articles, or Hamilton's speeches, did to change the vote can't be said, but ratification won in the New York convention by three votes.

The Constitution did not provide for a popular vote for President and Vice President. Instead, the state legislatures appointed Electors to do the voting. The people first chose Electors by vote, in some states, in 1824. In a time of slow communications, the Electors served the practical purpose of simplifying the voting. Today we have a fair idea of the winners before we go to bed on election night. Before the introduction of telegraphy, no one could know anything of an election's outcome until the sealed votes of the Electors had been opened in Congress. States remote from the capital waited a couple of weeks more to find out who won.

There was never any question as to who should be the first President. The Electors of every state voted for George Washington. He made a triumphal journey from Mount Vernon to New York City, where he was inaugurated.

Oliver Evans's high-pressure steam engine. Hopefully reconstructed.

10.
Inventions and Factories

TRADE UNDER THE CONFEDERATION

ENGLAND had made a good thing of selling manufactures and reselling her own imports to the American colonies, so as soon as the shooting stopped, in 1783, she set vigorously about getting the trade back. Her ships brought in quantities of everything the Yankees had lacked for seven years, and sold it all to them, regardless of profit, cheaper than the Americans could buy their own products. Metalware, pottery, woolen cloth, calico, tea, coffee, wine—it was all of good quality; it was all familiar; it was all bought up immediately.

This was more pressure than most American enterprises could stand. Many of them were born of the war, and all were paying higher wages than their English competitors paid. Congress, under the Articles, was powerless to help them with import duties. Scores of them quit trying, and a nationwide depression resulted. Other things contributed to it, of course. Merchants and financiers in any one state had difficulty trading and collecting debts in all the others. The lack of a national currency hampered them, and so did the floods of nearly valueless paper money that the states printed. Worse, though there could be no

national import duties, the states now set up trade-restricting tariffs against one another. Yet, in spite of all this, the country's incredible natural resources, and the released energies of men who saw that they could *make* opportunity, rebuilt some prosperity even before the Constitution was ratified.

COTTON CLOTH

The seeds of what we call the Industrial Revolution were sown in Europe in the 1600's, but their first growth showed in England in the 1760's. They found fertile soil there, as England's worldwide commerce created a demand for manufactured goods in greater quantities than the old hand methods could supply. The sea trade itself brought in money to pay for developing new ways and new machines. The English traders could sell cotton cloth anywhere, but all the hand spinners and hand weavers of England, and there were thousands of both, could not supply enough. In 1767, James Hargreaves multiplied the single spindle of the one-thread wheel by eighty-five, with his spinning jenny; and Richard Arkwright hitched a waterwheel to it. England was soon flooded with spun yarn, but her weavers still wove at the old speed. Then, in 1785, the Reverend Edmund Cartwright (he of the too-stiff springs) patented his successful power-driven loom. The Americans heard about these things, but the English guarded the details of them as state secrets. Neither the machines nor any models or drawings of them could leave the island—but the restrictions failed.

Young Samuel Slater got a job in a spinning mill in Derbyshire, England. Deliberately he studied all its methods and every part of every machine. Then, in 1789, he suddenly took his headful of knowledge to the United States. In partnership with a shrewd old Rhode Island Quaker, Moses Brown, and with the help of a carpenter, and a super-blacksmith (whose daughter he married), Slater reconstructed the Arkwright machinery. He spun so much yarn out of West Indian cotton that Brown had to slow him down. As had happened in England, there weren't enough weavers to use it all.

Francis Cabot Lowell went to England in 1811 to find out about power spinning and weaving. He was there two years. He examined all of the most modern spinning machinery, but he was never allowed to see a power loom. Undoubtedly he discussed the loom minutely with men who were familiar with it. When he returned, Lowell enlisted the help of Paul Moody, an expert mechanic, and the two of them started building cotton machinery.

Samuel Slater's soft yarn made good weft, but he couldn't twist it hard enough for warp. In addition to the more modern versions of Slater's machines, which he and Lowell built, Moody invented a successful warp spinner. Then, with no models to guide them, the two designed and built a loom. Its drive, from an eccentrically revolving cone, was so much better than the crank of Cartwright's loom that it eventually replaced the crank everywhere. In 1816, Lowell's mill at Waltham, Massachusetts, spun and wove its first cotton cloth by a completely mechanical process that started with raw cotton fiber. Soon, its machines were turning out four thousand yards of cloth every week.

Much of this cloth became calico when decorative patterns were printed on it. Men in little shops were still cutting the patterns on wooden blocks. They inked a block and pressed it repeat-

61

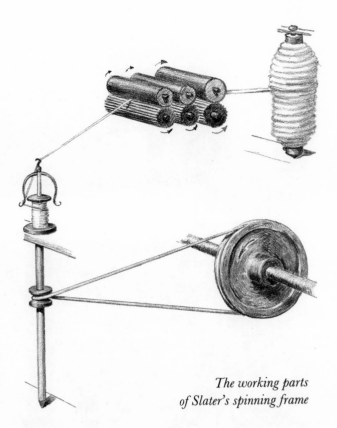

The working parts of Slater's spinning frame

edly on the fabric until the whole surface was covered. In the late 1790's someone succeeded in embossing patterns on a copper cylinder. With this as a roller, calico could be printed in a continuous operation. The quality wasn't as good as that of the old method, but the calico was cheaper.

MANUFACTORIES

Early enterprises, larger than craft shops, were literally manufactories, that is, establishments where things were made by hand. Many started as craft shops and simply grew larger. Each journeyman was able to do every part of the work, and in most factories each actually did every part of it. If a cabinetmaker's business throve, he took on more workers, but each man made a piece of furniture, complete, and then started on a new piece. In a sailmaker's loft, several men might work on a single sail, but each did whatever part of it needed to be done. Forty men might work in a shoe factory, each making one complete shoe at a time.

They might, that is, everywhere except in New England. There, back in 1750, a Welshman named Thomas Adams Dagys had broken shoe-

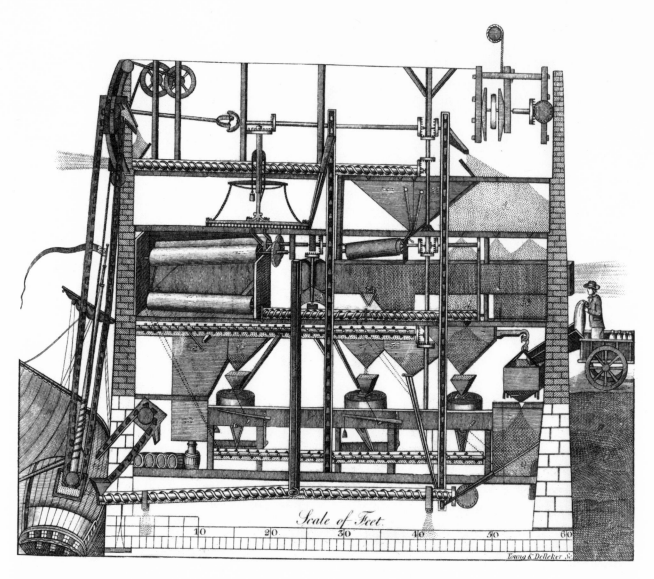

Evans's automatic flour mill. Plate VIII of his The Young Millwright and Miller's Guide, *1795*

making down into parts so that each worker did one part of it only. His idea was widely copied. Only leather cutters and packers worked in the small factory. Local people, who could not successfully have made a whole shoe, came there for piecework, which they did in their homes. Women "bound" uppers, that is, sewed them together; children pasted in linings; men put the soles on, at first by "whipping the cat" (sewing with two threads at once), later, soon after 1800, by pegging the soles to a welt with wooden pegs.

In 1792, by the way, the Philadelphia shoemakers started the first American labor union, and were the first to strike for higher wages. They got away with it the first time, but when they struck again, in 1805, they were tried and found guilty of criminal conspiracy.

THE AUTOMATIC FLOUR MILL

An authentic genius, the Thomas Edison of his time, turned up in Delaware. When Oliver Evans was only twenty-four years old, he built a machine to make wire teeth, for wool cards. These were square paddles covered with leather which was studded with hooked teeth. Both wool and cotton were dragged between two of them to fluff the fibers into slivers for spinning. Up to Evans's time, the teeth had been cut and bent, one at a time, by children. His machine made teeth at the rate of one thousand a minute. He soon taught the device to pierce the leather and set the teeth in it in rows. It could then make 150 pairs of cards a day.

Little is known about some of Evans's inventions. He applied for patents on a water distiller, an ice-making machine, a road scraper, and a wire-drawing machine, but that is all the record says of them.

In 1785, he reached clear into the twentieth century by designing an automated flour mill. It started with his dissatisfaction at the labor needed to move material in his own mill. When he had finished, wheat dumped in at one end was moved mechanically through the whole process, by power taken from a waterwheel, and came out the other end as flour. Its journey was accomplished by conveyors that anticipated nearly all that are used today. He lifted grain with a series of iron buckets fastened to an endless belt. He moved it horizontally on a flat conveyor belt, and also, with what he called a "drill"; this was a belt with cleats across its underside, to push grain through a trough. He also used the Archimedes' screw (a revolving spiral) to move grain horizontally in a half-round gutter, or upward in a wooden pipe.

When George Washington rebuilt his mill on Dogue Creek in 1791, he paid Oliver Evans for the privilege of installing many of these improvements. Apparently Evans's brother went to Mount Vernon to help with setting them up. Many large merchant mills installed the complete equipment. In one of them, Ellicott's Mill, on the Patapsco River in Maryland, it saved thirty thousand dollars a year while grinding 325 barrels a day.

THE HIGH-PRESSURE STEAM ENGINE

When Evans was a boy in Newport, Delaware, a local blacksmith's apprentice created a loud satisfying noise by heating a tightly corked gun barrel with a little water inside. Later, when Evans saw the English Newcomen steam-pumping engine, he was astonished to find that it made no use of this powerful expanding force of steam. Newcomen filled a large cylinder with low-pressure steam, and then created a partial vacuum by condensing the steam with cold water. This allowed some part of the normal atmospheric pressure to push a piston slowly through the huge cylinder. A counterweighted walking beam returned the

piston to its original position. This engine could pump water, but it was useless for anything else.

In the early 1780's, Evans designed a noncondensing steam engine, with a small cylinder in which the expansion of high-pressure steam moved a piston with force enough to do real work. Again, a walking beam did the returning, but Evans hitched it to a crank that rotated a flywheel. In 1786, he petitioned the State of Pennsylvania for a patent on this engine to drive mills and *carriages*. Perhaps it would have been granted if he had stuck to mills alone. As it was, a majority of the legislators assumed he was insane and turned him down. Five years later an Evans engine actually ran a mill.

In 1794 or 1795 a friend took the drawings of the Evans engine to England and showed them to some engineers. Richard Trevithick, who built a high-pressure engine five or six years later, may have seen them, but there was nothing about his design to indicate that he copied Evans's engine. These facts are labored a little here because it has been suggested on our side of the ocean that he did copy Evans, and on the other side of it that the two engines were invented simultaneously.

Evans started his business as an engine builder in 1807, in Philadelphia, and in thirteen years, he made fifty engines. One, probably the largest, he installed in the Fairmount Water Works, which replaced an earlier pump in the heart of Philadelphia that had been powered by a Watt engine from England. Evans's engine had a cylinder twenty inches in diameter; its piston made a five-foot stroke, under the pressure of nearly two hundred pounds of steam. On three occasions, the boiler burst.

Early manufacturers didn't rush into the use of steam engines. In 1812 there were but ten factories powered by steam in the United States. The foothills of the Appalachians are not far from the sea, but the rivers that run through them fall rapidly enough to generate waterpower. It was cheaper than steam in spite of lost time from freezing in cold weather, and the loss could be reduced by housing the waterwheels. Some of the big wheels, thirty feet high and ten feet wide, produced real horsepower. On some streams it was possible to set up half a dozen wheels, one below another, like steps. But in most of the old Northwest Territory streams flow gently. So, as it became populated, many of its new factories turned to steam as the only practical power.

THE *ORUKTER AMPHIBOLOS*

In Philadelphia, in 1804, Williamina Cadwalader wrote: "I have Today seen a waggon go through our Street without Horses—a piece of mechanism that charms me as I look forward to having a carriage that I can wind up and set ago-

Orukter Amphibolos

ing as I do my watch . . ." If, when Mrs. Ridgely received the letter, she thought her niece had slipped mentally, she was wrong. Oliver Evans was at it again. He had built a steam dredge for the city. To get it to the Delaware River, he put wheels under it and belted the power of its Evans engine to them. With what he must have intended as humor, he named the contraption *Orukter Amphibolos* (Greek for "amphibious digger"). Once he got his dredge to the river, Evans took its wheels off and did nothing further about automotive carriages. Incidentally, the dredge propelled itself in the water with a revolving stern wheel, three years before Fulton launched the *Clermont*.

Three or four men built small models of self-powered vehicles in the eighteenth century. The earliest full-size one known to have actually operated was Nicolas Cugnot's three-wheeled steam wagon, in Paris in 1770. In England, Richard Trevithick built two which ran. The first, built in 1801, burned up while he was having a drink at an inn; the second, built in 1803, made eight miles an hour on its ten-foot-high wheels. Evans thus rates third place in the world, and of course first in the United States.

THE COTTON GIN

In the six years between the end of the Revolution and the inauguration of George Washington, South Carolina added cotton to the rice and indigo that had made her planters rich. Water-powered spinning created a demand in England large enough to justify the tedious handwork of removing cotton seeds from the usable fiber. The bulk of the seeds in a boll of upland cotton is twice that of the fiber, which adheres tightly to them, and through which the seeds are scattered. In 1793, a twenty-four-year-old Yale graduate, Eli Whitney, visited a plantation and watched its slaves endlessly cleaning cotton. In ten days he devised a machine that would clean fifty times as much in a day as a slave could clean by hand.

Whitney's "cotton engine," quickly shortened to cotton gin, was operated by a hand crank. The crank turned a wooden cylinder studded with hooked wire teeth which were set in circumferential rows. A mass of raw cotton was dumped against the thin bars of a metal grid. The teeth on the cylinder, passing between the bars, hooked

The cotton gin

the fiber through them but left the seeds behind to fall into a hopper. When the fiber-laden teeth had made a half revolution, they met a rotating brush made with stiff bristles, The brush, turning at higher speed than the cylinder and in the opposite direction, swept the cotton from the teeth and delivered it at the rear of the gin.

Whitney patented his cotton gin, but it was so simple that a glance was all any mechanic needed to copy it. So Eli spent all his profits defending his rights in court. Soon, every cotton plantation had its own gin, and planters were looking for more land to raise more cotton—and for more slaves to hoe it and pick it. Charleston shipped twenty million pounds of it in 1801. Cotton was King, and it fastened the "peculiar institution" of slavery upon the South with a grip that only a bloody, fantastic war could loosen.

MASS PRODUCTION

Eli Whitney didn't stop with the cotton gin. In 1798, he started a gun factory near New Haven, Connecticut, where he made army muskets so accurately that a given part of any one of them would fit any other. This is now commonplace; it was near miraculous then. Thomas Jefferson, who hated factories and believed the United States should be forever an agricultural nation, wrote to John Jay about something of the sort he had seen in France. It is ironically possible that Jay may have passed the idea to Whitney. All modern mass production makes use of interchangeable parts, which began in Whitney's gun factory. Without them we would still be riding behind horses.

The system by which he made them was as important as Whitney's interchangeable parts. Instead of hiring expert gunsmiths he used unskilled labor, and taught each man to do one thing on one gun part. He thus originated what became known in England as "the American system," the base upon which modern industrial production is built. How much he owed to Dagys's shoemaking is open to guess. Whitney preferred men with no mechanical experience because they had nothing to unlearn. He created special machines to help them, and provided

Shaw caplock

gauges to check their work—if the part would fit the opening of the gauge, it would also fit the gun. The micrometer that would measure thousandths of an inch was still seventy years away. Whitney's gauges couldn't have been much closer to absolute accuracy than a hundredth of an inch, but in spite of their limitations, Whitney was able to pile the loose parts of ten muskets on a table in Washington, and assemble ten operating guns from pieces he picked up at random.

While we are speaking of guns: In the 1700's firearms were fired by flintlocks, and for more than half of the 1800's most of them still were. A chip of flint was held in a clamp on the side of the flintlock. Pulling the trigger allowed the clamp to snap forward and down. The flint struck the surface of the frizzen, a curved flange on the edge of the cover of the priming pan, which pan held a little loose powder. The blow simultaneously opened the cover and threw a shower of sparks that ignited the powder. Part of the flash passed through the touch hole, drilled in the side of the gun barrel, and set off the main charge. A flintlock missed fire about once in six tries.

Around the end of the eighteenth century, it was discovered that fulminate of mercury would ignite if it was struck a sharp blow. In 1807, a Scottish clergyman named Alexander Forsyth patented a quite dangerous device that used the phenomenon to fire a gun. In 1816, Joshua Shaw, an English artist living in Philadelphia, perfected his simple percussion caplock. Shaw drilled a steel cone, from top to bottom, and attached it to the side of a musket barrel so that its hole connected with the gun's touch hole. His cup-shaped copper cap, with a little fulminate in it, fitted on the cone. When the gun's hammer struck the cap, flame spurted through the touch hole and fired the charge in the barrel. Basically, this still happens in a modern cartridge. Some soldiers in the Civil War carried caplock muskets, but more of them still used flintlocks.

MACHINE TOOLS

The machine tools Eli Whitney built or modified were run by waterpower. Most of them have disappeared entirely, but his milling machine survives, the first practical one known. Its revolving

*Simon Willard
banjo clock*

Eli Terry pillar-and-scroll

England. Then, over there, Henry Maudslay put his mind to the problem and finished the job in 1818. His machine had changeable gears that would let it cut any kind of thread within the limits of its size. It could be built to handle huge press screws, or tiny screws for watches. So thoroughly did he do his work that, regardless of what or who went before him, Henry Maudslay must be said to have invented the slide-rest lathe.

CLOCKS

Clockmakers worked in this country from the middle of the seventeenth century, casting scrap brass and pewter into disks and small cylinders on which they filed the teeth of gears and pinions. They were strictly handcraftsmen, working in small shops with an apprentice or two. They sold only clockworks and faces. If the customer wanted a case, he had a cabinetmaker build him one. If he couldn't afford a case, he stood his clock on a shelf, high enough to give its driving weights room to descend, and let it run as a "wag-on-the-wall." Perhaps it was the four Willard brothers—Benjamin, Simon, Ephraim, and Aaron—who first tried clockmaking in a hand factory in Boston. By their time, gear-cutting devices had come into use. These could be set to space the required number of teeth around a brass disk, and would cut them accurately when a crank was turned. The Willards made only high-quality clocks—some tall grandfather clocks, but mostly shelf and wall clocks. They sold the smaller kind already cased, and handsomely, particularly Simon's beautiful "banjo" wall clock, which he patented in 1802.

Eli Terry of Plymouth, Connecticut, conceived the idea of mass-producing wooden clockworks with water-powered machinery. It is said that a word from Eli Whitney gave him the idea. He made four thousand sets of thirty-hour grandfather clockworks, with wooden gears and pinions, between 1808 and 1810. He sold these, without cases, for twenty-five dollars each.

Terry's factory aroused much curiosity by using one of the first "round" (circular) saws ever seen in this country. This was an English invention. When Terry realized that only one American

blades cut away metal to a controllable depth on a plane parallel to the machine's flat bed. After the machine had done its work, Mr. Whitney's men probably ground off a little metal from the parts that had to have accurate dimensions.

Most of the machine tools were developed in England, for the same reasons that the textile machinery was developed there. One of the most important was the slide-rest lathe. The operator of an ordinary machine lathe controls the cutting tool by hand to remove metal from a blank which his machine revolves. A slide-rest lathe cuts screw threads, and its rest, which holds the cutter, must advance on another screw at a fixed and predetermined rate, to control the pitch and the uniformity of the spiral thread. The French attempted this in the sixteenth century. In the eighteenth, slow improvements were made on the idea. In the United States, in 1791, Sylvanus Brown built a big lathe to cut the iron screws for sperm-oil presses. Samuel Slater's brother-in-law, David Wilkinson, patented a slide-rest lathe in 1798. He made nothing from it, but thirty years later Congress gave him fifty thousand dollars as an award for his public service. Similar more or less workable thread-cutting lathes were built in

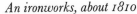

house in ten had a clock in it, he decided to make a clock cheap enough for most people to buy. So he sold his old factory to Seth Thomas, and started a new one to make his patented "pillar and scroll" shelf clock. This would run eight days, and strike with a loud clang. Peddlers sold them for fifteen dollars, complete with case. Demand was so great that Terry licensed Seth Thomas to make them also. Quite a lot of them, from both factories, still keep time, even though their wooden gears have become oval with age.

PIG IRON

Until after 1830 most American blast furnaces, for smelting iron, differed in no way from those of the 1600's. They were almost solid stone structures, about twenty feet square and thirty feet high, with sloping walls. Embedded in each was an egg-shaped chamber called the "bosh." A wide stack allowed hot gases to escape from the top of the bosh, and a much smaller hole at its bottom let molten iron run down into a square crucible, called the hearth. A blast of air, to blow the fire in the bosh, entered through a tapered pipe, just above the hearth. Its inner and smaller end was about four inches in diameter.

An iron furnace always stood at the foot of a

67

high bank, from which a wooden bridge could reach the top of the stack. Men trundled ore, flux, and charcoal across the bridge and dumped them in layers into the bosh. Flux was crushed limestone or oyster shells. The lime in either combined with impurities in the ore to form a glassy slag which could be raked from the surface of the iron in the hearth. The charcoal, of course, was fuel.

Shifts of ironworkers kept the furnace going, night and day, for thirty or forty weeks at a time. About every twelve hours they tapped the hearth by breaking a clay plug, to let the liquid iron flow into "gutters" scraped in the sand floor of the casting shed. Here it cooled into brittle pigs.

By 1775 every colony except Georgia had had ironworks, both blast furnaces and forges. Nearly all were small country enterprises, but even before the Revolution they made more iron than England did. Iron ore had always been melted by heating it with charcoal. The British Isles had run out of wood from which charcoal could be made; the colonies emphatically had not. In the years between 1709 and 1760, a father and son, both named Abraham Darby, succeeded in smelting iron with coke as a fuel. Other English ironmasters were reluctant, or unable, to follow their lead, and many of them shut down. If the English demand that resulted had not pushed American furnaces to producing thirty thousand

tons a year, it is doubtful that the colonists, even with help from the French, could have successfully fought the British army. The British were conscious of this, and they destroyed many furnaces.

All American ironworkers were exempt from military service. They made not only cast-iron cannon and cannon shot, bar iron which gunsmiths beat into muskets, and even a little steel for bayonets and swords, but also such simple necessities as camp ovens and cast-iron cooking pots. Nevertheless, the end of the war found American ironworks behind the times. It was not that they still used charcoal; they continued to use it for years, and charcoal made excellent iron. But the Americans still blew their furnaces with slow-puffing leather bellows, which the English had replaced with double-acting pistons in iron cylinders to deliver more air in a steadier flow. By hitching the new Watt steam engine to the pistons, instead of the time-honored waterwheel, they forced the air higher in the furnace stacks, and thus melted more iron ore in the same furnace.

After 1800 a few American ironmasters began using cylinders and pistons, instead of bellows, to blow their furnaces. They usually made their cylinders of wooden staves, like huge tubs, but they still moved the pistons in them with waterwheels that might take a full minute to make one

revolution. Though an improvement over the bellows because of volume of air and evenness of flow, these cylinders did not deliver the high-rising blast that steam gave to the English furnaces. When ice stopped their waterwheels, American ironworks closed down for the winter, and all hands cut wood for charcoal.

WROUGHT IRON

Forges, sometimes connected with furnaces, converted part of the pig iron into malleable wrought iron. They melted several pigs together in a finery, an open-hearth blast furnace, and workers stirred the melt with iron bars. This removed more slag and burned out some of the carbon. Purifying it raised the melting point of the metal, and it partially solidified into a soft mass. The forgers removed this "bloom," as it was called, from the furnace and "shingled" it with sledgehammers to compact it and to get out more slag. They next put the bloom under a water-powered tilt hammer which dropped its three-hundred-pound head repeatedly on it. The workers held the iron with tongs, and turned it over between blows. What resulted was an odd billet, called an ancony, shaped quite like a dumbbell, though with squared ends and shank. The crew

68

of a second, and similar, furnace, the "chafery," reshaped the ancony into "merchantable bar iron," eight feet long, three inches wide, and an inch and a half thick.

An English act of 1750 forbade the American colonists to increase their processing of bar iron. They went ahead anyway, rolling and slitting as much as they could sell. They often hid new rolling-and-slitting mills under gristmills, taking power from a waterwheel that was ostensibly grinding corn. The rolls and the slitters were commonly mounted near one another on the same pair of shafts, though the power was seldom great enough to allow both to be used at the same time. Established mills which didn't have to hide, often got more power by using two waterwheels turning in opposite directions, one for the upper roll and one for the lower.

All the machinery came out of hiding after the war, and went on working, unchanged, for twenty-five years or more. The four-inch-wide rolls, turning toward each other, flattened hot bars, and elongated them. A "passer" and a "catcher" used tongs to pass a bar between the rolls, time after time. When they had reduced it to a strip a quarter of an inch thick, or less, they could run it through the rotating ring-blades of the slitter and divide it into a dozen or so nail rods. In 1817, a mill in western Pennsylvania imported rolls with a series of progressively deeper grooves in them that could make round rods. In the 1820's there were eight such mills in Pittsburgh, most of them steam powered. Earlier, in 1810, Isaac Pennock installed very wide rolls in his mill to supply the increasing demand for boiler plates. Up to then, American iron could be formed into sheets only by repeatedly beating it with a broad-faced tilt hammer on a large flat anvil.

NAILS

Almost from the discovery of iron, nails were handmade, by tapering one end of a hot iron rod, cutting off a nail's length, and then "upsetting" a head on the cut-off end. A Yankee found a faster and cheaper way. He used big bench shears to scissor slivers off the end of a flat strip of wrought iron. These got the name of cut nails. They were square in section, tapered, and either two or three inches long. They had no heads, but they served well for inside trim, and for holding down floorboards. In 1803, a Mr. Odion invented a foot-operated machine to cut nails like these so fast that they could be sold for only two cents a pound more than the iron cost. The machine's blade cut just slightly off a right angle to the edge of the strip, and the operator turned the strip over after each cut. He had to use hot metal for the three-inch nails; the two-inch ones he could cut cold.

GLASS

A glassblower worked at Jamestown in 1609; and Salem, Massachusetts, had a "glass house" in 1641. Jan Smedes' glassworks, in New Amsterdam, lasted ten years, from 1654. His, and the one Caspar Wistar started in 1740 in New Jersey, and the flamboyant "Baron" Stiegel's factory in Pennsylvania in 1766, were all European glass factories, transported complete. Their craftsmen guarded trade secrets from Americans. Even as late as 1785, the workers in John Frederick Amelung's factory, in Maryland, were German immigrants. They made some of the finest "American" glass. By Amelung's time, though, some men who had learned the trade on this side of the Atlantic were making glass. The Revolutionary War was still being fought when Robert Hewes started his Temple Glass House, up in New Hampshire. Seven years later he moved south and opened the Boston Crown Glass Company to make windowpanes.

Until 1827 all American glass was "hand blown." The blower thrust his long blowing iron (a tube) into the hot furnace and collected a parison, a glob of molten glass. Applying his mouth to the cool end of the tube, he blew the glass into a thick-walled bubble. Reheating at the glory hole as necessary, he could alter the shape of his bubble, elongating it by swinging it, or teasing a neck on it by rolling it on an iron table. When he had shaped it, an apprentice attached a rod, called a punty, to the outer end of the bubble, and the "wetter-off" cut it loose

Crown glass

from the blowing iron with a wet blade. The 'prentice reheated the glass and took it to a gaffer, an expert, who shaped the bubble further with tools and turned it into the wineglass or bottle that it was destined to be. Cheaper bottles and tumblers could be made complete by blowing the glass bubble inside a hinged iron mold.

To make common sheet glass, for windows, the blower elongated his bubble to a somewhat conical shape, which the wet knife halved lengthwise. Flattening the halves on an iron table made sheets of them, but the iron dimmed the luster of the glass. Crown glass, such as Mr. Hewes advertised, was very thin and kept its luster. In spite of showing some wrinkles, called striations, it sold at premium prices. For it, the blower created a large bubble, transferred it to a punty, and then spun it in front of a hot fire with the punty resting in a forked support. As it spun, the bubble flattened, and the hole in it, where the knife cut it from the blowing iron, enlarged. Quite suddenly, with what is described as a fluttering sound, the bubble opened completely, and what had been the hole became the edge of a circular sheet. Still spinning, but backing away from the heat, the sheet was cooled enough to stiffen and hold its shape. It was then tempered, as all glass must be, by being moved slowly through a leer, which is a long annealing oven, hot at one end and cool

at the other. Nine factories are known to have made glass by 1800, two of them west of the Alleghenies in Pennsylvania.

Encouraged by the isolation resulting from the War of 1812, forty-four new glassworks appeared by 1814. Half of them failed in the next year or two, because Britain revived her old tactics and dumped glassware at prices below cost. It was good stuff and Americans snapped it up. Congress rushed to the rescue with high tariffs on imported glass, which did little good until about 1820.

Soon after that a glassworker named Robinson invented a machine that would press glass into shape in molds without any blowing. It was perfected with the help of a remarkable man, Deming Jarves, the manager of the Boston and Sandwich Glass Company's factory on Cape Cod. Jarves encouraged every man in his plant to experiment. He also paid good wages for a forty-hour week, and continued to pay them full-time through the frequent depressions. All other employers *knew* Jarves was insane. You worked men seventy-two hours a week, and you fired them as soon as demand slackened. Incidentally, Jarves's factory

was among the earliest to be powered by steam.

It was good manners at this time to cool one's tea or coffee by pouring a little at a time from the cup into the saucer. You drank from the saucer, extending the pinkie of your right hand to show how elegant you were. But the wet cup had to go somewhere, and not, heaven knows, on the white linen tablecloth, so a fancy little

70

plate was provided. The Sandwich works made many kinds of glassware, but its most famed product is these cup plates, their underside crowded with raised lacy patterns to yield a satisfactory sparkle. The central feature of the design was often patriotic—an eagle, or a portrait of a national hero. The plates sold at retail for five cents each; frequently they came free with half a pound of tea. Today, you will be lucky if you can buy one for ten dollars; the rare patterns run into hundreds of dollars.

COAL

Near Pottsville, Pennsylvania, Philip Ginter built a fire up on Mauch Chunk one day in 1791 and "set fire to the mountain," not just the dead leaves and underbrush but the hill itself. Philip had found "stone coal," as they called anthracite then. But finding it wasn't selling it. Coal, however well it burns when hot, ignites less readily than wood or charcoal, and people were chary of it. Blacksmiths covered their prejudice against the stuff with objections to rebuilding their forges, to put grates in them. Coal demanded grates in fireplaces and stoves, too, so householders stuck to wood. Even Oliver Evans, after experimenting with coal on a grate, seems to have dropped it there.

Of nine wagonloads hauled to Philadelphia, as late as 1812, only two were sold. Josiah White and Erskine Hazard bought those two to try in the furnace of their wire mill. They poked at the coal, and peered in at it every other minute, but they couldn't make it catch fire. Disgusted, they slammed the furnace door and left. An hour later one of their workmen found such a fire as that furnace had never held before—the cast-iron doors were red hot.

Hazard and White knew they had something. They leased Mauch Chunk Mountain and went into the coal business. By 1820 they were selling coal in Philadelphia for $8.40 a ton. Their mine was high on the mountainside, so they built a road to get the coal down to the Lehigh River by gravity. The mules that pulled the empty wains back up the hill rode down in them with the coal, at fifteen miles an hour. This made them sick; nevertheless, after one ride, they refused to walk down, so the management slowed up the wains. Scows brought the coal as far down the Lehigh as Allentown. From there it traveled overland in wagons. The company deepened the channel in the river, and built sluice gates, known as "bear traps," to catch enough water to float its scows in dry spells. In 1829, the new Lehigh Canal, paralleling the river, carried the coal all the way to Easton. Three years later another canal took it on to Philadelphia.

Sandwich glass cup plate

11.
Money and Some Foreign Affairs

TO ESTABLISH American credit at home and abroad, Alexander Hamilton wanted Congress to pay off not only fifty million dollars' worth of Confederation bonds, which had been issued to pay for the Revolutionary War, but also twenty million in bonds issued by the states to pay for confiscated Tory property. Hamilton also wanted Congress to charter and support a central Bank of the United States. He was a Federalist; he believed in encouraging industry and commerce, and in a strong central government, run by men of affairs. His constant opponent was Thomas Jefferson, who favored an agricultural nation, with strong state governments, controlled by the votes of the common people.

The Constitution authorized the establishment of a national capital, but made no mention of its location. Jefferson, who never forgot he was a Virginian, urgently wanted the capital to be on the Potomac River. Neither man could be sure of persuading Congress against the opposition of the other, so they privately traded support for

support. Hamilton got his redemption and his Bank, Jefferson his southern capital. The two agreed that the government should move to the District of Columbia in 1800, and that Philadelphia—not New York, which had expected the honor—should serve as the temporary capital until then. Congress concurred.

Most people had given up all hope that their Revolutionary bonds would ever have any value. Speculators, gambling that they might be worth something, had bought up sheaves of them for pennies. The cities heard a rumor of redemption before the rural areas did, and agents with bags of real jingling cash rushed to the country to buy all the bonds they could find. James Madison made a strong effort in Congress to get at least part of the payoff for the original owners, but his motion was defeated. Possibly it was because many congressmen were buying bonds as heavily as their credit would let them.

One of the speculators who profited enormously by redemption was perhaps the gaudiest character in American history. He was a glover by trade, with a little shop in Newburyport, Massachusetts. No one has explained where Timothy Dexter got the money to buy his hoard of securities, but there is no doubt that he had it. He became wealthy overnight, and immediately went to extremes to display the fact. He "ennobled" himself as "Lord Timothy Dexter of Newburyport, Earl of Chester, first in the East, first in the West, and the Greatest Philosopher in the known World." He rode in a coach with six horses and outriders, built a mansion, and filled its grounds with painted wooden statues of all his heroes. Withal, he was a shrewd bold merchant, and there was always about him the wry suggestion of a tongue in the cheek.

The bonfires that celebrated the United States' first president were hardly cold when the country thrilled to the news of the French Revolution. Here were brothers, doing what we had done. Even the removal of King Louis's head, and the subsequent Reign of Terror, failed to shake the faith of most Americans in *"Liberté, Egalité, Fraternité."* The Anti-Federalist Party began to call itself the Republican Party. The name was its only resemblance to the present Republican party.

When the French beheaded their king, England and Spain declared war on them, and President Washington announced the neutrality of the United States. Federalists favored England; Republicans favored France. The English navy stopped American ships at sea in an effort to keep supplies out of France. At the same time, French privateers preyed on American ships. France was furious because the United States wasn't fighting on her side, in accordance with the 1778 Treaty of Alliance. But George Washington was a Federalist; he and his cabinet held that the treaty wasn't made with Republican France. When John Adams became President, in 1796, he sent a commission to Paris to try to calm things down. Talleyrand, the French foreign minister, demanded a loan of $250,000 as the price of merely negotiating. Charles C. Pinckney replied, "Millions for defense, Sir, not one cent for tribute." The United States echoed his words, sang the new song "Hail Columbia," and started building the six strongest frigates in the world. The war that almost happened evaporated in

1800, because Napoleon Bonaparte, who had become First Consul, turned his attention elsewhere.

The Bank of the United States was founded, in part, with government money, to serve as a stabilizer for the nation's weird finances. Banks were not new. Something called "The Fund at Boston," which worked like a bank, had been established in 1681. Just a hundred years later, Robert Morris started his own private bank in Philadelphia, calling it, rather grandly, The Bank of North America. It proved useful in re-establishing commerce and industry in the city. The states started chartering other private banks, which in turn started printing paper money, known as "bank notes." The banks were supposed to redeem these, on demand, for their face value in metal. All banks printed more notes than they could have redeemed even if they had had all their assets in cash, which they never did. The more solid ones backed their issues with mortgages and promissory notes, seldom readily collectible. "Wildcat" banks often had little more than ambition and a willing printer. As a result bank notes, like Continental currency, had more bulk than value. But, up to the point where panic started and everybody suddenly demanded redemption, few people bothered about the worthlessness of the paper.

One purpose of the Bank of the United States was to issue notes, backed by solid metal in the vaults, that would be actually redeemable, and hence would keep their face value. The Bank also took in the notes of state banks, and frequently demanded their redemption. This, though sound practice, disturbed many people, especially bankers and mortgagees, who wanted things left alone to work themselves out.

The shortage of currency continued to be a heavy drag on American business, above all, the shortage of small coins, which had been chronic

Copper cent, 1792, actual size

73

for 140 years. As colonies, Massachusetts, Maryland, and New Jersey had all issued coins. Massachusetts actually stamped her own "N.E." and "tree" coins. Six of the new states issued coins between 1776 and 1788. Most of these were cents, with a few half cents. Even the Confederation Congress coined pennies. In 1787 it ordered three hundred tons of them, supposedly stamped from the copper hoops of powder kegs sent over by the French for the Revolution. Collectors call these coins "Fugio cents"; on their face appears a sundial with the word *Fugio,* "I fly," plus the inscription "Mind your business." Abel Buell, who had once done time for counterfeiting, engraved the dies.

As Secretary of the Treasury, Alexander Hamilton made a thorough coinage survey. He issued a permit for the continued circulation of foreign coins (they circulated until 1857). On the Secretary's recommendation, Congress authorized a mint in Philadelphia which, though now in a new building, is still there. Its first coins were issued in 1792: a silver half disme (five cents), a disme (dime), a large copper cent, and a curious small copper cent which had a plug of silver in it, to bring its actual metal value up to its face value. The silver dollars that the mint issued two years later had more silver in them than the Spanish silver dollar had. So anyone who got one kept it, and the coins failed to serve their purpose. Congress stated officially that an ounce of gold was worth fifteen ounces of silver, but it was actually worth more than that, so the first gold coins vanished entirely.

Continental bond

Copper
Fugio cent

Small bank note

Silver disme

front

back

Silver dollar. "HUNDRED CENTS, ONE DOLLAR OR UNIT" *was stamped on the edge of the coin.*

12.
Turnpikes and Travel

BY REVOLUTIONARY times some trade moved by road on short hauls, and it would have been possible for a foolhardy wagoner to "jag" a load from Boston to Savannah. But for almost twenty years after 1776, there was no paved road in this country, except for some streets in the larger towns. By then wagoners, hardy but not foolish, were hauling three-ton loads from Philadelphia to Pittsburgh at a hundred dollars a ton. The road they used had been cleared by Colonel John Forbes through western Pennsylvania, to reach the French at Fort Duquesne.

In the North, in winter, people preferred to travel and haul on runners, because snow made the roads smoother. They sometimes found themselves stranded by a sudden thaw. In 1796 (it must have been in early spring) one stage wagon took five days to get from Philadelphia to Baltimore, about a hundred miles. On such journeys the stage frequently upset, and the surviving passengers had to help to set it on its wheels again. Horses were reported as being mired belly-deep. When all else failed, passengers proceeded on foot to the nearest shelter, as the Father of His Country once did on a trip to New York. Even as late as 1800, Mrs. Abigail Adams, going to join her husband in Washington, found the road so bad

south of Baltimore that her coachman, detouring around morasses, lost it entirely.

POSTAL SERVICE

In 1800 there were but a thousand post offices in the United States. Mail arriving at one of them by coach or by post rider was held until the addressee called for it. Rural mail and mail for small villages with no post office was left at a store or an inn. Though a correspondent could pay in advance, and have his letter marked "postpaid" and autographed by the postmaster, few did so. No stamps existed. Up until 1847 an addressee commonly paid the postage when he received the letter. The cost was about twenty-five cents for a single sheet, twice that for two sheets. Actual weight was not considered, but distance increased the postage. Apparently a storekeeper would have had to pay for a left letter and hope to collect. After 1810, the writer could use a steel pen instead of a quill. He merely addressed the letter, with no return information, and gave it to the postmaster. There were no stamps or postal cards. The letter had no envelope. The sheet, about eleven by fourteen inches, was folded twice and

twice again, and was held that way with a blob of sealing wax. The elegant impressed the hot wax with an engraved seal. The inelegant wetted a gelatin disk, called a wafer, and used it for glue.

TURNPIKES

In 1792, the State of Pennsylvania chartered the Philadelphia and Lancaster Turnpike Company. This was a private corporation which sold its stock to the public for thirteen dollars a share. It was snapped up, partly because stockholders were not held responsible for the company's debts. This was a new idea which was quite generally thought to be an unfair privilege. The sixty-two-mile road that the company completed in 1795 was called a turnpike because the swinging gate that stopped travelers at each tollhouse was a long pole much like the pikes then used to raise the frames of houses. To the shareholders, these gates, which the public paid to have opened, were the important thing about the road; but to the public the important thing was that the road was graded and paved over its full length. This early turnpike paving was not macadam, as some writers have asserted. It was gravel spread over a foundation of sizable stones, to "support" the wheels of vehicles. The foundation stones either sank in mud, leaving a wallow, or were forced to the surface by traffic. John McAdam didn't publish his system until 1819. All of his stones were the same size, about as big as walnuts. He spread them in a thick layer, and shaped its surface to shed water. Keep the earth dry, he said; dry earth will support any load. Americans, having seen much evidence that wet earth would not, were easily converted.

The Lancaster pike pleased everybody, including its stockholders. By 1801, sixty-six turnpike companies had charters. Enthusiasm blinded a few of them, and they built turnpikes where traffic was too thin to support them. There exists today a meandering country road that links two much larger highways. It may carry fifty cars a day. It was never much more important than it is now, but old maps call it a turnpike.

Company charters specified toll rates, based on gates at ten-mile intervals. Rates varied somewhat from state to state. The pikes were free to church-goers; to doctors and midwives; and to anyone taking grain to a mill, or a horse to a blacksmith. Average tolls for ten miles ran about like this: one man on horseback, six and a half cents; a one-horse chaise, twelve and a half cents; a carriage with two horses, twenty-five cents, with four horses, thirty-seven and a half. Twenty driven cattle cost a quarter for ten miles; twenty sheep or hogs, half as much. If a freight wagon's tires were as narrow as four inches, its driver paid twelve and a half cents per horse. Wider tires cost less, on the theory that they damaged the roadbed less. In winter and spring, the weight limits of loads were governed by tire widths. This tire business seems to have been largely theory; a turnpike supervisor reported never having seen a tire wider than four inches. Many farmers resented paying toll. They "built," with their wheel ruts, shun-pikes around the toll houses. These were illegal, and users of them were fined if they were caught.

The turnpikes promoted roadside inns which became far more important to their local neighbors than motels are now. They served as clubs. They provided entertainment, news, gossip, discussion, and a place to trade. Travelers who stayed at them slept in any bed that had an empty space in it, but they were well fed. The innkeeper was a man of substance. Often he was the local magistrate and also an officer of militia; possibly he also sat in the state legislature. He didn't hesi-

tate to expel from his house any guest whose manner displeased him, as one guest, who later became the King of France, found out. This was Louis Philippe, Duke of Orléans. He and two younger brothers stopped at an inn in Winchester, Virginia. The boniface, Mr. Bush, welcomed them cordially. But when the Duke asked to have dinner served in their room, Mr. Bush became enraged: if they were too good to eat with his other guests, they were too good to stay in his house.

COVERED BRIDGES

Ferries were not only nuisances, they were also dangerous. In rough weather they often upset or sank, drowning people and horses. When they were near large towns—and almost all such had rivers to cross—the ferries created bottlenecks. The great rivers, the Hudson and the Delaware, were too wide and deep to be crossed by any bridge that could be built at the time, but smaller streams, like the Charles at Boston, offered better possibilities. In 1786, the Charles was, in fact, bridged on piles driven into the river bottom. Shortly after that, Philadelphia paralleled Grey's Ferry, across the Schuylkill, with a crude bridge of floating logs. It could be used for equestrians and foot passengers only, and could be drifted aside to allow boats to pass. It didn't survive long, and was replaced by what was called the Permanent Bridge. Timothy Palmer built it. He had been a shipfitter in Newburyport, Massachusetts. It was a fine bridge. Three arched wooden spans rested on stone piers that raised them high enough to clear the masts of small sailboats. Sometimes early bridges, taking off from low riverbanks, arched so high to clear masts that it was a feat to get a vehicle over them. The third Schuylkill bridge, the "Colossus," 1811, leaped the river with a single arch 340 feet long. It lasted twenty-seven years, and then burned. The Colossus was the first American covered bridge, but nearly all of its many descendants were flat spans.

With the exception of stone ones, all bridges at this time were wooden, and moisture would rot them. The sole reason for putting a roof and sides on a bridge was to keep its timbers dry. Stripped of its shingle and weatherboard skin, a covered

77

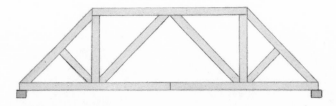

Queen post truss

bridge is revealed as a truss construction. A truss is a long frame stiffened by diagonal braces. The supporting sides of a covered bridge were such frames, made of heavy timbers bolted together. These trusses permitted spans far greater than the length of one log, or of several. Some existing covered bridges have spans well over a hundred feet long, supported only at their ends. In 1812, a truss bridge more than a mile long crossed the Susquehanna. Each of its twenty-eight connected spans stretched two hundred feet between stone piers built in the river.

Covered bridges soon crossed rivers in every part of the United States, including the new territories in the West. Private citizens built and owned many of the early ones, and charged toll. Vibration was bad for wooden bridges, so most of them had signs reading "Walk your horses." All covered bridges were dimensioned to let a load of hay pass through them. That was big enough. In that leisurely age, no one minded one-way traffic on a bridge. There is something oddly pleasant about driving a horse through the echoing tunnel of a covered bridge, something that has nothing to do with sentiment or quaintness.

RIVER TRAFFIC

Most of the turnpikes ran from river to river, as the Lancaster pike did; those that paralleled the flow did so only where the streams were too small to float cargo. Where large rivers ran, traffic on

Keelboat

them continued to be heavy. On the Hudson in the late eighteenth century, sloops ninety feet long brought barreled flour to Manhattan directly from the mill doors, where forty feet of water allowed them to berth. On the Delaware, until canals and railroads took over, a fleet of several hundred "Durham boats" moved freight north of Philadelphia. Sixty feet long, and but eight wide, these boats were originally built to move iron downriver from the Durham Iron Furnace, forty miles upstream from Trenton. When they multiplied as general freighters, more than two thousand men worked at poling them upstream, and guiding them down again through the rapids. The Durham boats earned an honored place in American history. It was they that on Christmas night in 1776 ferried Washington's soldiers across the river to take Trenton. Emanuel Leutze put the wrong kind of boat in his famous painting.

Logs floated down the Susquehanna as long rafts. Even in the far South, slaves guided big flatboats called "cotton boxes" down the sluggish currents of the Ashley and the Cooper to Charleston. But, because of their length and the great tonnage they carried, the Ohio and the Mississippi led all other rivers. In their part of the country in the early 1800's, roads were mere trails—"traces," as people called them—so nearly all passengers and freight traveled by water. After 1790, families with all their goods drifted down the Ohio in an unending flotilla. The swelling population of Ohio and Kentucky and Tennessee weren't sitting

on their hands. By 1800, hundreds of men had cleared farms and were raising more on them than their families needed. To ship the surplus upstream by poleboat and then back East by wagon was absurd. They built flatboats and floated the surplus down to New Orleans, where they sold both the cargoes, and the boats. The boatmen had a choice then; they could walk home along the Natchez Trace, or they could get jobs on keelboats, helping to pole them upstream.

A keelboat was long and narrow. A "house" to cover cargo took up most of its deck but left narrow cleated walkways on both sides for the polemen. A poleman carried his "settin' pole" forward on the deepwater side, crossed over, set his pole against the bottom, and walked the boat under him, crossing back at the stern. In front of the cargo house a stumpy mast held a square sail, useless in a head wind. Back aft, the "p'troon" (captain) steered with a tiller. The keelboat's cargo was much the same as that which the gundalows took upstream in the East, but it came from "N'awl'ns."

LOUISIANA

The French settled New Orleans in 1718. The Spanish got it, and all of the French claims west of the great river, at the end of the Seven Years War. Then in 1800 Napoleon glared at Spain, and she secretly surrendered the whole business.

78

Whoever held New Orleans controlled the Mississippi. The Spanish had amiably allowed Americans free trade through the port. Napoleon now proposed to close the river. This was a blow to the westerners because Marietta and Pittsburgh were now building seagoing vessels, and shipping cargoes not only to east-coast seaports but also to Europe. An Ohio River sea captain reported the incredulity of a British harbor master when the captain registered his ship's "impossible" home port, a thousand miles from the sea.

There was consternation in Washington, where Thomas Jefferson had begun his presidency in 1801. The West was out of touch with the nation, and its new wealth was draining down the Mississippi, instead of comforting eastern merchants. There was even danger of losing the West entirely. The President made the first move. He sent James Monroe to Paris to buy New Orleans. Monroe and Robert Livingston, our minister to France, could hardly speak when the French foreign minister Talleyrand offered to sell them not only the city, but *all* of Louisiana with it. That was about two thirds of all of the land west of the Mississippi. The two Americans had no authority to buy that much, but they had vision and courage; they grabbed the bargain for fifteen million dollars. It is highly improbable that Jefferson could have guessed that they would do that; but several months before Monroe left Washington, Jefferson had organized the Lewis and Clark expedition, to explore the Far West.

79

THE GREAT ROAD

New Orleans and Louisiana vastly enlarged the American West but did little to tie the westerners to the East; they could still sell, and more important, buy, downriver. The need was to put the two areas in closer touch with one another. So in 1806 Congress authorized a good road between them. Some said the government had no constitutional right to build a road, especially a toll road, but it built one anyway, and after it was in use the Supreme Court decided it was legal.

The National Road, at first called the Cumberland Road, ran from Baltimore to the Ohio River at Wheeling. Later, beginning in 1825, the road crept farther westward, across Ohio and Indiana. By then it had served its purpose of knitting together the two parts of the country.

Work began in 1808 and the improvement of an old road from Baltimore to Cumberland was finished by 1814. Beyond Cumberland a new road followed General Braddock's track, turning northwest into Pennsylvania about ten miles short of the western edge of Maryland. From a place called Redstone Old Fort, now Brownsville, a branch followed the Monongahela River to Pittsburgh. The first stagecoach reached Wheeling in August 1817.

It's startling to read that stumps, up to eighteen inches thick, were left standing in the roadbed, "rounded and trimmed so as to present no serious obstacles to carriages." This was supposed to be a good road, and compared to what is replaced, it was. The cleared right of way was topped with an inch of crushed stone covered with gravel. Milestones and tollgates were iron. Stone bridges spanned all streams. At Wheeling, a ferry crossed the Ohio to connect with Zane's Trace. Most people, and most goods, took to riverboats at Wheeling, and by 1817 a few of those were steamboats.

An epic waits to be written about the stream of life on the National Road. Most of it flowed at the slow pace of laden Conestoga wagons, of sorefooted wayfarers, of herded animals; but the scheduled stagecoaches, changing their four horses every twelve miles, barreled along steadily, day and night, at five miles an hour. These were real coaches, with padded seats and springs. Each one had its name painted on it, and its driver was a personage. Some of the more dramatic ones, like Montgomery Demming, who weighed nearly five hundred pounds, were famous in the East and the West.

People said that all America seemed to be moving west. Dominated by the coaches and the great six-horse freight wagons, vehicles of all descriptions crowded the Road: farm wagons carrying families and all they owned; chaises driven by businessmen; pushcarts trundled by those who could buy no wagon; even wheelbarrows. Droves of steers, pigs, horses, and mules, going east to market, sometimes crowded even the lordly stagecoaches off the road. People who made the trip remembered for their lifetimes its noises and its smells.

Migrating families usually camped at night on the cleared strips by the wayside. More prosperous travelers put up at inns. These were of two classes: the staging inns, where the coaches changed horses (in one minute flat) and where "Old Monongahela" whiskey cost five cents a glass; and the wagon inns, for the freighters, which sold drinks at three cents, two for five. In the first kind, a guest might hope for at least half a bed; in the second, he rolled in his own blanket, as at The George Washington in Benson Town, and slept on the floor of the public room with his feet to the fire.

Gideon Chestnut's shipyard

13.
The Seafarers
and the Countinghouse

SHIPBUILDING

THE little ship John Winthrop built on the Mystic River near Boston in 1631, *The Blessing of the Bay*, must have been the heaviest vessel of her size ever known, and the toughest—she was built entirely of locust wood. Otherwise she is notable only as the first of many American ships. Until well after the Civil War, every seaport on the Atlantic coast built wooden ships. They were also built in little coves where there was no port, and on the banks of rivers so narrow that a launched vessel ran clear across the stream and had to have her stern dug out of the mud on the other side. Timber had become scarce in England, so ships could be built cheaper here than there. Shortly before the Revolution a third of the British merchant fleet was American-built. This overseas trade didn't revive quickly after the war, and didn't reach anything like its old level until the big clipper ships appeared in the 1850's.

In the Confederation period the largest ships were built in Philadelphia, the fastest on the Chesapeake Bay, the greatest number in Massachusetts. New England merchants hedged their risks by trusting their ventures to several small craft rather than to one large one. The largest merchantman out of Salem was only about 125 feet long, and the ships that town sent to China were seldom more than 100 feet. This was partly because Salem harbor was too shallow to float larger ones. Also, a superstition claimed that a too large hull would break in two in a heavy sea.

THE LAUNCH OF THE *ALICE*

Things are stirring in the small shipyard of Gideon Chestnut, at the edge of Standish village, on this bright September day. Since early April, Mr. Chestnut's shipwrights have worked on the hull of the brig *Alice,* designed for the West Indies trade, and she stands now on the ways, ready to be launched.

The yard is a cluttered lot lying between the Shore Road and the harbor, giving off pleasant smells of new lumber and tar—not asphalt but good pine tar. The clutter is largely wood: timbers in piles; timbers on blocks for shaping; two-inch planks, piled and also scattered; short pieces of all dimensions, cut off and left lying; and chips everywhere. The whole place is paved with chips: bright, golden new chips scattered and heaped over gray weathered chips.

Two sheds for supplies stand near the road and a third is on the fitting dock (it is a wharf, really) that extends a hundred and fifty feet into the

Hanson's ropewalk

harbor. Once afloat, the *Alice* will be moored there to receive her finishing touches, and the complex rigging that will support and control her sails. Two sets of stocks, with their "feet in the water," slope up the bank from the harbor. They look very much like extremely wide railroad tracks. The completed hull stands on one of them; on the other, between the *Alice* and the fitting

dock, is the newly laid keel of a small sloop. Her stem and sternpost stand at the keel's ends, propped upright. Windlasses for raising timbers on tripod derricks are set up alongside the stocks wherever they are needed. Between the stocks stands the long wooden steam box, with its brick-enclosed boiler beside it. The shipwrights soften planks in it so that they can bend them to fit the curves of a hull. Thick curved timbers, like stems and frames (ribs), are shaped from several straight pieces and scarfed together. Pieces with short radii, like the knees that support deck timbers, are hewn from wood that grew crooked naturally.

The resemblance of the stocks to railroad tracks comes from the long timbers laid, like railroad ties, side by side to form an inclined plane. These are the foundation on which a ship is built. The new sloop's keel is pegged to the stocks with temporary treenails. The shipwrights have now pulled the treenails from the *Alice*'s keel. They have also laid wooden rails on the stocks, and have built a cradle under the hull, conforming to its curves. The cradle rests on the rails and will slide on them when it is released. The men have removed all of the many shores, long and short, that propped the hull, and now only the cradle keeps it from falling over sideways. Two props, called dog shoes, prevent the cradle from sliding too soon. All these things were done yesterday, and the men who built the *Alice* got their first good look at their handiwork—no greyhound of the sea, small but sturdy and competent—brave, with her black tarred planking and the bright yellow band from stem to stern below her bulwarks. Mr. Seth Whitman, Standish's one rich merchant and benevolent dictator, who will own the *Alice,* wanted her to have carrying capacity.

Tupper's sail loft

Caleb Somers's forge

So she has a broad U-shaped bottom and a round "apple" bow. Her beam is somewhat more than a quarter of her length. Speed is secondary. If she makes nine knots with the wind behind her, Mr. Whitman will think her fast.

This morning the workmen have raised the rails an inch or so off the stocks by driving wedges under them. Doing so, they have lifted the cradle and the hull too. The brig's keel is now clear of the stocks, and all her weight is supported by the cradle. The men have also greased the top surfaces of the rails with tallow and soft soap, and have carefully suspended the two weights that, falling, will knock down the dog shoes and allow the cradle to slide.

All the while that the carpenters were shaping timbers with broadax and adz and bolting them together, and bending planks and pegging them to the frames, other Standish citizens have been at work on the *Alice*. Four of Job Williams's looms have woven hemp into canvas for her sails; and now sailmakers in Tom Tupper's loft are cutting those sails and sewing them together. In Nathan Hanson's ropewalk, a shed three hundred feet long, his men are spinning the marline, and laying the last of the ropes and cables for the *Alice*'s rigging. Caleb Somers's smiths have finished all her metal fittings, and now, working with two fires and two derricks, are shaping and welding her heavy anchors.

But none of these shops is working this morning. Along with everybody else in Standish who can walk, the workers are in the shipyard to see

the launching; some three hundred people have gathered. Mr. Whitman has set up free rum for all comers. His special guests are drinking punch, Madeira, and French brandy. These guests include Mr. Henry Wilkins, the Boston merchant who acts as Mr. Whitman's agent there. Mr. Wilkins's arrival yesterday, in his scarlet chariot drawn by four black horses, created almost as much stir in Standish as today's launching. His hat, too! Standish has never seen one like it. It is stiff and shiny, with a tall crown. The Reverend Tobias Small, minister of the Congregational church, is present, and so is the whole Board of Selectmen, with their wives. All of the master craftsmen whose shops have contributed to the *Alice* are guests, clinging together and watching their manners. Captain Lemuel Tilbury, who will command the brig, is there, and so, of course, is Gideon Chestnut, who looks frequently at his thick watch and tries to conceal his nervousness. Accidents can happen; ships can stick on the ways. . . .

The more important men have spoken at some length, using rather high-flown language and many classical quotations. The watch in Mr. Chestnut's perspiring hand shows less than a minute to noon as the Reverend Tobias concludes his prayer for the success and safety of the *Alice* and commends her to the care of God. As the chorused "Amen" dies away, Gideon Chestnut shouts:

"Stand by!"

The crowd stops breathing. Then:

"Ho!"

Two sharp axes, swung in unison, cut the ropes. The falling weights knock down the dogs. . . . For an instant there is silence. Then a creaking, and a slight movement.

"I name thee *Alice*," Peg-leg Duckett yells, as he smashes a bottle of rum on the stem. As the oldest sailor in the village, Peg-leg is automatically the sponsor. Very slowly the brig moves away from him, but quickly gathers speed, and rushes down the incline. The rails smoke and the cradle bursts into flame. Everybody, from Mr. Wilkins down to the smallest urchin, shouts. With a great splash, the *Alice* plunges into the little harbor and floats away, stern first.

Two longboats lying in wait catch lines thrown from the vessel's deck, and a dozen straining oars slowly check her speed. As the crowd drifts home

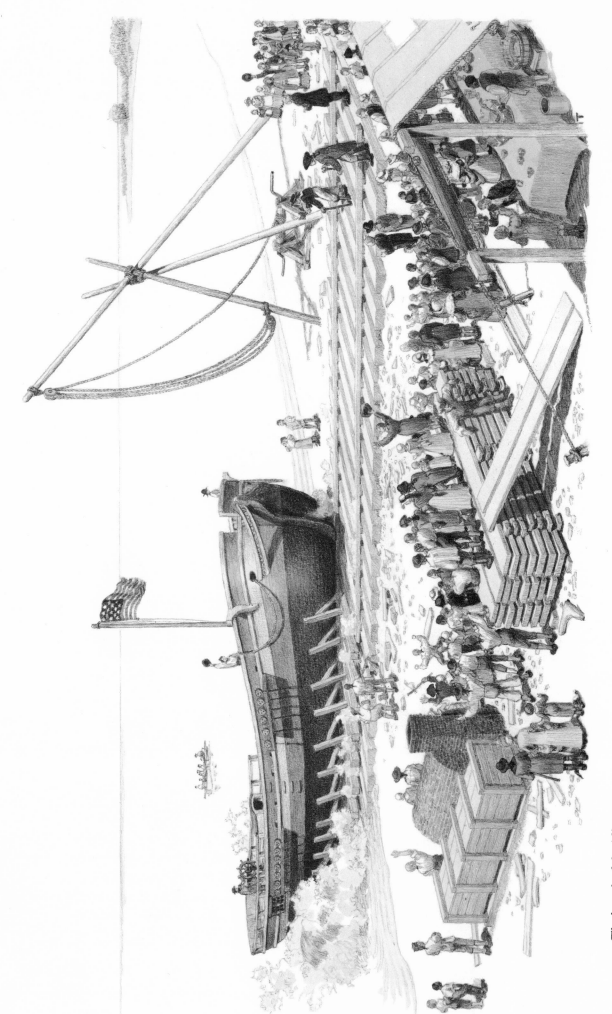

The launch of the Alice

for dinner, the rowers start moving the brig, almost imperceptibly, toward the fitting dock. It will take them a couple of hours to get her there.

SAILING VESSELS

The full-rigged ship was best for long voyages where the square sails could be set in the trade winds and left untouched for days. Except for the jibs and the little steering sail at the stern, called the spanker, all the sails on a ship were square and were set athwartship on three masts. Only a craft so rigged could properly be called a ship. Square sails could not be furled or unfurled from the deck. Men had to stand on footropes aloft and "hand" them, so a square-rigger needed a large crew.

Schooners have been mentioned earlier. The type evolved in New England: a small vessel that a few men could handle in shallow waters and in narrow harbors; a boat for the coasting trade but also sturdy enough for the open sea. The schooners of the time we are considering had but two masts, and normally all their sails were set fore-and-aft, behind the masts and parallel with the keel. Such sails can be raised and lowered from the deck. In later years big ships, called schooners, were given five, six, and even—in one case—seven masts. The typical coasting schooner's hull drew little water and was somewhat sharper than, say, a fishing boat. Its appearance of lying low in the water was largely the result of the six-inch-high "log rail," substituted for the chest-high bulwark of a fisherman. The very sharp, fast schooners of the Chesapeake Bay will be discussed later.

The variety of rigs didn't end with the ship and the schooner. Sloops, with a single fore-and-aft-rigged mast, came middle-sized and small, the small ones busy on bays and rivers. A brig, like the *Alice,* was a two-masted square-rigger. A brigantine, also two-masted, had square sails on her foremast only. So had a barkentine, but she had three masts; both her main and mizzen carried fore-and-aft sails. A bark had three masts also, with square sails on both forward ones. The size of the hull had something to do with the choice of rig, but not too much. A large hull that could be rigged as a ship could just as well be rigged as a bark. Whalers were usually barks.

85

In 1794, when the Yankees and the French were snarling at each other, Congress authorized the building of those six unusually large and, supposedly, fast frigates. Joshua Humphreys, a noted Philadelphia shipwright, had over-all charge of them. He designed three and built the *United States* in his own shipyard. She turned out to be very slow and was generally known as "The Old Wagon." If she still existed she might be the oldest ship in the Navy. As things are, that honor goes to the *Constellation,* launched at Baltimore on September 7, 1797, about a month before the *Constitution* took to water at Boston. Each of the frigates was built in a different port: the *Congress* at Portsmouth, New Hampshire, the *Chesapeake* at Norfolk, Virginia, the *President* at New York.

It's impossible to imagine citizens today building, say, a flattop and presenting it to the Navy, but it was different with frigates. The *Philadelphia,* the *Boston,* and the *New York* were built by and at the cities whose names they bore; Charleston built the *John Adams;* Essex County, Massachusetts, had the *Essex* built at Salem.

Sloop

Schooner

Brigantine

Barkentine

A full-rigged ship: the U.S. Frigate Essex

COMMERCE

In 1783 five American towns were large enough to be called cities. They were all seaports. Philadelphia, New York, and Charleston shipped local produce; Newport did a thriving trade in slaves.

Bark

Mr. Whitman's brig, Alice

But in Confederation times their combined sea trade was not equal to Boston's. Her only real rival was Salem, which wasn't a city at all. Other New England towns followed the sea too; they had to. Towns farther south exported wheat, lumber, tobacco, rice, indigo; New England grew only timber in any worthwhile quantity. She exported that as lumber, and used a lot of it to build ships, furniture, and carriages, which she exported. She also manufactured shoes and rum from imported materials; but the solid base of her export trade was dried fish and train oil. So we have to begin with fishing and whaling.

FISHING

The Revolutionary War stopped commercial fishing entirely and destroyed most of the fishing boats. When the New Englanders returned from the navy and the army (enlisted Marbleheaders manned the Durham boats that took Washington's men across the Delaware), they started fishing again exactly as they had done it before. They refitted what was left of their boats and built new ones just like them—tubby little heeltappers with old-fashioned high sterns. At first they fished where they always had, off the shore of Newfoundland, but soon they pushed farther, to the shore of Labrador.

Chiefly they caught codfish, but they also took pollack and mackerel. Clad in loose calfskin slops, cowhide boots, tarred canvas hats, and big leather aprons known as barvels, they fished over the heeltapper's rail with handlines. As the cod came aboard, apprentices took them over. They beheaded them, split them, rubbed salt into them, and stacked them in the hold. When the crew had "made a fare," that is, caught all the fish the boat would hold, they took them ashore and dried them on low flakes (platforms) usually made of poles and withes. Mackerel they pickled in barrels of brine.

Each man fished "on his own hook." He provided his own fishing gear, his food, his bedding, and bought his share of the salted clams for bait. In return he got a share of the money the fish brought. The owner of the boat got the biggest portion, or "lay," the skipper the next largest; the rest of the hands shared alike, except that a smaller share went to the apprentices and to the twelve-year-old boy who was the cook. A fishing boat made three fares a summer, sometimes four. In the 1780's this didn't yield enough to keep a family over the winter, and in 1789 Congress gave the fishermen a bounty of five cents on each hundred pounds of fish.

About then, the fishing towns began to build the larger boats that were needed to fish on the Grand Banks. In these Marblehead exported her fish directly to Spain, France, and the West Indies. The heeltapper faded and was replaced for inshore fishing by the Chebacco boat, so called after a town of that name, now called Essex. A Chebacco boat was pointed at both ends; she had no bowsprit. Her two pole masts carried fore-and-aft gaff sails, with no tops'ls, and her foremast was set as far forward as it would go, like a catboat's, to do the work of a jib.

The War of 1812 repeated the havoc of the Revolution, but once more the fishermen struggled back. They built the Chebacco boat larger, up to sixty feet long, and renamed it "pinkie" for its sharp stern. Such boats could run south on trading voyages in winter, and many did, but the fishermen had a new winter occupation: from November to April most of them pegged soles onto the uppers of shoes their wives had sewn together.

WHALING

In early colonial times most train oil came from codfish. Better stuff could be gotten by trying the blubber of seals and of all whales, including porpoises. When clarified train oil, more often called whale oil, was burned in a lamp, it gave a brighter

87

Heeltapper

light than a tallow candle. Though the stuff itself had a rank fishy odor, one finds no mention of any smell from a whale-oil lamp. Curriers used train oil to soften leather; before the days of petroleum, it oiled machinery. Clockmakers clung to it long after mineral lubricants came into general use.

After the early 1700's, whalers took liquid sperm oil from the head cavity of the cachalot, or sperm whale. It was brought to port in barrels. There refiners neutralized the oil with potash, and clarified it. Sperm oil gave a strong white light when burned, and hence brought premium prices. Soon after this oil was removed from the whale, a waxy substance precipitated in it. This was spermaceti. Candlemakers put the spermaceti into canvas bags and squeezed the free oil out of it with hugh wooden presses. They molded the residue into the best candles that have ever been made; they did not smoke or drip. When the need arose to measure the illumination delivered by gaslights, the light of a spermaceti candle was

Handlining for cod

taken as the unit called one candlepower. Modern footcandles and lumens are more accurate measurements, but they are still based on the candle.

Whales, as well as ships, were often stranded on the shoals around Nantucket Island. The Indians and the Quaker settlers on the island killed the whales for their meat and blubber. These were right whales. The oil from their blubber had value and so had their whalebone, or baleen. This is the strong, highly elastic material of the "sieve" that strains seawater from the plankton the right whale lives on. Soon the islanders began rowing out in whaleboats to kill the whales in deep water, and laboriously bent their oars towing them ashore. They ventured

Pinkie

farther in small sailing vessels. Then in 1712 Christopher Hussey stumbled on the first cachalot. His find led to longer voyages in larger ships, equipped with brick tryworks on their decks, so that blubber oil could be extracted and barreled at sea. Nantucketers, and soon mainlanders too, caught sperm whales along the coast of Brazil. By 1791 Nantucket and New Bedford whalers had rounded the Horn and were whaling off the coast of Chile. In another ten years the whole Pacific was Yankee whaling ground, and every little port from Long Island to Maine sent out a whaler or two.

In *Moby Dick*, Herman Melville described, once and for all, the cruel, bloody, reeking business of whale killing. It will not be repeated here.

The Browns of Providence had started a factory for making spermaceti candles in 1753. It took

Whale-oil lamp

the islanders on Nantucket nineteen years after that to discover the secret of how to make them; but the Nantucketers prospered without candles. They shipped whale oil to England in their own vessels, and brought back any kind of cargo they could pick up. The Bostonians held their famous tea party on the decks of three Nantucket ships.

The two wars did the same thing to whaling that they did to fishing; they destroyed the ships. Both times Nantucket, cut off from the mainland by enemy ships, nearly starved. In the later years New Bedford took over the lead in whaling, and the old lay system was perverted until finally a crewman could find himself owing more money to the slop chest than his share of a three-year voyage would pay. By then the decline of whale oil had started. A mixture of turpentine and alcohol, called camphine, though highly explosive, gave an even better light than sperm oil; and lard oil, from the four-footed "prairie whale," was far cheaper than the cheapest whale oil. The introduction of kerosene in the 1870's dealt the final blow to Yankee whaling.

THE MERCHANTS

They throve in every American seaport. Only the greatest plantation owners were richer, and the merchants had more ready cash than the planters had. A merchant trafficked in remote countries, as Dr. Samuel Johnson's dictionary prescribed, and he almost always owned the ships that did his trafficking. He also owned a warehouse to shelter the goods he traded in, and a countinghouse where his clerks did bookkeeping, and where he sold not only at wholesale but also at retail. He sold to his fellow townsmen, to upcountry storekeepers, and to other merchants in other seaports. He was a banker too. He loaned money at interest and invested in local enterprises. And he joined with other merchants to share the risks of insuring ships and cargoes and of insuring buildings against fire.

A merchant, particularly in New England, often acquired his whole fortune in his own lifetime, starting with the profits he made as a sea captain on a few voyages to remote countries. These "codfish aristocrats" completely dominated the smaller centers, like Salem and Newburyport.

Mr. Henry Wilkins's countinghouse

In such larger places as Philadelphia and Boston, they deferred to the heads of the older families, but nevertheless they were men of authority and were accepted socially.

In Philadelphia, New York, and Baltimore a few successful merchants held Republican ideas; in Boston and Salem they were Federalists almost to a man. It seemed to them that what was good for their trade was obviously good for the United States. They lived well in richly furnished houses that were mostly spanking new. They stocked their cellars with French, Spanish, and Portugese wines in hundreds of gallons. They owned fine horses, and their purchases supported coach-makers in every northern city. Their servants were usually Negro slaves, though the Philadelphia Quakers abjured them. His clerks worked long hours, but a successful merchant could

finish his day's business between a leisurely breakfast and his midafternoon dinner, which might last two hours or more.

SEA VENTURES

Some little sea trade with France and Holland continued through the Revolution, though many ships were captured or sunk. John Adams's effort to make a favorable trade treaty with England failed at the peace table. When the English poured their flood of long-missed luxuries into United States ports, the merchants swallowed their ire and bought—and sold. The British barred American foodstuffs from their West Indian islands, but the Yankees foxed them. They ran cargoes to Dutch, Danish, and Swedish islands, where local merchants bought them and resold them to Jamaica, Barbados, and Bermuda. Then the Yanks turned their ensigns upside down, ran right in to British island ports under "flags of distress," and landed with bribes in hand. The English governors declared a "condition of starvation" and bought the codfish.

At the same time, American merchants all along the coast started reaching across the Atlantic for trade. Since they could not trade with England, their captains and supercargoes bargained in continental European ports from Lisbon to St. Petersburg, far up the Baltic Sea. They even sneaked into the Mediterranean armed with forged British papers to fool the Barbary pirates.

THE CHINA TRADE

In 1783, Captain Hallet took the sloop *Harriet* out of Boston harbor and headed her southeast, with the idea of going to China around the tip of Africa. His cargo was ginseng root. Ginseng grew wild in New England; in China its forked root was highly valued as "the dose of immortality." When the *Harriet* broke her journey at Capetown, the British East India Company's officials there smelled competition in their profitable Canton market. So they gave Captain Hallet two pounds of fine green tea for every pound of his ginseng roots. He would have done no better in China, so he went home, vastly pleased his employers, and missed being the first American ship in the China trade. But the high price "John Company" paid to stop him alerted Yankee merchants to the profits that trade must yield.

Trade at Canton

Next year the *Empress of China,* out of New York, followed the *Harriet* and went on to Macao with her ginseng. Macao is at the mouth of a wide estuary, eighty miles downstream from Canton. The *Empress* brought back a highly profitable cargo of tea and silk. In 1786 the *Grand Turk,* of Salem, anchored far up the estuary at Whampoa and traded directly with the hong merchants of Canton. These men were designated by the imperial government to trade with foreigners. Houqua and others of them became the personal friends of American sea captains and agents, and over many years maintained a reputation for generosity and absolute integrity. In 1819, one of them, Pannkeiqua, was elected a member of the Massachusetts Agricultural Society.

It was hard to collect a whole cargo of ginseng, and there was a limit to how much of it even China could absorb. What else would the Chinese buy? Boston found one answer in the report of the remarkable American explorer John Ledyard who had made his way, alone and largely on foot, across Russia and most of Siberia. Ledyard described the Russian fur trade along the northwest coast of North America. Mandarins would avidly buy choice furs. In 1788 a group of Boston merchants sent two vessels, the ship *Columbia* and the sloop *Lady Washington,* to Vancouver Island. They were the first American ships to round Cape Horn. The crews wintered on the island and worked at making chisels out of the bar iron in the cargo. The seagoing Indians of the northwest coast, different in appearance and customs from all other Indians, were skilled workers in wood. They knew what iron was, but they had very little of it. They shaped their wood with sharp stones, shells, and beaver teeth.

In the spring, trade began cautiously with the Nootka, the Kwakiutl, and the Haida, none of them notable for friendliness. They coveted the shiny junk that the Yankees offered, but the chisels they had to have. For one chisel they would at first give a magnificent sea-otter pelt, worth $150 in Canton. But the Yankees were too anxious and showed it; the last pelts cost them eight chisels apiece.

The masters of the two vessels traded commands and sailed for Hawaii to rest, and to pick up sandalwood, "incense for heathen idols." John Kendrick, who took over the *Lady Washing-*

ton, liked the Pacific so much that he never went home. He bought the sloop, and spent the rest of his life trading back and forth between China, Hawaii, and the West Coast. When the *Columbia* left Hawaii, Captain Robert Gray took along as cabin boy a young islander named Attoo. The ship went on to Canton, traded her furs and sandalwood for tea, and continued westward around Africa to Boston. Gone almost three years, she had logged nearly 42,000 miles and had become the first American ship to circumnavigate the earth. Her voyage cost so much that its profits were not large, but Boston gave the *Columbia* a salute of twenty-six guns and staged a parade. Attoo marched with the rest, wearing a crested helmet and a scarlet-and-gold cloak made entirely of feathers. Surely, though, he looked no stranger to Boston than did Boston to Attoo. The *Columbia* went westward to the East again in 1790. This time she discovered the great river that is named for her—and returned Attoo to his poi.

Sealskins brought only a few dollars apiece at Canton, but a ship loaded with a hundred thousand pelts could turn a neat profit. Such a cargo could be had for the cost of slaughtering and skinning the animals and salting the hides—all done by the ship's crew. In their mating season, the seals went ashore on lonely islands. They were almost helpless on land; the sailors killed them with clubs. While her sealers worked on an island, the ship smuggled "Yankee notions" into some South American port and turned an added penny.

SALEM

The noted merchant Elias Haskett Derby, known as "King Derby," ran a school at Salem. Likely boys, usually from "good" families, entered his countinghouse at the age of ten. They learned bookkeeping and the values of all foreign coins; they learned the grades and prices of world commodities—tea, coffee, amber, ivory, silk, sandalwood, tin, hemp, copal rosin—along with American products—tobacco, indigo, naval stores (tar and turpentine), ginseng, and, of course, codfish. They also learned to dicker, with a hard eye for profit. At fourteen the boys went to sea on a Derby ship. They worked hard and observed

91

Trade with the Nootka Indians

trading in action. Of sailoring they had only the fine points to learn; they had absorbed most of it through their pores from birth. The best of them could move up fast, and many commanded ships before they were twenty.

Salem merchants gathered cargoes for their long-distance ventures by trading in the West Indies and along the East Coast. Wheat, tobacco, and salt pork could be had in the Chesapeake Bay, tar and turpentine in Pamlico Sound. The longer voyages were an extension of this kind of trading. Salem ships continued to follow the eastern route, around Africa, but they seldom went that way directly. Loaded with iron, pottery, salt fish, soap, candles, hams, flints, tobacco, furniture, and half a hundred other things, some of which were small "ventures" put aboard by local citizens, they went wherever there might be demand: along the coast of Europe; to the Atlantic islands off Africa, the Azores, Madeira, the Canaries. At each port they traded, usually with a cash profit, for articles that would be salable farther along. On most voyages the cargo changed completely several times. Beyond the Cape of Good Hope they touched at Mauritius, India, Ceylon, Malaysia, Sumatra, the Moluccas. Tortoiseshell sold well in China. It could be had from island natives, and these same natives would dive for mollusks that yielded mother-of-pearl. The Yankees themselves gathered edible birds' nests on cliffs ashore and waded on coral reefs hunting the cucumber-shaped sea slugs, called *bêche-de-mer;* both were delicacies in China.

Engaged in such a trading voyage, Captain Jonathan Carnes anchored in the open roadstead of "Bencoolen" (Bengkulu), on the southwest coast of Sumatra, to buy pepper and camphor. Ashore, he heard a whisper of wild pepper to be had from the natives farther north on the same coast. Knowing that his large ship couldn't reach the villages, he returned to Salem, got a shallow-draft schooner, and departed again, saying nothing about pepper or where he was going. With constant soundings, and with a lookout on the crosstrees, the schooner felt her way through gaps in uncharted coral reefs to visit huts standing on stilts along the shore. Carnes got what he went for. The whole cost of the voyage was $18,000; the pepper sold for $126,000. For a while no one else could find the wild pepper, but of course the secret leaked out. Salem became the

Sumatran wild pepper

world's pepper capital. From less than five hundred pounds a year before Carnes, the United States export of pepper jumped to more than seven and a half million pounds in 1805.

THE EMBARGO

England and her European allies started another war with France in 1803, with the object of unseating Napoleon Bonaparte. Again the two sides caught American shipping in their crossfire. Both boarded American merchant ships, and sometimes captured them. The British warship *Leopard* went so far as to attack the American frigate *Chesapeake* in order to search her for English deserters. To avoid war, President Jefferson persuaded Congress to declare an unprecedented embargo on all shipping in 1807. For a year, until the end of Jefferson's term, American merchantmen lay idle in their home ports. Merchants, especially in New England, howled with anguish. Farm prices fell; those of imported goods skyrocketed. But New England, and most of the middle states, gained in the long run by being forced to develop their manufactures. Philadelphia boomed. The southern states hardly noticed the embargo at the outset, but having no manufactures to develop, it did them lasting harm.

THE WAR OF 1812

It's true that deserters from the British navy took berths as sailors on American merchantmen. It's true that British men-of-war boarded American vessels at sea and removed such men from them. It's also true that the British frequently seized Yankee sailors, who hadn't deserted from anything. The Admiralty was hard up for seamen. It's further true that the United States government, and the people along the seaboard, were disturbed about this, but not so much as to put the matter beyond negotiation.

It was the "warhawks" of the new states beyond the Appalachians—Kentucky, Tennessee, Ohio—who howled with rage, and demanded war first and negotiation afterward. In spite of his assurance that they would not do so, Napoleon's ships were still seizing American cargoes on the high seas—but that could wait. The English had insulted American pride, and besides, they were inciting the Indians in the Northwest Territory and thus slowing the western advance of settlement. Henry Clay harangued the House of Representatives. The United States should take Canada at once, and then dictate stiff peace terms. Congress declared war on England, June 18, 1812, by only slim majorities in both houses.

The reluctance of the British army to surrender

Canada proved too strong for the American militia and its elderly generals to overcome. The Federalists of New England had so little sympathy for "Mr. Madison's War" that they did a good business selling beef across the border to feed the English soldiers. Though two of them were soon captured, the big frigates did well early in the war. But by 1814 the English blockade had bottled up all of our large ships in American harbors. An English fleet sailed unopposed into the Chesapeake Bay to land the troops that chased the President out of Washington, and burned his house and the Capitol. The White House got its name from paint put on to cover its smoke stains. But the British could not cope with Yankee naval superiority on the Great Lakes. It was a sorry little war that decided nothing, but it had some permanent side effects.

THE PRIVATEERS

As with most wars, a lot of people made money out of the War of 1812, notably the merchants who financed privateers. These were small armed vessels, privately owned but provided with official "letters of marque" permitting them to capture enemy merchant vessels as "prizes." A prize crew, put aboard a captured ship, sailed her into the privateer's home port. There she and her cargo were sold, and the proceeds divided between the owners and the crew of the privateer, by the same lay system that the whalers and fishermen used.

Privateering required courage and dash. It also required fast boats that could overhaul a merchantman or run away from a man-of-war. The little Baltimore clippers, developed on Chesapeake Bay, were the ideal craft for the job. Narrow hulled and deep keeled, they could carry more canvas than any other boat of their size (usually some fifty feet long, though a few were twice that big). The famous American clipper ships came along later and were quite different—larger, more full-bodied, and rigged with square sails on three masts. The clipper was rigged as a tops'l schooner: she had two masts, with standard fore-and-aft sails, but with two square sails on the upper part of the foremast. These were handy in running before the wind. A privateer's principal armament was a single large gun, mounted amid-
93

ships on a swivel so that it could be swung to shoot in any direction. On large ships, only very small guns were swiveled.

The clipper made so effective a privateer that it was copied by northern shipwrights, but the "nest of pirates," as the British Admiralty called Baltimore, built and harbored most of them, and the town's speculators grew fat on their profits. After the British navy swung into full action, privateering fell off; a lone schooner could do nothing against a convoy; but the clippers stayed in business as blockade-runners. Between 1812 and 1815 they carried two thirds of all American overseas cargoes. A clipper's capacity was small, but it had the same advantage over a ship of the line that a kingbird has over an eagle.

Privateersman ashore

THE SLAVE TRADE

England outlawed the African slave trade in 1807, and started trying to suppress it. By then the United States had begun a series of halfhearted gestures in the same direction. Naturally, Baltimore clippers moved into the trade after the war, and shortly they moved into slaver-catching as well—setting a thief to catch a thief.

For many years, Yankee and English ships had been buying slaves on the west coast of Africa, at Guinea mostly, and selling them to the sugar planters in the West Indies and to the rice and tobacco planters along the southern East Coast of the United States. The slavers bought their "black ivory" from Arab traders, and from some native Africans, who captured or purchased slaves in the interior of the continent. New Englanders did much of the early slave carrying; the Rhode Islanders especially, but also men from Connecticut and Massachusetts. At first the business was entirely legal and made one leg of the famous three-cornered trade: slaves bartered in the West Indies for molasses, which the Yankees distilled into rum, used to pay for slaves in Africa. Along the line, the slavers picked up a nice profit in Spanish dollars and in drafts on London for pounds sterling.

The operation of packing—literally packing—a hundred to three hundred prostrate human bodies in a vessel's hold, for a voyage that could last a month, is almost too horrible to think about;

*Privateer
clipper schooner*

The bloody slave revolt in Haiti, beginning in 1791, shook the confidence of slaveholders in the United States and started debates in Congress that ultimately produced the Act of 1807, which said it prohibited the slave trade. The slavers simply ran up the Spanish flag and went on trading. They smuggled slaves into this country and into the West Indies, and sold them openly in Brazil, which had no restrictive laws. Federal acts became tougher; slave trading was piracy by 1820, and carried the death penalty. But successive presidents—five of them, from Jefferson to Jackson—pardoned convicted slavers. After the War of 1812, the American and British navies cooperated in trying to wipe out the trade. Disgusted Yankee commanders often turned captured slave traders over to the British, who, they knew, would hang them. Clear up into the 1860's Congress was still passing resolutions about the suppression of the slave trade.

but men who passed for good Christians did it. Boston merchants would insure a slave cargo against loss due to insurrection, but not against loss by "natural" death. In the 1770's conscience began to trouble the New Englanders. They put a heavy duty on imported slaves, but remitted it in full if the slaves were re-exported within a year. In 1788 Massachusetts forbade the sale of slaves. New York, Baltimore, and Charleston all harbored slave ships, but Newport remained the slave clearinghouse for the nation.

Many individuals, of every religious sect, followed the lead of the Society of Friends and repudiated slavery. Those of them who owned slaves freed them, often at great financial loss. An increased population of free Negroes found freedom a hardship. They had suddenly to make their own way in the world and they had no training or experience for doing it. In 1816, the American Colonization Society was formed with the not-always-charitable purpose of sending freed slaves to the west coast of Africa. Slave owners feared the influence of the freedmen on their slaves. The Society actually deported enough people to found what became the Republic of Liberia. Aside from much internal bickering, the Society's trouble was that most of the freed Negroes did not want to leave. Nearly all of them had been born in the United States; they knew nothing of how to live in Africa; and even though they were not then citizens, they rightly considered themselves Americans.

ICE

Another trade, curious and much more innocent, developed through the efforts of one man, Frederic Tudor. In 1805, he shipped a cargo of Massachusetts pond ice to the West Indies. Boston ridiculed the idea, and sailors were sure that the ice, melting, would swamp the vessel. Most of the first shipment did melt because Tudor hadn't learned to pack it properly, but the boat still floated. By 1812 he had learned the trick of using sawdust and had a steady trade going. Gradually he extended his market to the southern United States and to South America. In 1833 he shipped a cargo to Calcutta, the first ice ever seen there. The trade flourished until the invention of ice-making machinery in the 1850's.

THE PACKETS

A packet was a vessel of any size or kind that maintained something near a fixed schedule over a fixed route. It carried passengers and any freight that anyone wished to ship. In its simplest form a packet line was a local enterprise, moving produce to a large center, or raw material to a factory; such a one would still carry passengers.

Even in colonial times sloops and schooners, advertised as "constant carriers," linked towns and cities along the seaboard. After 1783, lines with two or more boats made longer runs, from New York, or Boston, as far as Savannah; later, as far as New Orleans. These, and the four or five lines that connected northern ports, advertised "elegant" accommodations.

Until after 1817 a passenger to Europe selected a likely ship and then put up at an inn to wait for it to sail. The establishment of the Black Ball Line changed that. A regular packet now sailed from New York to Liverpool on the first day of every month, regardless of season or weather, and she sailed with or without a cargo or a full passenger list. The Black Ball ships were well built and fast. Cabin passage cost from $140 to $150, including bedding, meals, and wine. The passenger got a private stateroom, about six feet square, and the freedom of the main cabin. This was some forty feet long and served as both lounge and dining saloon. The trip to Liverpool averaged twenty-three days, running before the prevailing westerly winds; it took forty days to return against them.

The success of the Black Ball Line encouraged competition. Two new lines started in 1821: the Red Star out of New York, and one that Thomas Cope ran out of Philadelphia. The next year brought the Boston and Liverpool Line into the business, but it shortly failed, as did several later Boston lines, because of the old scarcity of outgoing cargo. A return cargo was easy to get. The packets put rough bunks into their holds, and brought over immigrants, permitting them to cook their own food in a galley on deck.

Though the steam-assisted sailing vessel *Savannah* crossed the Atlantic in 1819, the sailing packets throve for thirty years. Then steamships took over. The emphasis was always on speed, and to get it the packet masters drove their hands unmercifully. Soon, no self-respecting seaman would sign on one. The pay was low, hence the packets came to be manned by the dregs of the seagoing world; "packet rat" was as low as a seaman could fall.

Deluxe passage

The shop and warehouse of Duncan Phyfe on Fulton Street, New York

14.

The Changing Americans

GEORGE WASHINGTON took the oath as President on April 30, 1789, on the balcony of the Federal Hall, which was New York's city hall, taken over by the Continental Congress. Next year, as Jefferson and Hamilton had agreed, the entire government moved back to Philadelphia to stay ten years, and the President and Mr. Jefferson inspected the site of the new Federal City on the Potomac. Until 1846, the District of Columbia straddled the river, with about a third of its hundred square miles in Virginia. Though Washington was a Virginian, he chose sites for the Capitol and the "President's Palace" on the Maryland side.

When President John Adams and his wife moved from Philadelphia to their still-incomplete residence, on schedule in 1800, the population of Washington was 3,210. Pennsylvania Avenue, which connected their house with the northern wing of the Capitol (all that had then been built), was a narrow lane crossing a marsh on a causeway. A few boardinghouses stood near the Capitol, and the Adamses had a few houses and shops as neighbors. All between was open country; a

whole city, with endless public buildings, was waiting to be built.

Less than forty miles away, booming Baltimore, expanding to match its sea trade, had by then outstripped Boston in population. Most of its older houses were brick, as they still are, but the new ones, hurriedly built, were wood, painted in bright, cheerful colors. The town was the nearest seaport for the rich Maryland counties that surrounded it, and also for much of central Pennsylvania, which was even richer. Already mills on three streams that flowed into Baltimore's harbor were grinding wheat. By 1825 they would make the place the leading flour-milling center of the world. Baltimore introduced gas streetlights to the world in 1817. In 1829, it completed the first formal monument to George Washington.

Philadelphia remained the largest American city until 1810, but she was already settling into prosperous and complacent middle age. Boston, deeply convinced of her innate superiority regardless of size, was, as now, the metropolis of New England, and still reminded visitors of an old English town. New Orleans in 1810 was still, quite actually, a French town. Charleston, substituting cotton for indigo, continued to be urbane and lopsidedly prosperous. A twenty-two-mile canal to the Santee River, built in 1802, aided in getting rice and cotton to Charleston's wharves. New York lost much of her old Dutch look in the great fire of 1776. Now she was losing more of it as old buildings were torn down, or given new roofs and new façades.

ARCHITECTURE

Wealthy merchants of all the seaports wanted mansions in the city, and other mansions in the country. They also wanted new exchanges, new banks; and as public officials, they wanted new courthouses, city halls, and statehouses. Here was an opportunity for architects, and they seized it. People felt that America should have a style of architecture that would express her democracy. Though today we might have different ideas, it was then obvious to everybody that the conventions of the ancient Greek and Roman democracies filled the bill. On its face there was an absurdity in this: for a hundred years the Georgian style, based squarely on what was known of this classic architecture, had dominated colonial building. But all of Georgian architecture had come from a single source, a book by a first-century Roman named Vitruvius. He described five fixed orders of architecture, and builders used those or nothing. Then, in the 1760's, came news of the discoveries at Herculaneum and Pompeii, and also the first precise descriptions of actual Greek architecture. Had these things happened even a hundred years later the civilized world would have heard of them within a few weeks; today the news, with pictures, would cover the world in twenty-four hours. In the eighteenth century, understanding had to wait for the careful preparation and publication of books; but in twenty years, American architects had realized that Vitruvius wasn't all of classic architecture; it varied from place to place, and even from building to building. Thus the new American style, though it showed many features similar to the Georgian, actually differed from it in both spirit and detail. It is generally spoken of as Federal architecture, or Classic Revival architecture.

97

Thomas Jefferson was a "gentleman architect," a true amateur, who took no fees for his work. He started the Federal style with his state capitol at Richmond, Virginia, in 1793. He based the design on a Roman temple at Nimes, France, known as the Maison Carrée. Mr. Jefferson preferred the Roman style. He imposed it on the University of Virginia; on homes for his neighbors, around Charlottesville; and on his own Monticello, where he actually made the inside inconvenient in order to make the outside properly classical.

Charles Bullfinch returned to Boston from Paris and London in 1787. For two years he had saturated himself with the Classic Revival, especially with the delicate style of the Scottish architect Robert Adam. Adam had developed this style from what he had seen of Pompeii, and of the ruins of the Roman emperor Diocletian's palace in Dalmatia. Like Adam's, Bullfinch's buildings were light and delicate. They stood out in somber old Boston like deer in a cow pasture. He made windows larger, with slender muntins between their panes. He let light into dark halls by framing entrance doors with glass. He introduced curved stairways, and even some rooms that were oval instead of rectangular. These created engaging curved bays in the outside walls.

The great woodcarver Samuel McIntire, who was also a master builder though not a trained architect, came to Boston and examined Bullfinch's houses. Then he went back to Salem and built mansions in the same style for the rich merchants there. These were not rigid copies of Bull-

Mr. Jefferson's capitol at Richmond

style can be found in Ohio, Indiana, Illinois, and Michigan.

That the same Classical Revival throve in Europe, also, took a little bloom off the style as an expression of Americanism; but nobody noticed. Actually, even while they talked independence, the Yankees kept glancing over their shoulders to see what England was doing, and what England thought of how they did things. The style affected more than buildings. It dictated the shapes and ornaments of silverware, of carriages, of furniture, and of women's clothes. It could not quite manage to shape the changes of men's garments, but it had no trouble at all in draping statues of George Washington in Roman togas, worn over the Continental uniform or over nothing at all. Even homespun Ben Franklin chose a toga for his statue on the Philadelphia library.

Delicate elegance was the watchword. Silver hollow ware flirted with the spare shapes of Pompeian vases and was ornamented only with a little engraving. Carriages became very light in England. One of them, called a curricle, had its horses hitched to it under a classical Roman yoke. The more elegant of American carriages became somewhat lighter, plainer, and better sprung, but common sense forbade driving anything really dainty over American roads.

finch, but they were as good as his, and the carved ornaments in them were much better.

Benjamin H. Latrobe was born in England, and was trained there as an architect. He saw the first book that described the proportions and details of ancient Greek buildings in Athens, and from then on, nothing was really good to Latrobe unless it was Greek. In 1799 he built the Bank of Pennsylvania in Philadelphia to look as much as possible like a Greek temple. That started the "Greek Revival," which lasted almost to the Civil War and spread as far westward as Iowa. Residences, as well as courthouses, were wooden copies of Doric temples, and hang the inconvenience. Few small cottages carried the temple idea so far that their chimneys and back steps embarrassed them, as the one illustrated is embarrassed.

Naturally, many lesser architects followed the leaders, some of them very ably; but listing them would serve no purpose, and discussion of their work belongs to technical books. One, though, should be mentioned: Asher Benjamin worked in Boston and absorbed Charles Bullfinch's ideas. He wrote (and drew) *The Country Builder's Assistant* and three other handbooks which spread the Federal style through New England and westward. It is due to Benjamin that good examples of the

FURNITURE

Following the designs of the Englishmen Thomas Sheraton and George Hepplewhite (who owed their ideas to Robert Adam), chairs and tables acquired slender legs and dainty carvings and inlays. The fragile openwork backs of chairs were either square or shield-shaped. The most notable producer of this Federal furniture in America was a dour Scot named Duncan Phyfe, a cabinetmaker of rare taste and skill. His early work was "bespoke" for individuals. When his little shop on Fulton Street in New York couldn't meet the demand, Phyfe expanded it into a manufactory, employing a number of journeymen. But he supervised their work personally and strictly and so kept the quality high. When fashion changed, and Napoleon's Empire furniture, based on Greek

98

vase paintings, became the rage about 1810, Phyfe shifted his men to that. They made it handsomely, with more distinction and restraint than the French models. Then, in the 1830's, American taste faltered. Machinery was the rage, and the public would buy nothing that was not made by machinery. Phyfe faced the loss of his thriving business. So, snarling with rage, he bought steam-driven band saws and set his men to cutting out clumsy curlicued "butcher furniture," as he named it.

One Federal ornament among many deserves to be singled out. In America, this was the day of the eagle. Its image, carved in wood, spread its wings over doorways; gilded, it topped mirrors,

Greek Revival house in Michigan

clocks, and courthouses; stamped on cakes of soap, it replaced the "Windsor crown"; with all members extended, like a dead crow nailed to a barn door, its talons grasped arrows and olive branches on the Great Seal of the United States. After six committees wrestled with the problem, from 1776 to 1782, the Continental Congress adopted the bald eagle as the national emblem. Bald in this case meant not hairless but piebald,

that is, black and white. Benjamin Franklin belatedly denounced the eagle as a coward and a thief; he preferred the wild turkey as a symbol, but nobody listened to him.

THE APPAREL REVOLUTION

The Federal period was marked by radical changes in the clothing of men, women, and children, not only in the United States, but in the whole Western world. Previously sudden innovations in dress had been confined to the garments of one sex, as when Charles II decreed the knee-length "vest" for men. This time everybody was affected (eventually), though not all in the same way or from the same impulses. Bare arms? Who, since the fall of Rome, had seen a woman's arm bare above the elbow in public? Hard hats? Who had seen a man wear any hard hat except an iron one?

MEN'S CLOTHES

Wigs appeared in England in the 1660's. Men started wearing skirted coats and three-cornered cocked hats about 1685, in the reign of James II. From that time until (but not because) Washington was inaugurated, the clothes of prosperous men changed only in detail. Then, within twenty years, they underwent a revolution, the effects of which are still visible in our long trousers, in the tails on our full-dress coats, in the starched collars and white ties we wear with those coats. The changes that began in the 1790's had already appeared in Europe. Naturally, the young dandies (people were beginning to call them "bloods" in-

Hepplewhite

Sheraton

Empire

Band-saw butcher

1780's   1790's   1800   1810

Federalist   *Republican*

*The dates
on the drawings are
approximate,
and there was
much overlapping.
Many men
clung to tailcoats
until after 1850.*

stead of "macaronis") wore the new styles first. Conservative men adopted them slowly and avoided extremes. James Monroe clung to knee breeches until he died in 1831, the last President to wear them in office, the last of the "cocked hats." Men who worked with their muscles took to the new styles only when, in the course of time, they got them at second hand, but the rising "middling sort" bought them new, and by 1830 only a sharp eye for the quality of cloth could tell an artisan from an alderman.

Mention has been made of the stiff round hat that Mr. Henry Wilkins wore at the launching of the *Alice*. Such hats were seen before 1790, at about the time that some men lengthened their tight nankeen breeches to reach the tan tops of short black boots. The best hard hats were castor, that is beaver fur, felted, stiffened with shellac, and brushed. Summer hats of the same shapes were made of straw. The first ones had quite low, and slightly tapered, cylindrical crowns, rising from fairly wide flat brims. Later the crowns grew tall and were frequently "belled," that is, wider at the top than at the bottom, and the brims dipped fore and aft, and rolled upward on both sides. So popular did the tall hat become that soldiers wore an adaptation of it, and a drawing made from life about 1824 shows a frontiersman wearing one. Later versions, with a silk nap, were

worn in the early years of the present century.

Most older men, and all young men who were not clergymen, gave up wig-wearing by 1800. The clerics, who at the outset had scorned wigs and preached against them, now clung to them. English judges and lawyers still wear wigs in court in our time, but there seems to be no evidence that legal wigs survived at all in America. Since before 1776, many men, including General Washington, had preferred to wear their own hair dressed like a wig. When the younger men cut off their long back hair, many older ones left it, and pinned the hank up to the crown of the head, often with the ribbon still attached.

A rabid Republican brushed his hair forward, so that he looked "as if he were backing into a hurricane." As soon as the French Revolution broke out, American Republicans, feeling a fellowship, began to copy Jacobin fashions. Since French proletarians wore slops, like Silas Whittle's, sympathetic Yankees went into "trowsers," calf-length at first and loose, but soon lengthened to the ankle and tightened; in fact they became so tight at one point that they had to be buttoned down the sides. Breeches, with silk stockings, persisted as evening wear for a long time; they still are worn at royal functions in England. Around 1820, a startling sign appeared at one of the assembly balls: GENTLEMEN MAY NOT DANCE WITH-

1812

Soldier

Naval Officer

1820

1830

OUT BREECHES. The dressier Republicans wore narrow coattails. Since the Federalists wore theirs broad, and continued to wear breeches rather than trousers, it became possible for a time to know a man's politics at a glance.

Except for the tails, coats differed only in being single-breasted or double-breasted, with the difference carrying no political significance. They were all cut straight across in front, just high enough to show a line of straight-cut vest, which, on a Republican, was likely to be striped. Much was made of the coat collar, and the wide lapels were cut into quite fanciful shapes. Gentlemen who were not naturally endowed with large chests frequently remedied the deficiency by wearing two or three vests, one over the other. This was done so widely that vests of single thickness were made to look like two or three. We may assume that these were for the barrel-chested.

Hanging from under the edge of all short vests was a fob, a heavy seal on a wide black ribbon. A watch anchored the hidden end of the ribbon as a rule, but so important was the fob that a man who owned no watch would wear one. Tailors still make a perfunctory little pocket below the waistband of a man's trousers for the fob he no longer wears. As long as they clung to knee breeches, Federalists continued to fasten their shoes with silver buckles; pantalooned Repub-

licans tied theirs. Incidentally, William Young, of Philadelphia, made the first shoes specially shaped for right and left feet in 1800. When trousers prevailed over breeches, after the end of "Mr. Madison's War," most men took to very short boots. The pants legs hid the boot tops, and in the twenties, many men wore a strap under the instep to hold the trousers down. This was of practical use on horseback. Most trousers were buff, yellow, or white, and made of lightweight materials: nankeen, drill, corduroy.

Along with cocked hats and knee breeches, the neck band, with its lace fall at the throat, and also the lace worn at the wrists, faded away. It seems probable that the Republicans first replaced the band with a neckerchief. This was a large white handkerchief, folded as a triangle and tied behind, under the coat collar. A man tucked the edges of the triangle under his vest and let the loose fold puff out. Shortly, someone reversed the thing and tied it in a large bow in front. Then a padded "pudding" was created to fill the vest triangle. Usually white but sometimes black, its extreme versions came up over the wearer's chin and suggested that some accident had befallen his neck. About 1809, men started letting their whiskers grow in front of their ears, the first hair on fashionable masculine faces since Charles II's time. Below these sideburns, the points of a "dickey" emerged

Pigtail and Nivernois hat   *Disheveled crop*   *Neckerchiefs*   *Pudding and pinned-up queue*   *Chitterling*   *Black stock*

modestly above the pudding and menaced the cheeks—the first starched collar since the ruff was abandoned in the early 1600's. At the same time, the pudding sprouted a jabot, known as a "chitterling," from under its front. The coat collar grew excessively high and stiff, and so did the dickey. The two together so restricted their wearer that he had to turn his whole body to look sideways. The dickey persisted well into Victorian times and acquired a padded black stock, with a flat made-up bow, to be worn with the long frock coat that appeared just before 1830.

Unless the weather was very warm, a gentleman wore a cape to an evening party to protect his clothes. Traveling in winter, on horseback or not, he put on a long riding coat. It buttoned to just below the waist, and was split up the back far enough to allow its skirts to spread smoothly on both sides of a horse. This coat had a turnover collar and two capes, a short one under a shorter one, covering its shoulders. Long double-breasted dress overcoats appeared in the 1820's, pinch-waisted and fur-collared, with sleeves that covered half the length of the fingers. No man hesitated to wear a shawl in a carriage or, in bitter weather, to wrap an incredibly long muffler twice around his neck, with one end hanging in front and the other floating behind.

The changes of fashion affected military uniforms much more quickly than new styles usually do. Soldiers went into tight trousers, and chest-padded tailcoats, barnacled with spherical brass buttons and topped with stiffened collars three and a half inches high. A black leather stock served as neckwear. The tall hat of the rank and file was a varnished leather "tar bucket" with a visor, and a heavy chin strap that hung across the face just below the soldier's underlip. Most of these hats displayed a plume, like a bottle brush, sticking straight up from the front of the crown. The headgear of officers followed that of the emperor Napoleon, set athwartship, or of the Duke of Wellington, set fore-and-aft.

Tars in the navy stuck to their wide canvas slops, blue roundabout jackets, and flat varnished hats. Officers turned out in black pumps, white stockings and breeches, blue tailcoats, and huge "half-moon" hats, ill-suited to the quarterdeck in a gale.

BOYS

There is overwhelming evidence that colonial children over six, in families wealthy enough to have portraits painted, wore exactly the same kind of clothes their parents wore. People saw nothing absurd about a seven-year-old boy in a wig, or a girl the same age in stiffened stays and mitts. The first break seems to have come in the 1780's. One-piece and two-piece suits for boys still exist from that time that are quite different from the clothes their fathers wore. Both have ankle-long pantaloons, which men would not wear for years. One two-piece suit is made of calico. It has a waist-length body with long sleeves, and a collarless round neck which was covered by a wide, sometimes ruffled, white shirt collar. There is a one-piece suit of linsey-woolsey with the same kind of sleeves and neck, but the flaps of its pantaloons are held up, both front and back, by horizontal rows of large buttons at the level of the armpits.

102

Suits like it appear in a number of portraits. Some similar suits, for very young boys, had sleeves gathered at the wrists and pantaloons gathered at the ankles, and displayed narrow white ruffles at both places. When a boy was about ten, he went into calf-length nankeen trousers, an ordinary shirt with a neckerchief, and a jacket, cut roundabout, or made with silly-looking short tails. Over hair cropped about three inches long, he wore a cap shaped quite like that of a modern naval officer, with a brim of varnished leather, and often with a long tassel attached to the center of its crown. Failing a cap, he had a round hat of felted wool. Some of the hats in old woodcuts look like hand-me-downs from adults.

WOMEN

In 1793, the popular Duchess of York appeared in London wearing a dress cut on Greek lines, with a high waist and a flowing narrow skirt that reached the ground. It was a modest garment,

The Greek dress, about 1797

with a high neck and long sleeves. All the ladies of London scrapped their stays, their bustles, and their bouffants, and followed the Duchess. As "the Greek dress," it turned up in Paris the next year, at the end of the Reign of Terror. But the French version missed the ground by some five inches, and had short sleeves and a daringly low neckline. In this form it was quickly brought to

103

America, where the ladies made detachable sleeves for it that reached nearly to the fingertips. They also produced a "modesty piece" to fit close around the neck and spread over the shoulders and upper chest, but not everybody wore one. These dresses became known as "the naked fashion," because little was worn under them. They looked charming on slim young girls. On

Outdoor clothes, 1800

their comfortably buxom mothers, the effect was less enchanting.

Such "Directoire" dresses were made of thin material, muslin usually. It was customary to wear a filmy scarf with them. It was also usual to wear the same thin dresses in winter. A high-necked, long-sleeved jacket, called a "spencer," could be worn on the street, but it was no longer than the waistline of the dress, and since that was only a little below the armpits, the spencer wasn't much for warmth. The one refuge was a cashmere shawl, six yards long, two yards wide, and vastly expensive.

Obviously the proper shoes to go with this dress would be sandals, but the ladies didn't carry authenticity quite that far. They compromised on heelless slippers which they tied on with ribbons, crisscrossed, sandalwise, around their ankles. Shoemakers made a few of the slippers of kidskin (one advertised "rips mended free"). Most ladies made their own slippers of silk, apparently with no added soles.

When the Greek dress came in, the Reign of Terror was still fresh in everybody's mind, so a gruesome memento of the guillotine seemed an appropriate coiffure. Female candidates for the guillotine's surgery had had their locks crudely shorn before the operation, so American ladies cropped theirs, too, and rumpled them *à la victime*. The style passed shortly, and wigs moved in to cover up the mess until it grew long enough to be arranged in flat curls, bound with proper classical fillets.

Empire, about 1805

The high-waisted style lasted for nearly twenty years, with constant variations. About 1805, it sprouted a train, achieved a waistline that was high beyond belief, and became the "Empire" dress. Ladies began to wear neck ruffs, sometimes attached to the top of a modesty. Dress materials began to have a little more body; some Empire dresses were made of satin. About 1817, though the waist stayed high, the skirt began to flare a little, and deep borders of ruffles, or fur, appeared

Poke bonnet and muff, about 1817

above its hem. Sleeves came into fashion, puffed at the shoulders. Huge muffs, two feet square or more, became necessary, and so did umbrellas, which, when not open, were carried handle-down by the spike. This was the heyday of the poke bonnet, plumed and beribboned, and nicknamed the "coal scuttle." It wasn't a new idea, but it suddenly flared into popularity and became perhaps the most engaging of all female hats. Its offspring was the great American sunbonnet, skirted to protect the neck, its brim stiffened, later with cardboard but in early versions with thin wooden slats. Sunbonnets are still worn by some farm women.

Sometimes fashion is obviously influenced by events, great or small. If an event influenced the next change—and the final one as far as the span of this account is concerned—it is hard to find. Does the Monroe Doctrine of 1823, or the visit of the Marquis de Lafayette in 1824 explain why ladies put their waistlines back where they agreed

Pantalettes and ribbons, after 1825

with nature? Or why they squeezed them as small as fortitude could stand? Their hair went into clownlike puffs; their sleeves and their hats became enormous; ribbons sprouted everywhere; and they turned their umbrellas right side up.

GIRLS

As they still do, the dresses of little girls reflected the trends of their mothers' styles, but at enough distance to allow them to look like little girls. The

classic styles brought about the charming short-waisted dresses that Kate Greenaway made famous—long after they had ceased to be worn. When the waistline returned to its normal level, girl children turned out in ribbon sashes, below puffed sleeves, and above full skirts that were short enough to show their ruffled ankle-length pantalettes. Their mothers wore these pantalettes too, but theirs were usually invisible except for momentary glimpses.

YANKEE MANNERS

Before the Revolution, wealthy colonists tried to establish themselves as an aristocracy, but a powerful upper class needs an oppressed and dependent lower class, which, except for the Negro slaves, did not exist in America. Even the most feckless failure always could, and usually did, pack up and try somewhere else. An established farmer or a prosperous artisan might respect a man of property and education, but he took no orders from him without wages. So, even before 1776, the gentry tacitly admitted an equality unknown in Europe. After 1783 all of the rank and file and most of the "better sort" made deliberate efforts toward at least a surface equality. Servants became "help" and "hired

hands," and the words "master" and "mistress" went out of style, except in the South.

Plenty of near-aristocrats clung to what privileges they could, and as they still do, people who had had money for thirty years looked down upon people who had made it more recently. Yet European visitors in the eighties reported in blank astonishment that men of substance toiled beside their field hands, and hobnobbed freely with them as they all ate their dinner together under a tree; that a man of note might cultivate the company of a packet captain, or affably buy a drink for the stage driver, who had invited his distinguished passenger to ride the coveted seat beside him on the box.

The newly prosperous sought to get a veneer of gentility from etiquette books, such as *The Compleat Gentleman,* by Henry Peacham, or Lord Chesterfield's *Letters to His Son.* This last book held its place as a social guide far into the nineteenth century. As a result of a surge of false modesty, some of His Lordship's precepts were denounced as immoral, and a purified version, *The American Chesterfield,* appeared in 1827. Children read handbooks of manners and pious moral maxims, many of which masqueraded as story books, but one was frankly titled *The Parents' Assistant.*

The French Revolution affected American manners in two different ways. One, to speak broadly, influenced Federalists, the other influenced Republicans. The presence in New York and Philadelphia of dozens of aristocratic French refugees heightened the polish of urban society. Chevaliers were commonplace in New York streets; a count or a marquis could be found at any inn, and even dukes and princes were not unknown. Though some of them were arrogant, most of them had the kind of natural manners that result from consideration for other people, and are worth copying. The Frenchmen were also worldly, and it may have been due to them, as well as to the decline of religion, that the old standards of strict moral behavior weakened and were replaced by form and pretense.

As the Republicans copied French revolutionary clothes, they also sought to copy the, to them, admirable leveling that the Jacobins achieved so forcefully. When the Constitution was ratified, the Federalists urged pompous titles for government officials. John Adams wanted the President addressed as "His Elective Majesty," and the Senate sergeant at arms was to be "The Usher of the Black Rod." Now, the Republicans went the other way and wanted to abolish ordinary titles of courtesy. Mister, Sir, Doctor, the Reverend, smacked of servility; all men should be addressed as "Citizen." The levelers had a little trouble with a word of address for women: "Citizeness," and even "Citess," were tried and found wanting. The whole nonsense blew away as the grandiose titles had.

LANGUAGE

Good or bad, speech is a part of manners. Americans started to rearrange the English language almost as soon as they got here. They borrowed words from Dutch and German settlers. They invented names for new plants and animals, or absorbed and changed the Indian names for them. They evolved local dialects, which isolation tended to preserve. Country people and frontier people seldom heard educated speech, and ridiculed it when they did. Pronunciation became slovenly: *thar* for "there," *cheer* for "chair"; *his'n, her'n, your'n, our'n,* all suggested by the sound of "mine" and "thine."

Especially in the back country, people still used old words that had died in England. Almost their only written guide was the King James Bible, and they hewed to it. *Jeans, molasses, andiron, trash* are

Coach passengers

all words they embalmed; so are the verbs *to whittle, to wilt, to guess.* New American words had gusto and originality. A small violet, which tends to appear in unexpected places, they called *Johnny-jump-up,* and it keeps the name. We use their words without noticing them. *Strenuous, clumsy, spurious* were once slang. Benjamin Franklin thought *to advocate, to progress,* and *to oppose* were barbarous Americanisms. And by the way, George Washington introduced, if he didn't coin, *to derange.*

The religious revival known as "The Second Great Awakening," which seems to have begun along the Ohio River in the early 1800's, created a new awareness of morality that quickly became a self-conscious and spurious prudery of language. All reference to the body and its natural functions became "indelicate." Absurd euphemisms appeared. Women ceased to have legs—they had limbs—and even these were mentioned only under stress. Pants became *inexpressibles. Shirt* or *corset* could not be uttered in mixed company. Even the word *woman* was avoided; it was replaced by the much uglier *female.* References to sex, in animals as well as in humans, were taboo: a bull became a *cowbeast,* a stallion, a *stablehorse.*

WOMEN

A woman had no rights under early United States laws. She was the ward of her husband, or of her nearest male relative. Yet parents seldom arranged marriages; the bride chose her own husband, presumably on the basis of romantic love, but sometimes with an eye to her own advancement. Though a fond father might give his daughter a munificent wedding present, he almost never gave her a formal dowry, as fathers did in Europe. Many a young man, of course, found himself more deeply affected by the charms of a maid with a rich father than by those of prettier girls with no prospects.

Early marriages were the general rule. An older daughter, all of fifteen, found herself almost a servant in her parents' big family, and got out as soon as possible. Her swain owned his farm, or at least his own labor, so they quickly set about raising a big family, whether in country or town.

Divorces were more common here than in Europe, and easier to get, but divorced people were less acceptable socially then they are now. Early frontier divorces were often nothing more formal than a mutual agreement to disband, and marriage was often just as casual.

The new American idea of a man dividing his estate among his children, instead of leaving all of it to his oldest son, was beginning to cut down family fortunes, and the old attitude toward women was beginning to change. Even without legal rights, an American woman had more freedom, and more responsibility, than any European woman. Remarkably, she also got more consideration from all classes of men. A respectable woman could safely travel anywhere alone, a thing impossible abroad. In spots, women were also grasping a little independence. Some were taking jobs in factories, and though they were grossly underpaid, their wages were their own.

BEHAVIOR

In all parts of the United States except in New England, the War of 1812 somehow whipped up a surge of nationalism. Whatever was American became good because it was American. This extended to manners. Editors urged the dropping of "imported superfluities of etiquette," and

readers with no etiquette to drop hailed the idea with joy. Americans would have "republican" manners, which turned out to be no manners at all. Respect for ladies survived, even when the behavior of the "ladies" did not entitle them to it. A visitor, who, it must be admitted, saw little good in any Yankee, reported women and children rudely thrusting themselves into the best seats on stages, and glowering from them upon their fellow passengers. Servants became increasingly independent. Strangers didn't wait for introductions before beginning conversations on a familiar basis, nor did they hesitate to ask other strangers personal questions. Table manners in taverns were spectacular. Men ate in silence, with their hats on, and helped themselves by spearing food across the table. Every man carried his own toothpick (the wealthy had gold ones) and made open use of it at the table. A French marquis bought a dinner at an inn for two casual acquaintances. When they had eaten, both departed with no word of thanks or farewell.

Only the most elegant men shaved themselves every day, and the idea that ladies and gentlemen should keep themselves clean at all times was still a novel one. In England, Beau Brummell was persuading a daring few to try it. But, even though they neglected bathing, most cultivated people were particular about clean linen. Their wool and silk clothing became deplorably soiled, however. Some fullers, whose regular occupation was finishing newly woven cloth, undertook dry cleaning. They used turpentine to dissolve grease and dirt, and for days afterward the garment advertised its new cleanliness with an acrid smell.

Most men smoked, many took snuff, and nearly all chewed, also. To light a pipe or cigar it was necessary to be near a fire; a "chaw" of tobacco or a pinch of snuff didn't have to be lighted. Dangerous and undependable matches existed after 1827, but few people had seen them or would pay their high price if they did see them.

of classic taunts, went to it "rough-and-tumble," without rules and with few holds barred. Kicking and biting were normal; nose twisting and eye gouging were not rare. If one warrior got a real stranglehold on the other's throat, bystanders would usually "persuade" him to desist. If there were no bystanders, there was one less warrior. Men frequently fought with knives, the six- or seven-inch blades held like swords rather than like the daggers they were.

Men spoke to one another bluntly and, as we have seen back in Benson Town, hated their

Encounter at Bladensburg

Men wouldn't smoke in a room with ladies, though a good many of the ladies themselves enjoyed a pipe in private. But a man wouldn't hesitate to chew in feminine company, and eject streams of "ambeer" into, or nearly into, the spittoon that was provided in even the most elegant homes.

PERSONAL COMBAT

Democracy was interpreted by nearly all Yankees as complete personal freedom, which they stood ready to defend. All classes of men would express with physical combat their resentment of any kind of slur or even a contrary political opinion, the style of battle varying from class to class. On the frontier and often in the rural East, combatants, after a proper exchange

enemies openly. The right of free speech was interpreted by editors as the right to call people names in print. Every so often an irate subscriber would arrive at the newspaper office appropriately armed to horsewhip the editor. Prepared, the editor would wave a four-pound pistol, harmlessly as a rule. Competing editors also took out after each other. As Mr. Philip Hone was shaving one morning in his house on Broadway, facing City Hall Park, in New York, he saw the meeting of two editors from his window. William Cullen Bryant, the poet, attacked William L. Stone with a whip. Stone was able to capture the weapon, and went off with it in his hand. Mr. Hone went on shaving.

A gentleman was tetchy about his "Honour." He challenged any other gentleman who insulted it to meet him in a duel. When the traducer was one he considered no gentleman, he simply beat him with his riding whip, if he was able to do it. A gentleman challenged by an "inferior" was considered justified in refusing to fight, as John Randolph of Roanoke did when General James Wilkinson challenged him. Randolph did meet Henry Clay, near where the Pentagon is now; both men fired and missed, probably on purpose, but honor was satisfied. The whole dueling business was governed by an elaborate set of rules usually called "The Code," or "The Tipperary Articles"; it had been constructed in Ireland. Dueling was of course the absurd survival of the medieval idea of trial by combat, which theoretically placed the decision directly in the hands of God; innocent weakness would strike down guilty strength.

The causes of duels were much the same as the causes of rough-and-tumble fights: politics, women, debts, and insults, but the insults usually grew out of other causes. Arguments built up to a point where one man said to another, "You lie!" Since it was assumed, on dubious grounds, that a gentleman could not lie, this demanded a challenge. A friend of the insulted party, his "second," presented the traducer, most politely, with an invitation to fight. The Code allowed the challenged man to choose the weapons; he also appointed a second of his own. From then on the two seconds managed the show.

In France, many duelists fought with rapiers, but Yankees preferred pistols. These were specially made in matched pairs for dueling. Dawn was considered a good, romantic, uncomfortable time to fight a duel. The seconds inspected the guns to see that they were identical and that no one had tampered with them. It is rumored that they were sometimes "adjusted." When all was ready, the two armed gladiators stood back to back. On command, they walked away from each other a counted number of paces, wheeled, and fired. Though the pistols could, and sometimes did, kill, the sport was not quite as dangerous as it seems, and many duels ended with nothing worse than powder smoke, or a little spilled blood. The pistols were smooth-bored and fired one spherical lead ball. Hence they were not accurate weapons. Also, it was snap shooting by men who were usually nervous about being shot. In America's most famous duel, fought in 1804,

Alexander Hamilton's shot went wild, and Aaron Burr wounded him, fatally.

Dueling was illegal in most states, but sheriffs, and even judges, who often had "been out" themselves, tended to be lenient. Duelists eased things by crossing state lines to fight. A spot near Bladensburg, in Maryland, was for years the almost official congressional dueling ground. The custom died hard, but public opinion turned against it, and the time came when intelligent men made light of challenges, sometimes by choosing ridiculous weapons, and finally the dreadful absurdity was laughed to death.

FOOD

We picture an early Yankee citizen as full-blooded, sturdy, and energetic, but travelers' reports fail to bear us out; they describe him as white-faced, sickly, and listless. The travelers blamed his food and his eating habits. Most people ate as much as they could afford, or as much as they could possibly hold, far more than any modern man except Diamond Jim Brady. They bolted the food down as fast as they could, and chewed it only as much as they absolutely had to chew it. They ate quantities of animal fat, and despised green vegetables, calling them "grass" or "fodder." One account includes in the menu of a dinner in a prosperous home "two dishes of butter." This was almost certainly eaten "neat," as cheese might be; though a backwoods woman, quoted elsewhere, said, "The children like a little bread with their butter." The plain people had strong prejudices against "fancy food." Martin Van Buren was hurt politically when he was accused of using public money to raise such things as cauliflower, celery, strawberries, and raspberries.

There were market gardens on the outskirts of large towns; people ate some vegetables, but thoroughly "softened" by cooking, and "flavored" with fat salt pork. Fresh fruit was perishable and suspected, along with salads, of causing cholera. Most people ate fruit anyway, though it was considered especially bad for children. Not surprisingly, there was much scurvy and rickets. In summer, milk would sour in two hours. It was sold in towns from large cans, carried on push-carts or on a neck yoke, and it was poor stuff. City cows never saw grass. They lived in stables and ate distillery mash. The diet of the city poor was especially bad. Their meat was largely "blood pudding" and "fatback" (salt pork). The pudding was beef blood and pig blood cooked with meat scraps and stuffed into sausage skins. With it, poor people ate bread and molasses. In the 1790's a blight hit the wheat fields of the middle states, and for several years, bread was made of half rye flour and half cornmeal. This "rye an' injun" was always prevalent in New England, where wheat grew poorly.

Most adult men still started the day with a "draft" of hard cider, beer, or whiskey-and-water, taken on arising. Breakfast, often eaten late, after two or three hours of work, was a heavy meal featuring, perhaps, salt fish, cold ham, hot bread (often cornbread), tea, and coffee. A good inn would add chicken and boiled beef or mutton to that. Dinner was eaten at two or two-thirty in the afternoon. A prosperous family would load its dinner table with eight or ten items of food for an ordinary meal, all of them major dishes, served in

Milkman, redrawn
from a woodcut in the book
The Cries of New York

quantity. Some of the fare seems repetitious: for instance, boiled goose and roast turkey at the same meal.

Though the famous French gourmet Anthelme Brillat-Savarin once relished a Connecticut farm dinner of mutton, vegetables, and cider, he and other Frenchmen deplored American cookery

in general. For his part, the average American firmly believed that the French lived on frogs and salad. One Yankee host thoughtfully served soup with whole green frogs in it to a French admiral. Americans who went to France learned to like the food. Mr. Jefferson liked it so much that he brought a French cook home with him. The refugees from the Terror had a beneficial effect on cooking in wealthy homes; and the tavern of "Black Sam" Fraunces was a culinary oasis in New York, and remained so for many years.

The problem of getting fish, meat, and fowl on the table while it was still fresh plagued people everywhere. Even in winter a chicken could spoil in eighteen hours; in warm weather, four hours would do it. Ice, cut from ponds and kept in covered pits, was expensive and there was no practical way to make use of it for home storage. In 1800, Thomas Moore, who lived in Maryland near the new capital city, covered a tub with rabbit-skin insulation and filled it with ice, in which he submerged a tin storage pot. The results encouraged him, and three years later, he patented a home ice chest. It was a double-walled wooden box, insulated with charcoal, or ashes, between its walls, and with a tin ice holder inside, near its top.

People recognized its value at once, but the high cost of ice held back its use. Then, in 1827, Nathaniel Wyeth invented a new ice cutter. It looked somewhat like a plow, with a saw-toothed blade in place of the share. A horse pulled it across a frozen pond and men followed to break out the cakes with pinch bars. Coupled with an improved above-ground ice house, built like Moore's box, it reduced the price of ice 60 percent. By the mid-thirties an ice chest was "as much a necessity in a kitchen as its stove."

The necessary stove was newer than Moore's icebox. It wasn't until 1815 that William T. James made and sold the first practical cookstove. Until its advent, and in many houses after its advent, town women cooked in open fireplaces, just as Bertha Whittle did. With a stove and the new short-handled utensils, they had to learn all over again, but most town women readily accepted the new method because it used less fuel. The stove could not broil or roast meat as well as a fireplace could, but it was neater; handling pots on it was much easier; and there was no spit to be turned.

Converting a kitchen from open-fire cooking to stove cooking meant closing up the fireplace with a brick wall and buying a new set of utensils. Most householders sold their old long-handled pots, skillets, and gridirons to a junkman, but often the prosperous merely gave them decent burial behind the new stove wall. Many utensils in museum collections came out of fireplaces reopened by restorers and wreckers.

The long-term preservation of food by sealing it, hot, in airtight containers, now generally called canning, was known by 1800, though nobody at that time knew why it worked. Scholars had observed bacteria through microscopes, but they had not yet connected them with disease or fermentation. By 1819, two plants in New York City sold preserved food in glass jars; probably quite dangerous stuff. The practice increased, and the first tin cans for food appeared in the 1830's.

ELEGANT DINING

A formal dinner in a wealthy home seems to have been an ordeal for hosts and guests alike. It lasted three or four hours. We catch glimpses of the agony of hostesses over the interval of stilted palaver that preceded the meal. This seldom improved much at the table. The menu seemed endless. In very grand houses the plates were real porcelain: Spode, Worcester, or Chinese export. Simpler homes were proud to own blue-printed Staffordshire pottery, or cream-colored Wedgwood with a fringe edge of green. This was politely called "china." Plates with American scenes on them became popular. They were made for the Yankee trade in England, in France, and in China. Spoons were silver. Very elegant knives and forks were steel with silver handles; bone or stag-horn handles were more usual. The knives had round tips, and up to about 1820, the forks had three tines; after that grander forks with four tines appeared.

There was no ritual of service plates, or the serving of what restaurants now call "appetizers." Normally a seated guest found his dinner plate waiting for him, though in cold weather all the plates would stay in a warming rack on the hearth

Wyeth ice cutter

until they were needed. The guest found a single fork lying, points down, on the white tablecloth at the left of his plate; at its right, a knife. Perhaps three spoons lay crosswise beyond the plate. There was no napkin. Colonial housewives had provided them, fresh for every meal, even when there was no company, but that was when people ate with their fingers. When forks came in, it was assumed for some time that napkins had lost their usefulness. They hadn't, so people quite casually wiped their fingers and their mouths on the edge of the tablecloth.

The most genteel ate with the fork, apparently using the left hand, as the English still do, but many well-mannered people raised food to their mouths on the knife blade, and defended their right to do so. As late as 1836, the wife of a Harvard professor wrote in an etiquette book, "If you wish to imitate the French or English, you will put every mouthful into your mouth with your fork; but if you think as I do that Americans have as good a right to their own fashions as any other country, you may choose the convenience of feeding yourself with your right hand armed with a

steel blade; and provided you do it neatly and do not put in large mouthfuls or close your lips tight over the blade, you ought not to be considered as eating ungenteelly." This was a rearguard action; by that time the fork had won the battle.

When napkins went out, finger bowls came in and persisted through the first decades of the nineteenth century. England clung to them through the thirties after they were abandoned here, for reasons that Mr. Philip Hone made crystal clear. He had been publicly criticized by the English actress Fanny Kemble for not providing finger bowls. His good manners would not let him reply, but he explained himself in his private diary: "I think it unseemly . . . washing their hands, rinsing their mouths, rubbing their gums with the finger, and squirting the polluted water back into the bowl." Mr. Hone was an ex-mayor of New York when Miss Kemble was a guest in his house in 1832.

When the napkin recovered its status it was customary to fold it around a guest's serving of bread, concealing the bread entirely. This laid a trap for the uninitiated; they sometimes flipped their bread onto the floor. For a large dinner party, the table was spread with two white linen cloths, one over the other. No flowers decorated the table; sometimes a silver epergne served as a centerpiece. The servants removed the top cloth at the end of the main onslaught, and served a collection of sweets on the other one. These might include, at one meal, pudding, tarts, custard, French pastries, and ice cream—the last two items recently introduced by the refugees. Ice cream created a furor and quickly became so popular that it was hawked on New York streets. Even with a hand-cranked freezer, making ice cream was a chore. Before 1850 it was worse;

someone had to rock the can by hand in the ice-and-salt mixture.

When the sweet course was removed, the second tablecloth went with it, and the servants placed decanters of port and Madeira at the corners of the table. Bowls of fruit and nuts went in the middle, and each guest got a fruit plate and two wineglasses. This was dessert. The name wasn't applied to the sweets until sometime after 1845. The ladies stayed at the bare table only long enough for a single glass of wine. This was supposed to be as much as the "weaker vessel" could stand, even though everybody knew that most women carried small flasks of rum in their reticules (handbags). The men lingered for several glasses of wine before joining the ladies.

The hostess served tea and coffee, often with cake, in the withdrawing room. The tea is reported as so strong as to have been bitter, and the coffee so weak that it looked like tea; so the hostess customarily put a spoon into each coffee cup to identify it. Tea drinkers got their spoon on the saucer. If for nothing else, the spoon was needed to place across the top of the cup as a signal of sufficiency. The guests drank both beverages from the saucer.

Naturally, tea had been unpopular just before, and during, the Revolutionary War. After the war it was so expensive as to be a rare luxury, but the growth of the China trade brought the price down. Then everybody drank it every afternoon; there were even tea parties in the evening. Old diaries monotonously note with whom the diarist drank tea, or who drank tea with the diarist. Since dinner ended at five or later, and tea always followed it, additional guests often came for tea only. In the country, people who were asked for tea expected supper, and got it.

Worcester

The Tea Water pump

15.
New York City

TWO FIRES, in 1776 and in 1778, destroyed the whole western side of New York, burning three quarters of its buildings. The town rebuilt its burned area after the Revolution, but though thriving, it didn't spread rapidly. In 1803, with a population of sixty thousand and exports totaling some twenty million dollars a year, it still occupied only the southern tip of Manhattan Island, and had no town houses north of Hester Street.

Geography, more than enterprise, made New York. As a site for a city, Manhattan Island has advantages over any other in North America, and is hardly matched in the world. The last of the glaciers dropped its huge terminal moraine some five miles south of the island's tip and created the Narrows. These protect a magnificent harbor in which whole fleets may anchor. The Hudson River, flowing past the island, also flows past rich farmlands and mineral deposits, and is navi-

gable for sizable ships for 145 miles northward. Useful tributaries to it penetrate far into New Jersey. To the east, Long Island Sound provides a protected waterway to the north shore of Long Island and to southern New England.

The early New Yorkers were fully conscious of their town's possibilities, and though its later development may have somewhat exceeded their expectations, they prepared for it as well as they could. By 1811 the town commissioners had planned and surveyed all the streets as far north as 155th. In the 1840's John James Audubon still had his farm there. The commissioners ran 155 streets east and west, but only a baker's dozen in the directions most people travel, north and south. They provided no parks whatever, giving as the reason the fact that Manhattan "is embraced by the sea." Even the spacious parade ground they mapped was all but eliminated, leaving only Madison Square as a vestige. Central Park was a

The corner of Wall Street and Water; at the left is the Tontine Coffee House.

happy afterthought, long after, but soon enough to save a little of the natural rolling terrain; everything south of it was leveled.

In 1811, Greenwich Village, which now seems far downtown, was an actual country village entirely outside the city, and what is now its Washington Square was a neglected cemetery for paupers. Yellow fever made Greenwich grow. Every summer, city dwellers who could afford it moved out there to escape the disease. During the worst epidemic, in 1822, not only people, but stores, banks, and even the post office, moved to Greenwich and enlarged the place permanently.

More than a mile of warehouses, fronted by slips and wharves, lined the East River in 1800.

Radishes

The Hudson side of the island was steep and rocky, and deep water came right up to the shore. This made wharf building difficult, so few were put there before the 1830's. The commerce that needed all these warehouses supported merchants and shipbuilders, and also created a class of businessmen who insured ships and cargoes and acted as brokers and agents. One day in May 1792, twenty-four such men met under a buttonwood (sycamore) tree at Wall and William streets and signed an agreement to act together as a group. Their immediate purpose was to sell the bonds that would finance Secretary Hamilton's redemption project. They didn't know they were starting the New York Stock Exchange. The group made its headquarters at the Tontine Coffee House, at Wall and Water, a short distance east of the buttonwood tree. Within a few years Wall Street became the financial center of the nation.

115

Even in 1825, with a population of 166,000, the town didn't reach above Fourteenth Street, and most of it was concentrated in what had been the little Dutch village, its unburned East Side still showing its origin. This, too, burned in 1837. The Dutch had laid out one wide street, Broadway, running straight north from their fort. The rest of the narrow streets simply accumulated wherever men, or cows, wore paths. Though time has made some changes, this pattern is still stamped on them. Rough cobbles paved them in the early nineteenth century, and oil lamps set on posts tried bravely to light them. Where there were any sidewalks at all, they were necessarily narrow and were interrupted every whipstitch by projecting cellar doors. The streets were filthy, and cluttered with their famous roving pigs. Householders owned the pigs and marked them as their property, but they roamed at will to scavenge a living. Riots met all official efforts to dislodge them, and they went on scavenging almost to the time of the Civil War.

Not all New York citizens behaved themselves, so the city hired watchmen who patrolled fixed beats all night. Unlike Philadelphia's watch, these

Scissors grinder

were policemen. A smaller group of constables handled trouble in the daytime. The watchmen wore thick leather hats. They carried clubs, and lanterns for peering into dark corners. The wards of the town had names, not numbers, and each ward had its watchhouse. The watchmen dealt with thieves, and with the looters who always rushed to the many fires. A lookout in the cupola of the jail rang a bell when he sighted a fire, and the watch repeated the alarm through all the wards. Volunteers fought fires, but they worked under the direction of a professional "chief engineer." There was no rivalry of fire companies such as existed farther south. The engineer got no salary, but he was paid for any repair work he did on the fire engines.

HAWKERS

Manhattan's great drawback was the shortage of good drinking water. Most people had wells and

Tea rusk

pumps but they yielded unpleasantly brackish water. Way back in 1700, people who wanted drinkable water brought buckets, or barrels on pushcarts, to the "Tea Water Spring." It was then outside the town, near the eastern edge of Collect Pond; to give it a modern address: the west side of Park Row between Baxter and Mulberry. After 1800 the city leased the spring to a man who put a pump over it and sold the water. Vendors bought most of it to peddle at a penny a pail from horse-drawn tank carts. With increasing population around it, Collect Pond became a cesspool, and seepage from the pond polluted the spring. The pump was condemned and the pond filled in. But the need for good water remained, and the carts, with TEA WATER painted on their tanks, supplied it until 1830 from good springs farther north.

Aaron Burr headed a group of men who saw possible profits in supplying water. They got themselves chartered as the Manhattan Water Company, built a spring-fed reservoir, laid six miles of wooden pipe, and by 1799 furnished all the water they had to about four hundred families. The shortage wasn't fully relieved until after 1837, when the city tapped the Croton River and brought water through an aqueduct to the reservoir that still exists at the upper end of Central Park. There was also a high-walled distributing reservoir on Murray Hill, just where the New York Public Library is now.

In addition to "tea water," all sorts of goods and services could be had in the streets. Small boys cleaned sidewalks and steps for small sums. Tinkers and scissors grinders rang bells to advertise themselves. Carters purveyed "clean Rockaway sand" for the floors of taprooms, restaurants, and private kitchens. Other carters sold straw, or cattail fluff, for stuffing mattresses and pillows. "Ay-rabs" sold food in the streets, to be taken home or eaten on the spot: clams and oysters from Staten Island, shad from the Hudson, wild pigeons at a few cents a dozen. In addition to those who sold fresh milk, some men peddled buttermilk from a can on a wheelbarrow. Onions, which came by sloop from Connecticut, appeared on the street in ropes two feet long, their tops "tied to a wisp of straw with twine string." Yeast, called "east," came from a pail that the vendor had

Bull's Head Tavern

filled with beer-vat sediment. Pathetic little girls sold bunches of radishes, even to people who didn't like radishes.

In view of the reported prejudice against fruit, a remarkable variety of it seems to have found a market. A collection of old woodcuts, *The Cries of New York*, shows men selling "water-milyons" from wagons. A woman carries Weehawken wild strawberries in small baskets, hanging by their handles from long horizontal poles. A juvenile cherry seller is equipped with a balance scale to weigh them out. Oranges, lemons, and limes travel in flat baskets; and a wheelbarrow load of "pines" (pineapples) attracts carriage-trade customers.

Hot food was offered, too: South Carolina yams; baked pears; green corn, boiled in the husk and salted to taste by the vendor. At three o'clock the tea rusk man started his rounds (his rusk was sweet bread, toasted); two hours later he sold hot muffins for supper. Hot gingerbread was available at all hours.

There were also professional buyers: of old metal, and of rags and old rope. Rags were the only known raw material for making paper. Old rope, picked apart, was oakum for caulking ships. Much of the picking was done in prisons and almshouses. New York still had a debtors' prison, but for a fee of fifty cents a debtor could live out-

side the actual building, as long as he stayed (boarded) within a fixed area.

GETTING AROUND

In 1816, Peter Cooper, the iron founder and philanthropist-to-be, ran a grocery store in little Bowery Village on what is now Third Avenue, at Seventh Street, outside the city. When he moved, he kept the land, and years later gave it to Cooper Union, which he founded. The Bowery acquired a bad reputation in later years, but in the early 1800's it was the marketplace for the East Side as Broadway was for the West Side. Originally the lane to Governor Peter Stuyvesant's *bouwerie* (farm), it now led into the Boston Post Road, which wandered up the island to King's Bridge across Spuyten Duyvil. This was the route of the eastbound post riders and of the Boston stagecoaches. In 1805, two local stage lines ran over it from The Bull's Head Tavern, on the Bowery, to the little village of Harlem.

When General Washington re-entered New York, at the end of the Revolutionary War, he waited at the Bull's Head until the British completed their evacuation of the city. In spite of being on the edge of the stockyards and hence serving as headquarters for the drovers and

Coachee

York and Paulus Hook, New Jersey. It was eighty feet long. Each of its hulls was ten feet wide, and they lay ten feet apart. The single paddle wheel turned between the hulls, with its engine mounted on the timbers that joined them. A deck covered the whole craft, except for the operating well in the middle. Fulton reported carrying eight carriages, twenty-nine horses, and one hundred people, on one trip, and claimed that three hundred more people could have gone along. With a reversible engine, the boat didn't have to turn around. Either end nosed into a slip, and it unloaded onto a floating pontoon that was connected to the shore by a hinged bridge. A second ferry was needed in two years. A year after that, a steam ferry crossed the East River to Brooklyn. In 1816, the city opened Fulton Street to join the two ferry slips and permit through traffic.

Rich New Yorkers owned stately equipages for formal occasions. Some of them were coaches which seated four; some were chariots, built like coaches but seating only two. No doubt the old Beekman coach, now in the New-York Historical Society collection, still rumbled over the cobbles, though it was more than fifty years old. Models changed more slowly then. Barouches had become popular for transporting the wealthy on casual errands. They seated four, and had collapsible tops. A family carriage for the merely prosperous might be a coachee, or "curtain coach," so called because it had rollable leather curtains instead of glass windows. The seat for the coachee's driver was built into the body of the vehicle at the same height as the passenger seats, and he had the protection of the vehicle's roof. This was an innovation; a coach driver had

butchers, the Bull's Head was a rendezvous for dashing young men; and being the first inn they came to, it was a popular lodging for New England visitors. After 1826, the Bowery Theatre stood right across the street. By then the Bowery offered beer gardens for the pleasure of the increasing German population, and shops whose clerks patrolled the sidewalks to collar customers and drag them inside.

Until the Brooklyn Bridge was finished in 1883, the only way to get on or off Manhattan Island, except at its northern tip, was by ferry. Ferries continued to carry all traffic across the Hudson until the Holland Tunnel was opened in 1927. Crossing with oars or sails was at best slow, and at worst dangerous. The ferries didn't try it at all in very rough weather. In the early 1800's travelers bound south crossed the Hudson by boat and boarded their coaches on the Jersey side, where they later boarded railroad cars.

In 1809, after his *Clermont* had succeeded, Robert Fulton built a twin-hulled steam ferryboat and ran it across the Hudson between New

Picnic

a separate seat out in the weather, high above the front axle. Elegant young men flourished around in varnished chaises with C springs and folding tops, or in one-man sulkies. Common chaises were everywhere, and the great American buggy was just making its first appearance about 1826. Youths seeking attention labored to ride the new velocipedes, or "swift walkers." These were wooden bicycles propelled by the rider's toes pushing against the ground. One of them appears on page 7. In winter, whenever there was enough snow to allow it, heavy commercial traffic as well as pleasure traffic took to runners.

Livery stables had vehicles for hire, and also saddle horses, not for riding in the park, but for going places on the streets. A "cab" with a driver could be hired on the street, too. Usually it was a standard chaise, but there seem to have been some "cabriolets" which were like chaises but had a folding seat for the driver mounted over the dashboard. About 1827, Mr. A. Brower began making regular trips on Broadway, carrying passengers for a fixed fare in a large carriage. It proved too small, so, in 1829, he introduced the "sociable," a closed coach mounted on high springs and capable of carrying ten passengers. This, also, was inadequate, and two years later he lengthened both his route and his vehicle. The new one was called the "Omnibus"; it carried twenty, at twelve-and-a-half cents each. Mr. Brower soon had so many competitors, who drove so madly, that the newspapers demanded traffic control.

Newspapers came and went. Often they were founded by politicians for the spreading of their opinions. Alexander Hamilton founded the *New York Evening Post* for that purpose in 1801. Only the largest cities had dailies. They went to regular subscribers only, at six cents a copy. Until after 1830, when papermaking machines became common, all newspapers were printed on handmade rag paper. Steam rotary presses appeared in 1835; until then each sheet was printed separately on a hand press. Even then, and long afterward, compositors hand-set all the type letter by letter.

AMUSEMENTS

The idea of a special playground for city children had occurred to no one; children played in the

streets or on vacant lots. That they played tag and hide-and-seek is certain; such games are instinctive. Girls rolled hoops and jumped rope and surely played some form of hopscotch. The boys, and perhaps some girls, too, played "tipcat" with a stick bat and a double-pointed wooden peg just as they do now. This might be called a ball game with no ball. Balls were hard to come by, and such as existed were costly. No one made rubber balls; "caoutchouc" was still a curiosity. Balls for "town ball" and "stoolball" were covered with leather, like a baseball, and stuffed hard with oakum or with linen tow. Stoolball made use of an actual stool as a base, or wicket, defended by a batter. Town ball seems to have been much the same thing, perhaps without the stool.

New Amsterdam had had a bowling green, of which the name and a small triangular patch survive, but the Yankees had lost interest in the game. Possibly it was too slow for them. Young men played skittles, or ninepins, on short alleys at taverns. They also played billiards, especially in establishments run by Frenchmen. It was almost the French national game. They introduced it in the Mississippi valley and it became so popular in the new western states that heavy billiard tables were hauled over the mountains and rafted down the Ohio. It's hardly an overstatement to say that every inn with a yard had pins for pitching horseshoes. Old and young pitched them. Chief Justice John Marshall was a noted expert.

The Gavotte

Except in Puritan New England, dancing was always popular. George Washington once danced for three hours straight with Mrs. Nathaniel Greene. Large taverns had handsome ballrooms where well-to-do bachelors sponsored "Assemblies," or "Cotillions," at which marriageable girls were "presented to society." A few such still survive. These same bachelors got up informal "frolics," for which they drove the girls, with chaperones, to the country in chaises for a picnic, or for supper at a rural inn. In winter they went to the inns in sleighs, with hot bricks at their feet under the lap robes.

There wasn't a lot of entertainment for the general public; especially there was little that was free, so people made much of patriotic observances. Some of their holidays lost their luster and disappeared. Evacuation Day, November 25, commemorated the departure of the last British troops, in 1783. Ratification Day, July 26, celebrated Alexander Hamilton's reversal of the majority in the New York legislature in 1788. The

Fourth of July had due attention, also. Parades celebrated all these holidays, and the whole populace turned out for them. At night there were illuminations. These survive now only as electric candles in windows at Christmas. When every window in an otherwise dimly lighted town had real candles in it, and bonfires burned in the streets, the effect was lovely, though dangerous. Any auspicious occasion produced an illumination: a victory, a peace treaty, a new President, governor, or even mayor. The Negroes of New York seized upon the old Dutch celebration of Pinkster Day, seven weeks after Easter, and made it their own. They took over the town and staged a riotous carnival. When it eventually became more riot than carnival, it had to be abandoned.

Christmas, though it called for an oversize dinner, was still a religious holiday. Only children received presents, and in New York preserved the Dutch custom of hanging up their stockings for St. Nicholas to fill. Professor Clement Clarke Moore, who lived in his square ancestral mansion near

120

Greenwich Village (incidentally, his house had quite small chimneys), designed the modern picture of a fat Santa Claus. In 1822, he wrote " 'Twas the Night before Christmas" for his children. His original title, "A Visit from St. Nicholas," has been forgotten; so, oddly, has his description of Santa Claus as a pipe-smoking midget dressed completely in fur.

New York gentlemen preserved the custom of paying short calls on New Year's morning, and sometimes it took two days to complete the rounds. Since they drank a little punch or eggnog at every house, they were usually somewhat bemused by noon.

Men raced horses informally almost from the time the first horses were brought in. Southerners were particularly keen about the sport, and organized annual meetings in colonial times at Charleston, Williamsburg, and Annapolis. By 1800, boatloads of enthusiasts traveled from Philadelphia and New York to see the Charleston races, and just possibly to bet on them. Public racing began on Long Island in 1820, and the East River ferries were loaded to the gunwales with fans. In 1823, one hundred thousand people saw the great Eclipse outrun the southern horse Sir Henry. These were not youngsters such as are now raced, but full-grown horses. Trotters also competed at Jamaica, not pulling sulkies but under saddle. The first racing wagons, with four wheels, appeared in the 1840's.

Professional pugilism was still to come, but there were plenty of impromptu fistfights to cheer up the crowds in the streets. Cockfights—or chicken fights, as they were called—were legal and popular. Bullbaiting, and more rarely, bearbaiting, which opposed bull terriers to the larger animals, attracted male spectators. A handful of "eccentrics" objected to them on the basis of cruelty.

Commercialized entertainment began in New York at about the same time that racing started there. The theater had been long established; this was entertainment at a lower level than that, though above the animal combats. In effect it was a circus with no menagerie: acrobats, slackwire artists, clowns, tumblers, jugglers. The same performers appeared in late summer at the agricultural fairs, which had started in New England

and quickly spread through the other states.

Peculiar to New York, and partly taking the place of public parks, were its pleasure gardens. Several of them competed in the eighteenth century, but gradually all fell by the wayside except the best of them, Vauxhall, named for the London gardens. It started in 1750, and remained popular, in several locations and under several managers, for almost seventy-five years. In 1806, Joseph Delacroix moved it, for the last time, to the old Barclay estate, which ran from Broadway east to the Bowery, above what is now Fourth Street. A man named Sperry had run a nursery there. Delacroix improved Sperry's gardens, planted flowers, built summerhouses and seats, and set up a large equestrian statue of General Washington. He charged an admission fee of two shillings, but it included a glass of ice cream or of punch. Fireworks were free of necessity, and music was free as a rule, but equestrian shows, theatrical performances, and special exhibits cost extra. Vauxhall exhibited America's first diorama, a representation of the parade with which New York celebrated the first Ratification Day. It was painted on a long strip of canvas which moved past the spectators, off one hidden roller and on to another. So important were the Vauxhall Gardens, that the city forbore to cut streets through them. The long block on the east side of Broadway north of Fourth Street remains unbroken nearly to Eighth.

Replacing Federal Hall, which stood on Wall Street facing the head of Broad, New York's "new" City Hall was finished in 1812. The handsome building still serves its original purpose. The small park in which it stands was originally cluttered with other municipal buildings—a watchhouse, the jail, the poorhouse. At that time the nearest approach to a public park was the Battery. A pleasant place to stroll had been made there by filling in shallow water at the tip of the island. Refreshments were sold in a roofed pavilion surrounding the flagpole, and a band played there at times. Just off shore stood Castle Clinton, built as a fort in the War of 1812, and converted afterward into a music hall. It was reached by a bridge. In later years, as Castle Garden, it became the gateway through which thousands of immigrants entered the United States.

The Park Theatre

16.
The Arts

THE THEATER

COMPANIES of English actors performed plays in all of the larger towns except Boston, and in some of the small ones, before 1750. They traveled from place to place by water; inland towns saw no plays. The larger ports had theaters, properly laid out, with stage, pit, and boxes, but usually constructed like barns, and very drafty. In villages, the audiences assembled in halls, or in the tavern ballrooms.

After 1800, all the cities, even Boston, had theaters properly built for their purpose. Though smaller places depended largely on resident repertory groups, the improvement of roads brought them occasional "big-name" actors like George Frederick Cooke (good even when drunk), Edmund Kean, Charles Kemble and his daughter Fanny. All of these were English, and they brought along English supporting actors. Bit parts were sometimes taken by local amateurs, whom the program identified only as "Played by a gentleman for his own amusement." Most of the few American professionals are mere names without renown. But the "Mr. Jefferson" who played substantial parts was a native, and was also the grandfather of that Joseph Jefferson who enchanted *our* grandfathers in the role of Rip Van Winkle. An American star appeared in 1806:

John Howard Payne. He is now known only as the author of "Home, Sweet Home," but he was an outstanding actor and also a successful playwright. He played Hamlet; he also played Romeo to the Juliet of Mrs. David Poe, who was Edgar Allan's mother. Payne was the first American actor to play a leading part on the London stage.

An American theater of the 1820's was arranged much as later theaters were, with an orchestra behind a rail below the footlights, seats on the floor behind the musicians, and more seats in balconies. The Park Theater in New York had four balconies. It was the arrangement of the audience that differed from later times. Our "orchestra" was their "pit," as it had been since Shakespeare's day. Only men sat there, and not the best behaved of men, since these were the cheapest seats in the house; the basic fifty-cent admission fee entitled the holder to a pit seat. Mixed company sat in the balconies, at twenty-five cents additional for the upper two, and at seventy-five cents additional for the box seats in the lower two—these seats had backs. The theater reserved no seats by number, so people often sent servants to hold seats for them. The doors opened at four-thirty in the afternoon; the performance began at six-thirty.

The audience got a "double bill" for its money. The main piece—comedy, melodrama, or tragedy

(in five acts)—was followed by an "afterpiece," usually a broad farce with music; the actors called it a "burletta." In the interval, the management presented a divertissement in the form of music or dancing. When Madame Francisguy Hutin danced at the Bowery Theater wearing a short ballet skirt and tights, the press described the impact of her costume: ". . . the cheeks of the greater portion of the audience were crimsoned with shame, and every lady in the lower tier of boxes left the house."

Mayor Philip Hone laid the cornerstone of the Bowery Theater in 1826. Seating three thousand people, it was the largest and finest playhouse in the country. Its pit seats had backs, and its stage was lighted by gas jets. Even that harsh English lady Mrs. Trollope found its scenery and machinery as good as those of a London theater.

Camera lucida

She objected, however, to men sitting in the front rows of the pit with their hats on, and to others who dangled their legs over the box railings. Her criticism was effective. Some months after her book appeared, a man who purposely stretched his legs thus was rebuked by the audience.

A merry protean Irishman from Perth Amboy, New Jersey, William Dunlap, was manager and producer, first at the Park Theater, then at the Bowery. Dunlap had studied painting in Benjamin West's studio, and had spent much of his free time haunting the backstages of the London theaters. In New York he worked to improve the quality of his productions. He introduced better scenery and costumes, and was able to tone down, a little, the bombastic excesses of the actors. When he became discontented with the quality of the plays themselves, he wrote new ones (not much better), and personally translated French and German plays. Dunlap made the German dramatist Kotzebue as popular in New York as in Berlin.

THE PAINTERS

Dunlap knew intimately his fellow students at West's "American School" in London, and those painters who were there before him, and after, he came to know in this country. All who had worked under West's benign influence belonged to a brotherhood for life. Most of what we now know of these men's biographies comes from a book Dunlap wrote, *The History of the Arts of Design*. Like many books about art, it is actually about artists.

Photography was about to startle the world and ruin portrait painting as a trade, but the wildest guess didn't yet suspect it. Since every man was sure that posterity would want to see his face, most of West's pupils were portrait painters. They were a remarkable group: John Singleton Copley, whom we lost to England, but not before he showed us how portraits should be painted; Charles Willson Peale, who believed that painting was a trade like any other, a better one than the saddle making he first practiced (accordingly, he taught his whole family to paint, and very well they did it); Gilbert Stuart, who made a good thing out of copying his own sketch of George Washington, and who painted many another

124

worthy, up and down the seaboard, suavely, and sometimes, perhaps, a little mendaciously. Thomas Sully, who grew up in Charleston, was especially good at romantic portraits of pretty girls. Among many, he painted Rebecca Gratz, of Philadelphia. Washington Irving described her so vividly to Sir Walter Scott that Scott made her into the Rebecca of *Ivanhoe*. Sully painted men, too, Edgar Allan Poe among them. Washington Allston, another South Carolinian, studied in London and Rome. He had literary taste, and was the friend of Coleridge, Lamb, and Washington Irving. After a seven-year residence in England, he settled in Boston. John Vanderlyn, a New Yorker whom Aaron Burr sent to Paris to study under David, throve there, but never did

Silhouette cutter

very well in this country though he painted many portraits here.

All these men painted wealthy people at what were then high prices, but much plainer people wanted their faces recorded, too, and they found painters to do the job. These were the limners, and this was their heyday. Most of them had had no training, or only so much as they could get by an apprenticeship under a limner who lacked training himself. Few comprehended perspective, or the modeling of form with light and shade; they simply looked at faces and tried to duplicate them. The best of them painted honest likenesses, which often reveal more about their subjects than fancier portraits do.

The limners traveled through the country in summer, on horseback, or in light wagons. Some are said to have carried pre-painted canvases, finished except for the heads. Limners didn't stop at portraits. They could turn out an inn sign, or

125

a representation of a farmstead, detailed down to the last hen, to go over a parlor mantel. Some of West's pupils started as limners, as he had, himself, and at least one of them finished at the trade. After William Dunlap left the theater, he became a traveling limner.

From 1797 until 1814, Charles St. Mémin, a Frenchman, traveled through the eastern states drawing crayon portraits with a camera lucida. This is an ocular device with which an artist can see the image of his sitter apparently projected on the drawing paper. He has only to trace it. St. Mémin was a trained artist; he traced skillfully. His men have character. He almost always drew the profile, and only rarely drew a woman.

There was another way to get a portrait that cost even less than the fifteen or twenty dollars a limner charged, and many people took advantage of it. This was the silhouette. There were silhouette "parlors" in large towns, and there was always a silhouette booth at a county fair. All silhouettes were profiles. The artists simply cut them out of black paper with scissors, and with remarkable skill.

Almost all professional painters did portraits, even though they specialized in other fields. Bumptious John Trumbull's specialty was large historical pictures. Our forefathers regarded this department of painting far more highly than we do. A large and dramatic "battle piece" was a nine days' wonder to people who had never seen a movie. They would pay to get a look at it, and painters made money that way. The eighteenth century liked its historical figures shown in Roman costume, even though they were still alive and had never worn such an outfit. Trumbull followed Benjamin West's lead, and presented his soldiers in the uniforms they actually wore. He knew what battles looked like. An aide to Washington, he fought in the Revolution until he got his feelings hurt because his commission was dated three months later than he thought it should be. Even so, he didn't render his battles realistically; his soldiers died with affecting grace; his generals commanded with operatic gestures. This accorded with the new romanticism.

Still other painters had interests that went beyond portraits. Thomas Cole tried being a limner in Ohio, and found the market flooded. In the early twenties, he came east to Catskill, New

York, and painted the romantic pictures of the Hudson gorge that led a whole group of painters to do the same. Robert Fulton—"Toot," his friends called him—was a better than competent painter. He, too, studied with West. In 1800, he painted "The Battle of Moscow," the first panorama ever shown in Paris. Fulton never gave up painting entirely. Samuel F. B. Morse studied in London under Washington Allston, from 1811 to 1815, and made his living painting portraits, though he hated doing them. Some of his work hints that he might have succeeded with historical pictures, and Van Wyck Brooks suggested that if he, instead of Trumbull, had been commissioned to paint the large pictures for the Capitol, Morse might have left the invention of the electric telegraph to someone else.

Peter Smith's toggle press

THE WRITERS

The Articles of Confederation didn't mention copyright, so the states had to settle the matter for themselves. For complete protection a writer had to copyright his work separately in every state. Congress enacted a national copyright law, under the Constitution, in 1790. It protected American writers for a total of twenty-eight years, but gave no protection whatever to foreign writers. Yankee publishers had already issued some European books without bothering about royalties; now, with a growing market, they went into piracy on a large scale.

Four translations of Goethe's *The Sorrows of Young Werther* had appeared here before 1800. For the next forty years publishing boomed.

Tristram Shandy, Tom Jones, The Vicar of Wakefield were all pirated many times. Nineteen editions of *Robinson Crusoe* sold out, and Richardson's sentimental novels *Pamela* and *Clarissa Harlow* were each reprinted forty times. All without a penny paid to any of the authors. Eventually responsible publishers began protecting foreign writers by contracting for their books, and then copyrighting them here in the firm's name. No other legal protection for foreigners was possible until 1891.

Philadelphia remained the center of publishing, but a dozen other towns, large and small, from Portsmouth, New Hampshire, to Pittsburgh, published books. Compositors still set all type by hand, and pressmen still pulled the handles of hand presses. But some of the presses were now made of iron instead of wood. These were more accurate than the old ones, but they worked in exactly the same way. In 1822, Peter Smith improved the mechanical advantage of the press handle, using a toggle instead of a screw thread. His iron press could print a whole sheet of paper at one impression. The older presses had to take two bites at a full sheet. Smith's press could almost double the production of a printshop. Binding made the bottleneck in publishing. Bookbinding methods were still medieval. They produced fine results, but very slowly. The binders sewed the leaves of a book to cords, which they tied through holes punched along the edges of the binding boards. They finished the job by pasting leather, or cloth, or paper, over the boards. Late in the 1820's someone invented case binding. Semiskilled women could cover the boards in advance, and simply glue them to the spines of the books, much as the job is done today.

American writers faced a bad situation: foreign books came free—and foreign books were better then theirs. But some Americans did get published, and it has never been necessary that a book should be good to be popular. Hugh Henry Brackenridge wrote a huge six-volume novel called *Modern Chivalry*. He got the first two volumes published in Philadelphia; then he went to Pittsburgh to practice law, and issued the third volume there, in 1793. Willam Wirt's *The Letters of a British Spy*, quite a good book, was a best seller. Wirt also wrote a biography of Patrick Henry in which he invented the famous phrase, which has crept into some history books, "Give me Liberty or give me death!" The runaway best seller of its

day, outselling *Pamela* and *Clarissa Harlow* together, was *Charlotte Temple,* by Susanna Rowson, who ran a finishing school for young "females" in Boston. The book was intended to warn her charges, and others like them, of the hazards of the gay seducer who loves and runs away. All the young ladies loved it. They blushed, and wept over it, and slept with it under their pillows. First published in 1791, it ran through two hundred editions.

In the early 1800's, in tune with the idea that Americans were as good as anybody, and probably better, newspaper and magazine editors demanded a ready-made American literary tradition, wholly independent of Europe. The writers mourned that we had no history, no romance, no manners, and undertook to create an American literature by imitating the British. A real epic was unfolding around them in a magnificent setting, but they saw only crudity, and did not understand crudity as subject matter in itself. In a sense it did become that, though not in writing that is first-rate literature. The Reverend Joseph Doddridge had written his memories of a youth on the Pennsylvania frontier; Dr. Daniel Drake would shortly write about his boyhood in a Kentucky cabin. Neither account was printed until long after it was written. So it was with diaries and letters; some of the best writing of the time lay hidden in them.

The bud that would be the flowering of New England had barely shown color. By 1812, the stripling William Cullen Bryant had written "Thanatopsis," but few noticed it. Even as late as the thirties, Emerson found "not a book, a speech or a thought" in Massachusetts. Shortly he would himself supply all three. In the late twenties, Hawthorne was beginning to scribble in Salem, and Thoreau was keeping his eyes open

in Concord, as he drove the family cow to pasture.

It was in New York City that the first sprouts of a genuine American literature reached the light. Washington Irving was the youngest son, and evidently the darling, of a prosperous mercantile family. He knew every inch of his "queer, old, topsy-turvy, rantipole city." He also knew the Hudson valley, and its homegrown yarns, through long visits at Tarrytown to the Dutch family of his friend James K. Paulding. When he was only nineteen, Irving wrote a series of articles under the pen name "Jonathan Oldstyle," for the New York *Evening Chronicle.* Perhaps they appeared only because Irving's brother, Peter, owned and edited the paper, but they attracted favorable attention, notably from Aaron Burr, and from William Dunlap, both of whom knew a hawk from a handsaw. In 1807, Irving and Paulding, who was a talented writer and versifier, collaborated on a yellow-backed magazine they called *Salmagundi.* It poked amiable fun at the town and its people, and was popular for the year it lasted.

Irving began *Knickerbocker's History of New York* as a satire on a pompous guidebook written by Dr. Samuel L. Mitchill, but he quickly left the good doctor in the lurch and aimed his good-natured shafts at the stolid Dutch settlers of the town. If he offended their descendants, he delighted everyone else. It is the proof of the book's quality that after more than 150 years it is still great fun to read. Here, at last, was a genuinely American book. No English models existed for Irving's stout Dutchmen, or for Diedrich Knickerbocker himself. The book's gaiety and charm certainly were not what the editors had in mind, but here was American literature nevertheless.

In England, Scott and Byron recognized the originality of *Knickerbocker,* and Coleridge sat up all night reading it. When Irving went over six years later, they and others welcomed him warmly. He stayed in Europe seventeen years, and long before the end of them, he had turned into what was actually an English writer, though the man himself remained American.

In 1819 James Fenimore Cooper published his first book, anonymously. It was *Precaution,* a conventional romantic novel which sank like a stone in the literary pond. Few read it then, and it's doubtful that any have lately. Cooper was born in New Jersey, but he grew up, a convinced aristocrat, in the central New York wilderness, where his remarkable father, Judge William Cooper, was creating a town in the midst of a forty-thousand acre estate. James went to school in Albany, and then, at the age of thirteen, to Yale. After college he went to sea for a while. Married, he settled down as a country gentleman. It is said that disgust with the novels he read impelled him to write.

Cooper put his own name on *The Spy*, published in 1821. It dealt with stirring events, set against backgrounds that Cooper knew, and was an immediate success. When he followed that formula, his books succeeded; when he departed from it, they failed. But the formula made him "the American Scott," and one of the most popular authors who has ever written in English. He encumbered all his books with trite moralizing, and often put strange literary language into the mouths of his rough frontiersmen.

That other American writers of stature followed the two trailblazers is obvious, but Poe, Melville, Whitman, the New Englanders, and some southerners belong to the thirties and forties, a new era that is beyond the limits of this book.

MUSIC

The American colonists did much group singing, in church and out. Even on the frontier, after the first raw years, a traveling teacher could always assemble a singing class. Local fiddlers played for

dances. Blissfully unconcious of even the existence of musical notation, they were spirited and rhythmical, nevertheless. Negro slaves brought the banjo, or at least the knowledge of how to make it, from Africa. Its plinking-plunking sound accompanied spirituals and hoedowns in the slave quarters, and long-remembered English ballads in lonely forest clearings.

The sons of plantation owners, and those of wealthy merchants, took up the flute or the violin. Their sisters practiced on the harpsichord, the spinet, or, from the early 1790's, on the new pianoforte. The tunes they played were European tunes. The Negroes seem to have produced the only original American music of these early days. When a white man wrote a song, he merely composed a verse to fit an imported tune, as Francis Scott Key did, in 1814, with "The Star-Spangled Banner."

The strings of early pianos were stretched on wooden frames, like those of a harpsichord. Soon the makers increased the range of the keyboard, and at the same time raised the pitch of the instrument. These changes required heavier strings and greater tension, more than the wood could take. In 1800, a Philadelphia piano maker, John Isaac Hawkins, braced the frame with metal strips. Incidentally, he also built the first upright piano with strings that started upward from the floor instead of from the level of the keyboard. In Boston, in 1825, Alpheus Babcock first built a piano with a cast-iron frame that could stand the strain of the strings. He went on to devise the method of crossing piano strings, so that the longest bass strings could take advantage of the diagonal of a "square" piano. For sixty years afterward most American pianos were cased in flat rectangular boxes.

Americans always liked to hear music. When it was discovered that they would pay to hear it, concert halls appeared in all large towns. Though many in the audiences were beguiled by spectacular gymnastics on the piano or violin, a taste for really good music began to take hold. Small groups met in homes to hear or to play chamber music, and larger groups financed serial concerts. The Handel and Haydn Society started in Boston in 1815; the Beethoven Society in Portland, Maine, in 1819. Both the New York Philharmonic Society and the Philadelphia Musical Fund Society maintained permanent orchestras.

17.
Schools and Colleges

THE THREE R's

THE planners of the nation saw clearly that, to succeed, a democracy needed educated citizens, yet they made no mention of schools in either the Articles of Confederation or the Constitution. They knew the people were opposed to federal control of education at all levels. Public schools were thus left up to the states, and most of their legislatures passed high-sounding statutes establishing them—but appropriated no money to pay for them. This forced each community to deal with its own school problem.

We have seen one solution, left over from colonial times—the village school, run by its master for his own small profit. Many communities set up similar schools of their own and hired a master, seldom a good one, and never a trained one. The first school for teachers was not started until 1823, in Concord, Vermont. At first, almost no women taught school, except the few who "kept" small "dame schools" to teach the very young their letters and the catechism. Nothing encouraged an able man to teach. The average hired schoolmaster got only twelve or fourteen dollars a month, with free board and lodging in the homes of his scholars.

Few of these local schools had any support

from taxes. Parents paid a couple of dollars tuition for each child for the thirteen-week session of six eight-hour days a week. Hardly more than a tenth of the nation's children went to school at all until after 1810, yet, surprisingly, though few read easily enough to do it for pleasure, most Americans could make shift to read and write. This was as much as many rural Republicans wanted their children to know. They harbored a profound suspicion of "book larnin'." Such people, and also the childless, saw no reason why their taxes should pay for "fancy" schools.

Aside from a few charity efforts, the first public schools started in cities. New York opened its first free school in 1806. Before 1830, some of the new western cities—Cincinnati, Louisville, Lexington —had such schools. Most Protestant churches sponsored primary schools that were more or less free. Religion had the strongest hand in all schooling throughout the country for the first half of the nineteenth century.

Schools increased before the supply of schoolmasters did. This led, in the late twenties, to the employment of some women, and to the introduction of the Lancastrian system. Joseph Lancaster, an Englishman, invented it and brought it to America. It set up lessons on a rigid rote basis, which the master taught to the older pupils.

These acted as "monitors" and drilled the lessons into the younger ones. It was claimed that one man could thus teach four-hundred children.

Until William H. McGuffey published his series of readers, beginning in 1836, no schoolbooks were graded to match the progress of the pupil. After the primer, everything was at one level, but the general quality was improving. The primer that Mathew Carey published in 1810 was better than the old *A B C With the Church of England Catechism*. After Noah Webster published his "Blue-backed Speller," he brought out a grammar and a reader. Arithmetic books repeated ancient problems, in terms of weights and measures that had passed from use a century earlier. Here is one from Walsh's *Mercantile Arithmetic*, published in 1807: "How much will 10 ferons of cochineal come to, weighing neat 724 okes, 73 rotalas, at 80 piastres per oke?"

THE ACADEMIES

Education beyond primary school was needed and the academies made shift to fill the need. They were never public schools, but neither were they quite private schools. Many were started in every state. Most had state charters and received some money from the state. The private side came from control by boards of trustees who, themselves, picked new members to replace those who had died or quit. Also, as at private schools, all students paid tuition, though they sometimes paid it in corn, hams, or wagonloads of firewood. Nearly all academies were located in the country or in small villages, hence most of them were boarding schools but accepted day students from

Master Tisdale's Academy at Lebanon, Connecticut

their neighborhood. Qualifications for admission were, quite simply, ability to pay tuition. Students got instruction at whatever level they needed it, from the elementary up. Tuition was vital; the state paid only about a third of the school's income. The teachers provided the real support, by working for next to nothing.

The academies advertised "training for life." This meant a smattering of education, pumped into the student by means of memorized passages from textbooks, recited in class. The academies taught Latin to those who wished to learn it, and many did; even a little Latin meant status. Most subjects were less pretentious—mathematics, perhaps in the form of surveying or of navigation; agriculture, handwriting, English composition, history, sometimes French or German. Few academies offered practical vocational courses; the old apprentice system still took care of trades.

Beginning in the 1790's, academies sprouted like mushrooms. They filled a need in their time, and by 1850, there were hundreds of them, scattered over every state and territory. A very few operating under the public-private system still survive but they are better schools than the old ones. Most dwindled away after the Civil War, when public high schools, located in towns, took over. Though a student could sometimes pay tuition by working, and though social position meant nothing, the academies were mainly for the prosperous. Many of them accepted girls as well as boys, and beginning in 1815, with Kentucky's Science Hill Academy, some were for girls only. In both cases the girls got the same "training for life" that the boys got. Here was a new thing in the world, greeted with ridicule. Up to this time, reading, writing, and a few "graceful accomplishments," like fancy needlework and a tune or two thumped out on the piano, were felt to be education enough for women. It had been solemnly stated by an "authority," that girls would go into a "decline," or even die, if they were subjected to hard study. Colleges for them were unthinkable, and there was none until Mount Holyoke was founded in 1837.

COLLEGES

Harvard opened in 1636, the first of nine colleges active before the Revolution. Dartmouth, 1769,

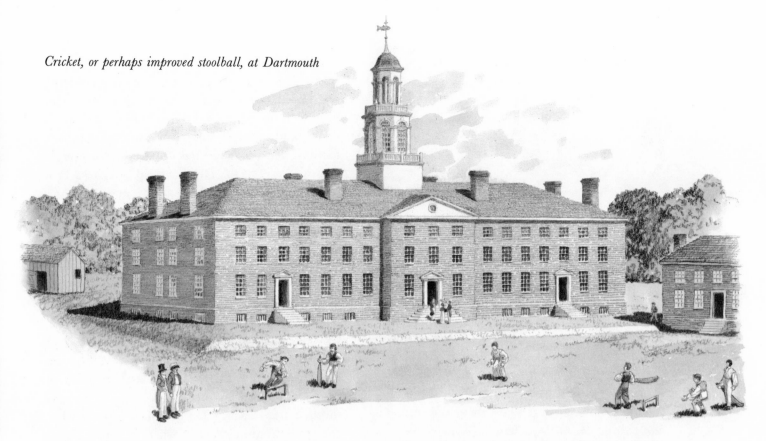

was the ninth. Several modern colleges, which trace back that far, were actually founded as small schools. All of the colleges suffered during the Revolution, and recovered slowly after it. Yale closed completely for a while. The end of the struggle found William and Mary with its president as the only instructor, and a few barefoot boys as students. Even as late as 1800, Harvard's faculty boasted only its president, three professors, and four tutors. All of the very early colleges seem to have been started either to instruct future clergymen or, like Dartmouth, to Christianize Indians. Both kinds had to make ends meet by taking in some prosperous students who fitted into neither group. Teaching strongly emphasized the classics, religion, and moral philosophy, with some rudimentary science.

Those states that had no state colleges founded them soon after the Revolution, six between 1783 and 1801. Even these had a strong religious slant. Scholarship and a liberal education were not thought of as ends in themselves but as means to other ends—in this case, the production of Christian citizens. The presidents of all the state colleges were clergymen, in fact, 90 percent of all college presidents up to the Civil War were clergymen.

When the churches had straightened themselves out after their war troubles, they began to attract new members. Popular interest in deism

waned; it had no emotional appeal. The evangelical sects absorbed many whose families had formerly been Church of England members. Methodist and Baptist missionaries traveled the West, stirred frontiersmen to a frenzy of religious enthusiasm, and started a needed moral reform. In the South they converted Negro slaves and small farmers. Evangelism became the religion of the Republicans. The more restrained appeal of Presbyterian and Congregational missionaries was less successful. The few Episcopalians hardly made a dent. Roman Catholics were still so scarce in the eastern United States that a New York museum could exhibit the wax image of a nun as a curiosity.

Competition arose between the sects. As a way of promoting themselves, they founded dozens of log-cabin colleges, especially in the new western states and territories. As schools these were generally not as good as the academies, and most of them faded away after a few years. There were far more of them than the population needed so they were all starved for students. The average enrollment has been estimated at seventy-five. Each begged its church for support, so that it could fortify church members, and add new converts; and at the same time it advertised to the public that it accepted all Christians, and would make no effort to indoctrinate them.

Most Republicans deeply suspected learned

men, and sneered at them as "edicated dam' fools." They demanded colleges, geared to teach "useful" subjects, that would serve a wider section of the public. Yet many of these semiliterate men were ambitious to place their sons in one of the "three learned professions"—medicine, the law, the ministry.

The Constitutional Convention considered establishing a national university, but decided to leave it to the future. All of the first six presidents favored it. Dr. Benjamin Rush urged it vehemently. In 1806, Joel Barlow wrote a prospectus for it, following the organization of European universities. But the project died on the vine; the people did not want their government to have any control over education. Such hope for it had been stirred in 1795, however, when Washington asked Congress for an appropriation, that Thomas Jefferson had urged the President to locate the school in Virginia. Jefferson was determined to have his kind of university in his home state. When this first try failed, he tried to persuade his alma mater, the College of William and Mary, to replace divinity and Oriental languages with law, medicine, and modern languages, and failed again. Not until 1825 did he finally found the University of Virginia at Charlottesville. His college was considered wildly radical at the time. It was strictly for secular education; all religious tests were omitted. It placed science, agriculture, and modern languages on a par with the classics. It relied on the honor of its students to maintain discipline. (We shall shortly see how radical this was.) Its professors governed it entirely, but they were required to teach the founder's Republican ideas.

College tuition during the period ran from $170 to $600 a year. In most cases it included bed and board, but not textbooks. A college president earned from $800 to $1800. With it he got a house, and the right to preach outside the college for pay. He was expected not merely to preside but also to teach, often several subjects. Professors received about $600 a year, and held their jobs only so long as their performance satisfied the president and the board of trustees. Tutors, sometimes called ushers, got $100.

Though college students ranged in age from thirteen to forty-five, most of them were younger than today's average, and they behaved accordingly. Much about their misbehavior is revealed by the rules with which the colleges hoped to control them. Every student had to memorize the rules, and recite them. They ran long—one of them had eleven chapters, with seven to twenty-three sections each. They specified exactly what the student must do and when he must do it: when he should arise, pray, eat, study, attend chapel, relax, and go to bed. The rules forbade misdeeds in such detail that only a selection of them can be given here. The collegian might not dance, gamble, drink, swear, fight, duel, play billiards, keep a dog, break furniture, strike a teacher, attend the theater. He was fined for infractions: three cents for missing chapel, three dollars for getting drunk. Three dollars was also the fine, at Harvard, for going to the theater in Boston.

Enforcement of discipline seems to have taken much of the faculty's time and energy. The president of Princeton chased some students up a tree one night. Some of the wilder student exploits are on record: firing guns from dormitory windows was commonplace, as was introducing cows and pigs into chapel and into professors' rooms. The stench of asafoetida, placed in a stove, would empty any building. Sometimes enthusiasm carried the boys away: two pounds of gunpowder in a hollow log made a firecracker that nearly blew up Nassau Hall; bowling a hot cannon ball in a dormitory severely injured a tutor. Occasionally real malice showed: a group of students horsewhipped several instructors at the University of Virginia. The honor system must have broken down.

The prohibitions against drinking didn't extend to beer, which was served to students in the "commons." There, the faculty ate at the "high table," and the undergraduates at tables set a step lower, on the floor of the hall. Food was usually poor, and the students expressed their disapproval of it loudly, and sometimes riotously. In some colleges students waited on tables, and helped the cooks to prepare food. Beer could be bought between meals at the "buttery," a little shop that also sold tobacco, sweets, paper, ink, quills (for pens), "wash balls" (soap), and "black balls" (tallow and lampblack for shoes).

No one had yet thought of organized sports, but college students enjoyed sports informally. They played sandlot cricket and football; they ran footraces; they swam; they skated; they boxed and fenced. To entertain themselves indoors, they formed singing clubs, Greek clubs, literary societies, and debating societies. The first Greek-letter fraternity, Phi Beta Kappa, started in 1776 as a literary society at William and Mary.

The full course of study varied from two to four years. Getting into college was easy; few, if any, questions were asked. Most students were not properly prepared, and had to be taught subjects they should have learned earlier. Study, like that in the academies, was largely monotonous rote. The student's recitation was criticized for omissions and deviations, while the ideas it expressed got short shrift. The reciting performance was believed to develop the mind, by exercise, as one would develop a muscle. Even so, the few good teachers could bend the method and actually educate the better minds in their classes.

In addition to languages, mild mathematics, theology, and ethics, colleges taught some history, geography, and the physics of Isaac Newton, who was believed to have said all that could ever be said on the subject. So impressive were his physical laws that they were believed to govern all nature, including man. So they were applied to something called "a science of society"; a few noticed that society continued its wayward course without regard to physics. In philosophy, along with the equally sacred principles of John Locke, students were taught "natural philosophy." In the main, it was Thomas Reid's "common sense," which he said was the judging of things self-evident, "the consensus of ages and nations, of the learned and the unlearned."

Engineering could be studied only after 1802, and only in the United States Military Academy, at West Point. Some of the larger colleges taught short courses in science. Benjamin Silliman offered minerology at Yale. A Columbia student could take botany or chemistry from the same Dr. Samuel L. Mitchill whose guidebook inspired Irving's *History of New York*. Dr. Mitchill lectured on the chemical theories of Antoine Lavoisier, which were as dramatic in their day as the fission of the atom is in the ours. Through the eighteenth century most chemists accepted Georg Stahl's theory, that fuel burned by losing a mysterious substance called phlogiston. Even Joseph Priestley, who had discovered oxygen, believed in phlogiston to the end of his life. He was as conservative in science as he was radical in religion. Lavoisier, troubled by the fact that the total products of combustion weighed *more*, not less, than the original fuel, asserted (correctly) that burning was the combination of oxygen with the fuel. This discovery went far toward forcing the complete overhaul of chemistry as a science.

Commons

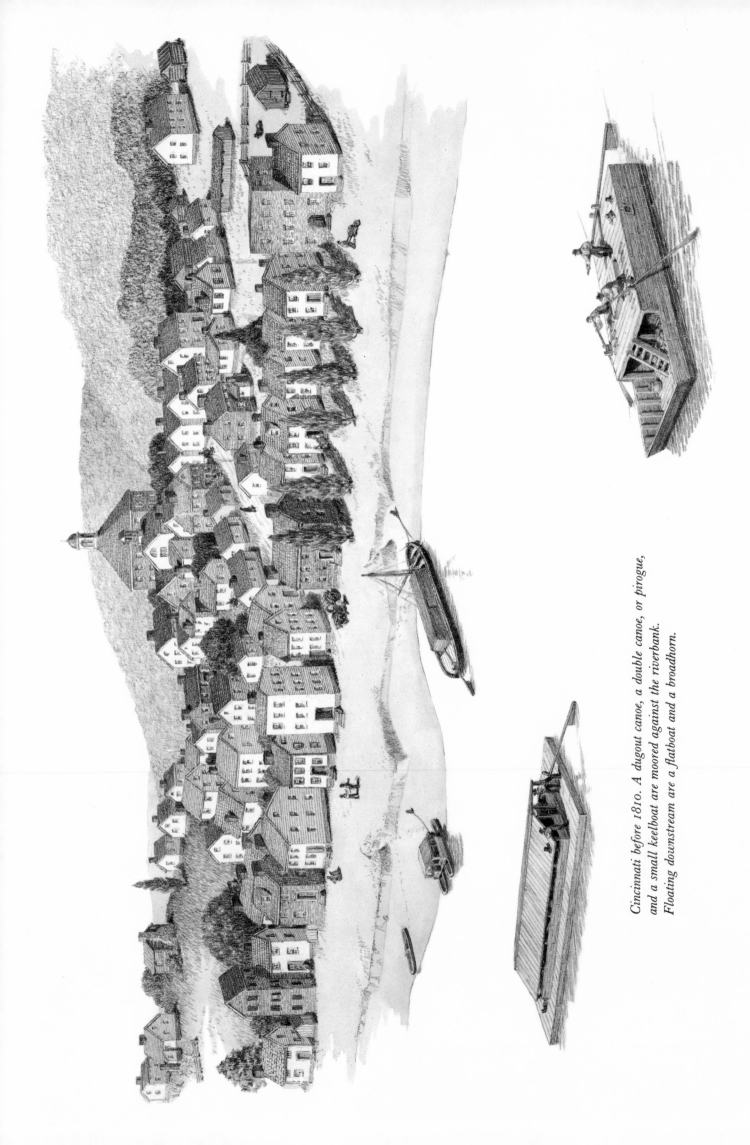

Cincinnati before 1810. A dugout canoe, a double canoe, or pirogue, and a small keelboat are moored against the riverbank. Floating downstream are a flatboat and a broadhorn.

Conner's Prairie (reconstructed)

18.
The Growth of the West

RICHARD CONNER was in Ohio, probably as a fur trader, soon after 1763. He met and married a white girl raised by the Shawnee Indians, Margaret Boyer. She is believed to have been captured by them at the age of six, in eastern Pennsylvania. Richard bought Margaret from the Indians for two hundred dollars. Two of their sons, William and John, grew up not merely with Indians, but almost *as* Delawares. Their parents had become closely associated with that superior tribe. As young men, the brothers both married Delaware wives, by simple agreement. William's wife, Mekinges, was the daughter of the strong chief John Anderson. The brothers both spoke several Indian languages fluently, and for years acted as interpreters. To the last, both of them kept the confidence of the Indians in spite of the chicanery of other white men.

In 1800, Ohio became a state, and all the rest of the Old Northwest was renamed the Indiana Territory. This included the present states of Indiana, Illinois, Michigan, and Wisconsin. Its total white population was about five thousand—seven hundred of it, mostly French, in Vincennes, with a couple of hundred at Detroit. The United States had taken actual possession of only a small southeastern corner of the Territory; nearly all the rest was held by various Indian tribes.

The Delawares were East Coast Indians in the 1600's. The Dutch "bought" Manhattan Island from them; and it was with them that William Penn made his famous treaty of peace. By 1751 the pressure of white settlement had pushed much of the tribe, along with the Shawnee, into southern Ohio. Fifty years later the Delawares had moved on into central Indiana, and with permission from the local Indians, bands of them had set up "towns" along the White River, some twenty miles north of where Indianapolis would rise. In 1802 William Conner established a trading post near the towns, four miles south of the present Noblesville.

An anonymous Frenchman helped William put up a double cabin, that is, two log cabins end to end under a single roof, probably with the covered space between them that was known as a dog run. One end was living quarters, the other was for trading and fur storage. No money was involved in the trading. The Indians preferred payment in knives, hatchets, beads, woven cloth—and whisky, if they could get it. If the trading post sold liquor, it did so illegally; this was Indian country. William's brother John could, and did, sell it at the store he started in 1803 on the Whitewater River, sixty miles southeast of William's cabin. John's store was just inside the ceded territory, hardly five miles beyond the western boundary of Ohio.

It was to John that William sent his accumulated pelts, overland, on packhorses. John forwarded them on a pirogue (two dugout canoes, lashed side by side) down the Whitewater, and up the Ohio to Cincinnati, a voyage of thirty-five miles. Cincinnati was not yet large. It had few more people than the five hundred it had had in 1800, but it was growing fast, and already killing hogs for the market as well as handling furs. By 1830 it would be the seventh largest American city. The fur buyers paid in good silver money. John Conner took his middleman's profit and sent the rest to his brother. In 1808 John moved his store, his wife, and his two half-breed sons twenty miles farther up the river, where he laid out the town of Connersville. Sometime in the next five years his Indian wife died, and in 1813, John married a white girl, Lavinia Winship.

With the Louisiana Purchase completed, President Jefferson envisioned farms in the vast spaces west of the Mississippi. But the Indian tribes still east of the river made a barrier. So the President ordered the governor of the Indiana Territory, William Henry Harrison, to make treaties that would allow white settlers to press westward toward a jumping-off place. John Conner was Harrison's interpreter. Between 1803 and 1805, the governor completed treaties with four separate tribes that granted the United States more than fifty-six million acres of land. Not surprisingly, he infuriated a lot of Indians.

The real Americans had just grudges against the white men. The settlers exterminated game, the Indians' only source of meat. Traders cheated them, and debauched them by selling them the whisky they couldn't resist. To gratify new tastes they acquired from the whites, they learned to steal. When caught, they were severely punished. But white men got light penalties, if any, for the same offenses. Above all else, the Indians were appalled by the speed with which government officials talked the tribes out of land. Congress pretended that each tribe was a "sovereign nation" qualified to surrender, by treaty, the land it occupied. The negotiation of these treaties was with a few individual Indians, who mostly acted on their own without even informal authorization from their fellow tribesmen. Thus the attitude of the warriors was, "You agreed to this. We didn't, so we're not bound by it." But once a

Touching the quill

couple of braves had been persuaded to "touch the quill," the deal was sealed as far as Washington was concerned.

Two Shawnee Indians, Tecumseh and his brother, known as The Prophet because of his supposed magical powers, believed that all the land belonged to all the Indians in common. Tecumseh preached this doctrine far and wide among the tribes and was partially successful in uniting them. He met with Harrison in 1808 and promised peace if the governor would take no more land, but threatened to get British help for war if he did take it. Harrison "purchased" two and a half million acres the next year. He actually paid the tribes some money, but not much.

In 1811, Harrison, anticipating trouble, led a thousand armed men to The Prophet's Town at the junction of Tippecanoe Creek and the Wabash River. Tecumseh was not there. The Indians attacked Harrison's camp suddenly at dawn. The Battle of Tippecanoe was indecisive, but the governor's successful resistance undermined the prestige of Tecumseh and The Prophet, and they were never able to unite the Indians fully. In the War of 1812, Tecumseh joined the British. He was killed when Harrison defeated fifteen hundred Indians and eight hundred British regulars at the Battle of the Thames, in Canada in 1813. That defeat destroyed the Indians' confidence in British help. They made no stand again until the desperate and pathetic outbreak, called the Black Hawk War, on the banks of the Mississippi twenty years later.

136

Thus the prime effect of the War of 1812 in the West was the opening of most of the Indiana Territory to settlement. The Treaty of Ghent, signed the day before Christmas in 1814, ended the war and did much for United States prestige internationally. This country became a nation, instead of a dubious experiment. The British, trying to hold on to their fur trade, demanded that the treaty create a buffer strip of Indian country south of the Great Lakes. The American commissioners objected, and got support from an odd source—the Duke of Wellington. He told the British cabinet that the English performance in the war gave them no right to make demands. Thus the Indiana Territory could be settled all the way to the northern border.

business, hurt when the Delaware towns were destroyed in the war, was reviving. In addition, Conner was raising good crops of corn on the "prairie" land around the post. This prairie was not part of a horizon-wide plain, but was merely a natural treeless opening in the forest, such as was called a "barren" in the East. William did not own Conner's Prairie, as this land came to be named. He had simply squatted on it and improved it with crude buildings and fences. He petitioned Congress several times to grant it to him, but not until 1822 was a limited patent, for 640 acres, issued to him and Mekinges jointly. He paid off his Indian children and got full ownership only shortly before he died in 1855.

Indiana had been a state for three years when

Settlers for Horseshoe Prairie

The war had slowed the westward movement of people. Now the dam broke and the Great Migration began. An endless flotilla of flatboats and rafts brought families and all their goods down the Ohio River. In 1812, there were less than thirty-five thousand people in the Indiana Territory; by the end of 1815 there were nearly sixty-four thousand. The next year, Indiana became a state.

By 1818 Connersville and John Conner's store, and the gristmill he had built, were thriving. He and Lavinia had been married five years and had had at least one child. One of John's Indian sons had died; the other had moved out. John was now a man of substance, and a member of the state legislature. His relations with his brother were still close and warm. They remained so for life.

William Conner, Mekinges, and their six children still lived at the trading post on the White River. William had formed a partnership with his only white neighbor, William Marshall, who, like Conner, had an Indian wife. Their fur

the first ripples of the tide of migration reached the White River. Five families came overland on horseback and in oxcarts, driving their cows and pigs along the trail by which William Conner sent out his furs. Though some of them were from the East, they had broken their trek with a long sojourn in Connersville. Their journey ended at a place they named Horseshoe Prairie, on the White River, just north of Conner's cabin. Though this was rougher living than they had known before, these people were not complete greenhorns. One of them, John Finch, was a competent blacksmith, gunsmith, and wheelwright. Another man was expert at building log cabins. But luck ran against them for a while. Worms ate most of their first corn crop. Wolves and wildcats killed their farm animals. In August nearly all of them were stricken with "ague" (malaria), and three died. William Conner helped where he could, and that winter he sold them corn from his crib, below the going price, or gave it free to those who could not pay. There was no mill; they had

137

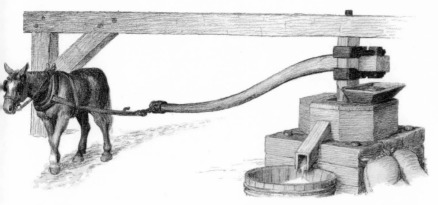

Horse mill

to pound the grain in a wooden samp mortar, as the Indians did. But there was game in the woods and fish in the river.

The next year things went better. The corn crop succeeded, and William Bush hewed out two small millstones to make a hand-turned quern which ground finer meal than the mortar could make. The settlers learned, no doubt from Mekinges, to gather wild nettles. Their fiber made an excellent substitute for flax. More people settled nearby, so, that winter, John Finch built a horse mill. Its operation was the same as the quern, but its stones were larger, and a horse turned them by walking a circle around the mill. Customers paid six cents a bushel for grinding their corn, and had to provide their own horse. The Finches also started a school, in which the teacher and all of the pupils were named Finch.

These settlers were certainly pioneers but they were greatly different from the earlier frontiersmen who settled western Pennsylvania and Kentucky. Most of these later people could read, and probably all of them belonged to some religious sect. If they were less prepared to deal with the wilderness than the earlier migrants, they dealt with a somewhat tamer wilderness. They also had the memory and the goal of a gentler way of living. And though they were twice as far from the east coast source of supplies as most of the earlier settlers had been, their local bases, Connersville and Cincinnati, were much more easily reached than, say, Benson Town had been from the mountain valleys. The first settlers of Kentucky might be said to have had no supply base.

In 1820, the year the Finches' school opened, the Indiana legislature appointed a commission of ten men to decide on the location of a permanent capital, near the center of the state. John Conner was one of the commissioners, and Gov-

ernor Jonathan Jennings came along to see the job well done. Not surprisingly all the men came from southern and southeastern counties; few others were settled. The group met at William Conner's trading post. To get there, Frederick Rapp, from Posey County, in the extreme southwestern corner of the state, had to make a wilderness journey of more than 165 miles. The commissioners all traveled on horseback, sleeping wherever they could find shelter, and camping in the woods when they could not find it. But they no longer ran much risk of being murdered and scalped in the night.

The governor, no doubt John Conner, and one or two others, stayed with William. The rest found lodging with the families at Horseshoe Prairie for the two weeks their work required. They examined several sites before they settled on the junction of Fall Creek with the White River, some twenty miles downstream from Conner's Prairie. They selected the site because several Indian trails converged there at a fording place, and because there was a good landing place for boats. None of these advantages was still an advantage ten years later. It took the commission but four days to reach its decision. The commissioners devoted the rest of the time to hunting and fishing, while they waited for surveyors to finish running the boundaries of Indianapolis. The name, by the way, aroused criticism and ridicule.

In negotiations held in 1818 at the blockhouse fort of St. Mary's in western Ohio, eight tribes, including the Delaware, had agreed to leave their Indiana land and move to new locations west of the Mississippi. Now, in the late summer of 1820, the Delawares gathered near Conner's Prairie to leave in a body for western Missouri. It was

obvious to everyone that Mekinges and her children would go with them. This was tribal law. William Conner would stay where he was, but Marshall elected to go west with his wife. The fur-trading partnership would have to be dissolved. Alongside Conner's bed stood a small stagecoach trunk, holding a little more than a cubic foot of silver dollars. He and Marshall divided its contents, and parted friends. Mekinges got sixty ponies, and she and her children retained a half interest in the Conner's Prairie land. This would be confirmed to them by the congressional patent.

In the late fall of the same year, William Conner married Elizabeth Chapman, the stepdaughter of John Finch. She was thirty years younger than her husband. At the wedding feast the most important dish, perferred to the venison and roast pheasant, was white bread made from wheat flour brought from Connersville for the occasion.

The ceremony which united William and Elizabeth was a civil one. It may be assumed that this was because there was no clergyman in the neighborhood at the time. The Moravians had been on the White River as missionaries to the Indians, but the efforts of The Prophet had defeated them. It isn't surprising that there was no church in so new a settlement, but it would be astonishing if no circuit-riding minister had visited it. These men, wrapped in their faith and large windproof capes, rode their horses into the remot-

est clearings, and preached wherever two or three could be gathered together. They married couples who had set up housekeeping informally, and christened children who had grown a full set of teeth. The fervor of the evangelistic revival that swept Kentucky and Ohio at the beginning of the nineteenth century seems to have abated a little twenty years later. Faith was still strong, but the camp meetings no longer aroused the emotional extremes of the earlier years. By 1825, Indianapolis had a Presbyterian church and a Methodist church.

None of the settlers at Horseshoe Prairie owned the land they lived on. It still belonged to the public domain, so in 1821 it was surveyed and offered for sale at public auction. Land regulations had been eased a year before this; a man could now buy as little as eighty acres. If it didn't bring more at the public auction, the squatter could then buy it, at private sale, for $1.25 an acre. An unwritten law held that none of his neighbors would bid against a squatter. This didn't help at Horseshoe Prairie. A man named Audrick announced that he was going to bid on all of it, and so did John Conner. Audrick promised to pay the settlers for the improvements they had made. Conner refused to do this, but announced that he would dam the river and build a gristmill, a sawmill, and a water-driven wool carder. These would raise the value of all the local land. There was some resentment against him. But he got the land and did exactly what he had said he would do. Audrick later turned out to be a ready promiser but a poor doer.

In 1823, William Conner bought a tract of land adjoining Conner's Prairie and built a two-story brick house on it that still stands. William and Elizabeth's first child, Lavinia, was born in the old cabin, some months before the house was built. Eventually there were nine more children.

OTHER PARTS OF THE WEST

South of Virginia, the Great Migration took a special form. Instead of small family groups, whole plantations, complete with slaves, animals, and cotton gin, left their exhausted land and moved over the mountains to exhaust more. They planted cotton and corn in large clearings, and year after year they increased the percentage of cotton. The plantations filled up Alabama, Mississippi, and western Tennessee. This wasn't healthy settlement. It created few towns, and almost no villages. The planters shipped their cotton to New Orleans and did their buying there. No middle class developed; the population was divided into rich planters, their slaves, and a scum of white trash.

In 1764, Pierre Laclède started a fur trading post where the Missouri and Mississippi rivers meet. It quickly became a French town, St. Louis, existing to buy furs. and to supply the *voyageurs* who brought them down the Missouri. Even after the Spanish acquired it, following the Seven Years War, it remained French. But just before

Cotton planter's bateau

1800, Yankee settlers, spearheaded by Daniel Boone, began coming in. They were not interested in furs. They headed for the back country and cheap land. Soon they outnumbered the French, whom the Louisiana Purchase turned into Americans. In 1812, Congress created the Missouri Territory and there followed a rush of cotton planters, who in eight years raised the price of land to eight dollars an acre (from ten cents), and

the population to the sixty thousand that allowed statehood. The planters demanded legal slavery in Missouri. The twenty-two states of that time were evenly divided—eleven had slavery, eleven were "free." One more slave state would give the South control of the Senate. The uproar that this created all over the country was quieted by the Missouri Compromise, which admitted Maine as a free state to balance the new slave state, and

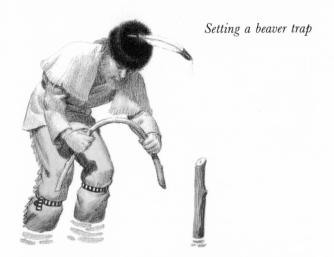

Setting a beaver trap

forbade slavery in all other western states north of Missouri's southern boundary.

Moses Austin, of St. Louis, got a huge grant of land in East Texas from the Mexican government, and died before he could do anything about it. Mexico confirmed the grant to Moses's son Stephen in 1821, on condition that he bring in three hundred families of settlers. In ten years, five thousand Americans had moved in and Stephen had a modest personal estate of sixty-six thousand acres. Again the cotton growers brought their slaves in. By 1826 the "Yankee" population had nearly doubled. It outnumbered the local Mexicans nine to one. By edict, these American settlers became Mexicans and Roman Catholics, but in fact they lived as they pleased, and soon were telling the Mexican officials what they would and would not do.

THE FUR TRADE

John Jacob Astor expanded his New York fur business into the Northwest Territory in 1800 with great success. His traders pushed on into the almost unknown Wisconsin area. In 1808 he be-

The Clermont

came the American Fur Company. At about the same time, a group of St. Louis men started the Rocky Mountain Fur Company, to send trappers far up the Missouri River. Astor was right behind them. St. Louis boomed. Both companies sent out yearly expeditions overland to buy furs, and to supply the "Mountain Men," the trappers who worked alone in the high valleys. These men met the caravans at a July "rondeevoo," spent all their beaver skins on a week-long binge, and then, in debt to the company, went back to the hills to trap more beaver. They were picturesque, but they were in no sense settlers. When the introduction of silk hats in the 1830's killed the market for beaver, the Mountain Men scattered. They had reduced the animal population and increased that of half-breed Indians, but otherwise they left the country as they found it.

LEAD

Julien Dubuque found lead ore in what later became Iowa, and in 1788 got a Spanish grant to mine it, where the city that is named for him stands now. Soon the metal turned up at other points near both banks of the Mississippi from a little south of St. Louis into the lower corner of Wisconsin and the upper corner of Illinois. The ore was in relatively pure form and lay near the surface of the ground. In 1827 a lead rush occurred. Prospectors pocked the landscape with trial pits. A man who found lead set up camp, dug his own ore, and smelted it on the spot. The resulting metal went to world markets by way of New Orleans. Unlike the Mountain Men, many who came for lead stayed to settle on the land.

141

WESTERN STRENGTH

The states and territories west of the Alleghenies grew, not only by the influx of footloose easterners, but also by the arrival of more and more Europeans, who landed at eastern ports and headed inland as quickly as possible. West was where the land was. All of these people continued to float most of the excess of their production down to New Orleans for sale. They wanted to buy everything from needles to steam engines, from billiard tables to scented soap. Eastern merchants, gnashing their teeth at the cost of wagon freight over the mountains, did their best to supply them. They could only mourn all the profitable export goods they couldn't touch. The West was just as anxious for closer communication as the East was.

Increasing people meant increasing votes, which gave the eastern politicians something to worry about. The Republican West voted for James Monroe in 1816, but he would have won anyway. The Federalists, accused of treason in the War of 1812, made a very poor showing, and the Federalist Party quietly died. Monroe was acclaimed even in New England when he went there. By 1822, western states held a fourth of the seats in the House of Representatives, and eighteen of the forty-eight in the Senate. In 1824, western strength gave Andrew Jackson, of Tennessee, a majority of the popular vote, but the electoral vote was so close that the decision was thrown into the House of Representatives. There Henry Clay, who described himself as "a Westerner with Northern ideas," put his enormous prestige behind John Quincy Adams, the son of the second President, and won the election for him. Clay had himself been a candidate, but had made a poor showing at the polls. He became Secretary of State, many said as the result of an "unholy bargain." All four candidates in this election ran as independents. Actually Jackson was a "Democratic-Republican," as the old Jeffersonian Republicans now called themselves. Adams, born a Federalist, had allied himself with the Republicans, but he acted like a Federalist. He urged Congress to start large interstate works, just as the country was growing suspicious of too much federal power. He saw public lands only in terms of government profit. The West, which disliked him for besting Jackson, despised him for that. He was deeply hurt.

STEAM ON THE RIVERS

Robert Fulton built the first commercially successful steamboat in the United States, but he did not invent the steamboat, even for this country. As far back as 1784, James Rumsey had demonstrated a craft that was poled up the Potomac by steam. Since it did move, however slowly, he must be credited with success. So, also, must John Fitch be. Twelve steam-driven paddles drove his 1786 boat at three miles an hour against the strong current of the Delaware River. Both

men kept trying; Rumsey used a pumped jet of water in 1787; Fitch, in 1789, got eight miles an hour, with paddle wheels. David Wilkinson, the brother-in-law of cotton-spinning Samuel Slater, built a steamboat "for fun" in 1794, and broke it up after playing with it for a while. In 1804, Colonel John Stevens achieved some success at Hoboken with a steamer driven by twin-screw propellers.

Fulton was familiar with these experiments. He knew James Rumsey and discussed steamboats with him. Chancellor Robert R. Livingston, one of Fulton's financial backers, obtained plans of Fitch's boats, and "Toot" studied them. He also studied the *Charlotte Dundas,* the highly successful paddle-wheel steamer that William Symington and Patrick Mills built in England in 1802. The *Clermont* much resembled this boat. Even Wilkinson's toy may have contributed something: Daniel Leach, who made Fulton's working drawings, had seen her.

Fulton supervised the building of his engine at the Boulton and Watts factory in England, in 1806, and Livingston persuaded the British government to release it for shipment. He was a notable man. He had been a member of the committee for framing the Declaration of Independence; he had been chancellor of New York State; and as minister to France, he had helped James

The Erie Canal crossing the Genesee River

Monroe to negotiate the Louisiana Purchase.

The *Clermont* was first known merely as "the steam boat," or as "Fulton's Folly." She was no beauty. Her hull was nothing more than a long narrow barge, to serve as a platform for her machinery. The story has been told too often, perhaps: the jeering crowd on the riverbank; the brave uneasy friends on the deck; the pop-eyed wonder and the cheers, as the little boat churned out into the stream and headed for Albany. She wasn't fast. It took her thirty-two hours to cover the 150 miles, but she got there a lot faster than the week it often took the sailing sloops. The *Clermont* commenced a regular packet service at once. One-way fare between New York and Albany was seven dollars. With good reason, people were afraid of explosions of the boilers of steamers. Many wouldn't travel on them—so many, as boiler after boiler blew up, that "palatial safety barges," for passengers, went into service on the Hudson in 1825. They were towed by the steamboat at the end of a long hawser.

Not long after the *Clermont*'s success, in the same year, John Stevens launched the *Phoenix*. She also had paddle wheels, but driven by a high-pressure engine he built himself. She was completely successful, but Livingston had wangled a monopoly on New York rivers, so in 1809 Stevens took his boat to Philadelphia. She went by sea, under her own power, and thus became the world's first oceangoing steamboat. The *Phoenix* had a long working career on the Delaware River. Stevens, by the way, had outlined the first patent law that Congress adopted, in 1790.

Fulton's monopoly didn't hold up in court, but the partners were looking beyond New York before the first fire was lighted under the *Clermont*'s boiler. When he described his success to his friend Joel Barlow in Paris, "Toot" wrote, ". . . it will give quick and cheap conveyance on the Missis-sippi, Missouri, and other great rivers." One of Fulton's partners, Nicholas Roosevelt, went west and engineered the building of a steamboat at Pittsburgh in 1811. She was run down the river and used in Louisiana. She could make only three miles an hour against the Mississippi's powerful current, but that was better than a keelboat could do, even with an upriver wind. It was many times faster than men could pole a boat upstream.

Steamboats multiplied on the Mississippi and the Ohio. As early as 1816, the *Washington* made a round trip between New Orleans and Louisville, Kentucky, in thirty-seven days. Each succeeding and better boat cut a little off the time; by 1840 an upstream trip took less than six days. The early river steamers were obviously helpful to the West, but they did little to tie it closer to the East. Those mountains still stood between the Ohio and the Atlantic. In 1818, a step was taken toward going around one end of them. A sturdy steamer (she also had sails), happily christened with the name the Indians gave her, *Walk-in-the-Water*, started regular service between Buffalo, on Lake Erie, and Detroit, with a stop at Cleveland. Travelers going west took the Genesee road up the Mohawk Valley, then turned west at Oneida, 180 miles across much of New York State, to Buffalo.

CANALS

Elkanah Watson had urged a canal through this Mohawk Valley as early as 1788. People had become aware of the advantages of canals. George Washington and Fielding Lewis surveyed one through the Dismal Swamp in 1762. It was completed in 1794, joining the Chesapeake Bay with Albemarle Sound. A canal avoided the rapids of the James River, at Richmond, by 1785. Others,

Packet boat

like the Santee Canal mentioned earlier, made shortcuts between rivers and harbors.

Many people, including Thomas Jefferson, thought Watson's bold idea of joining the waters of Lake Erie with the Hudson was absolute madness. But the powerful politician De Witt Clinton backed it. A survey in 1810 showed the job was at least possible. Then the war halted all progress. The federal government refused financial help, and Ohio and Indiana, which would benefit from the canal, failed to raise any money for it. So, in 1817, New York started alone. "Clinton's Ditch" was dug by newly immigrated Irish "broadbacks," helped by horses and mules. Ingenious machines gave further help. They were invented

*The first
McCormick reaper*

on the spot as need for them arose: oversize plows and root-cutting scoops; horse-powered stump pullers, mounted on enormous wheels. The stump pullers could also uproot whole trees of moderate size.

The finished Erie Canal was 363 miles long. It was twenty-eight feet wide on its bottom, and forty feet wide at the surface of the water, which was four feet deep. Between Albany and Buffalo, successive locks lifted boats five hundred feet. At Lockport a series of them, arranged like steps, accounted for sixty feet of this. Stone aqueducts carried the canal across the Genesee River once and across the Mohawk twice. Houses and villages sprouted along the ditch almost as fast as it progressed. And it speeded the settlement of all of upper New York State.

On October 26, 1825, water was let into the canal's last section, at Buffalo. At once Governor Clinton, as he had become, and a group of assorted dignitaries started south on the canal boat

Seneca Chief. A cannon fired as they left. Others, spaced along the whole route, repeated the salute as soon as their gunners heard it. The last gun, at New York City, fired an hour and twenty-five minutes after the first. The governor's party was greeted at all likely points with speeches and banquets. It reached New York in nine days, on the fourth of November, and was met by a flotilla of twenty-two decorated steamboats and unnumbered sailing craft. Amid cheering and ceremonial, the governor emptied a keg of Lake Erie water into New York Bay.

Both freight and passenger traffic was heavy on the canal from the first. Horses, walking along towpaths on the sides of the muddy ditch, pulled the canal boats; in the Hudson, steamboats towed them. Ordinary "line" boats traveled only in the daytime, but the deluxe "packets" moved day and night. The speed was a mile and a half an hour; the base fare for passengers was a cent and a half a mile. Though slower than coach travel, canal boating was more comfortable; a passenger might be bored, but he wasn't bruised. In pleasant weather, the ladies and gentlemen relaxed on the roof of the cabin, chatting and ducking bridges as they admired the scenery. The boats were about sixty feet long and eight feet wide, the right size and shape to fit into a lock. Even freight

Flagg's thresher

boats were housed over completely, except for patches of deck at both ends. Passenger boats had the enclosure divided into three parts—the forward cabin, restricted to women; the main cabin, where all the passengers ate and where the men slept (they growled at being wakened early so the crew could set up breakfast); and the small space aft, which was the galley and the crew's bunkroom.

144

Inclined plane on the Pennsylvania System

It is only a small exaggeration to say that the states of Michigan and Wisconsin were populated by way of the Erie Canal; so was much of northern Ohio, Indiana, and Illinois. It was common for fifty boats to arrive in Buffalo from Albany in a day. Steamboats and sailboats thronged on Lake Erie. Freight from New York to Ohio traveled a third faster than by wagon, and at half the cost. Except for cotton, New York City was a more profitable market for farm products than New Orleans was. River traffic on the Mississippi dwindled sharply, and New York boomed as never before. The canal even affected trade along the East Coast; Savannah could buy wheat from upper New York State cheaper than wheat grown in central Georgia.

The increasing acreages of wheat and other small grains demanded implements that would substitute horse power for man power. The use of the implements then increased the acreage. The prime lack was a machine to replace the line of cradlers that were needed to reap a field. In the thirties, Cyrus McCormick in Virginia and Obed Hussey in Ohio both built successful horse-drawn reapers. McCormick's won out because he constantly improved it. In its original version (1831), a "sickle-bar" of moving knives cut the straw near the ground, and long wooden blades knocked it down onto a platform. A man with a fork kept the platform clear. Workers gathered the straw and bound it into sheaves by hand. Later the reaper became a harvester when it was modified to bind the sheaves and drop them, complete.

David Flagg, of western New York, and Joseph

145

Pope, of Maine, both invented threshing machines. They were slow but they took less human labor than did beating the grain off the straw with flails. A horse, walking in a circle, powered Flagg's thresher just as one did John Finch's gristmill. His effort turned a toothed cylinder much like the one on Whitney's cotton gin. Its teeth dragged the kernels off the straw. The human operator appears to have held each sheaf and then discarded it, after the machine had cleaned it of grain, without the straw's passing through the mechanism. Today a single machine, the combine, both reaps and threshes in the field.

OTHER CANALS

Ohioans decided that if one canal was good in New York, two would be good in their state, and for a while they were. Both were authorized simultaneously in 1825; one, called the Ohio Canal, ran from Cleveland to Portsmouth on the Ohio River, and the other, the Miami, from Toledo to

The Rail Road from Philadelphia to Columbia

Cincinnati. They opened up the central part of the state, and the wheat shipped on them was better than eastern farmers could grow on their tired land. Indiana started a canal, too, the Wabash and Erie. It was plagued with bad management, financial troubles, and some thievery, but it eventually connected with the Miami Canal in Ohio.

The success of the Erie Canal alarmed merchants in other eastern states—New York would get *all* of the western trade. The long-projected but long-dormant Chesapeake and Ohio Canal was revived. The original plan had been to make the Potomac River navigable with short canals around rapids; now a continuous canal would follow the river until the stream turned southward beyond Cumberland, then, somehow, get to the Ohio from there. Digging started in 1828. Twenty-two years later the canal reached Cumberland and stopped permanently. Nevertheless, it carried mountain coal to tidewater into the early years of the present century. Many other canals, intended from the first to serve such local purposes, were dug in the eastern states at about this time.

The Pennsylvania System was more dramatic and was completed more energetically and quickly. It ran from the Delaware River to the Ohio, at Pittsburgh, and used any practical means to cover the distance. The first stretch was a horse-drawn "rail road" from downtown Philadelphia to the Susquehanna River, at Columbia.

From there a canal, with 108 locks in it, went to Hollidaysburg. There, passengers and freight were unloaded and horse-powered winches hauled both up a series of inclined planes—fourteen hundred feet in a mile. After a stretch on an ordinary road, they were lowered again, at Johnstown, and reloaded for passage on another canal. This one had sixty-four locks, sixteen aqueducts, and two tunnels. Eventually, steam engines hauled canal boats, built in sections, piecemeal, up the inclines. They traveled across the high ground on railroad cars. The final Pennsylvania System, though thirty-one miles longer than the Erie Canal, was much faster—four days from Philadelphia to Pittsburgh. Hence it did well.

STEAM RAILROADS

If anyone could have foreseen the future success of railroads, probably none of the canals would have been built; not even the Erie, which would have been too bad, since, much widened and deepened to twenty-seven feet, it is still valuable as the New York State Barge Canal. Merchants of Baltimore conjured up not only Philadelphia's ominous picture of an unchallenged New York but also a vision of little Georgetown, the eastern terminus of the C & O Canal, grown great on western trade that the National Road had been bringing to them. Their small river penetrated

only a few miles westward, but they used its valley for the first few miles of the Baltimore and Ohio Rail Road. Their intention was merely to create a smoother surface on which horses could pull cars faster and more easily than they could pull wagons on an ordinary road.

But Peter Cooper was a B & O board member. He had an old steam pumping engine, and using it, he "knocked together" an experimental locomotive in 1830. A later generation called it *Tom Thumb*. There was a steam railroad in England in 1825, and the English had built much better locomotives than Cooper's, but his was the first one made here. It pulled forty people at ten miles an hour. They tested it by racing it against a horse, and it was winning handsomely, but it broke down and the horse didn't.

Nevertheless, the directors had seen enough to convince them that a better engine was all they needed. They offered a prize of four thousand dollars for the best coal-burning locomotive that would pull fifteen tons at least fifteen miles an hour. Phineas Davis won with the *York*, named after his home town in Pennsylvania. The horses retired. The railroad reached Cumberland eight years before the C & O Canal did, and steadily pushed on westward. Steam railroads sprouted quickly all over the country. As early as 1832, William Conner was helping to promote one in Indiana. Few of them were as much as forty miles long. Their promoters wanted to move rural pro-duce into their towns. They had no interest in reaching any distant point, as the B & O did, or even any interest in connecting one town with another, as a rule. Still, with careful preparation, a through traveler could make some use of the "steam cars." He used stagecoaches to bridge gaps between railheads, and endured long waits in remote villages. At least such waits provided rest from the discomfort of hard benches, and gave the traveler time for darning the holes that flying sparks had burned in his clothes.

By 1842 it became possible to go all the way from Boston to Buffalo by rail, except for the ferry ride across the Hudson River. But the trip used ten different railroads, none of them with the least interest in making connections with any other. A through train, using the tracks of all ten roads, would not have been physically possible. The rails were not connected, and there was no standard gauge. Each road laid its tracks to fit its own locomotive, from about three feet wide to about six; even an inch of difference ruled out visiting rolling stock.

Slowly public demand forced, first, cooperation, then amalgamation of the little railroads, and passengers, but not cars, went through on something near a schedule. By the mid-fifties, railroads had put most of the canals out of business. Even the National Road, intended to reach St. Louis, expired halfway across Illinois, only sixty miles from its goal.

York. *Each car had its own brakeman.*
The flat iron rails rested on courses of granite blocks.

19.
"Old Hickory"

IN 1828, John Quincy Adams ran for reelection as a National Republican. This party rose from the ashes of the Federalists. It would later be tagged Whig, and still later would become the Republican party of our time. Adams's opponent was again Andrew Jackson who believed wholeheartedly in the rule of the people by the people. He was a Democratic-Republican, but would soon change the name of his party to plain Democratic. Both men seem to have left campaigning largely to their supporters, who did a bitter and vicious job of it. One newspaper went so far as to attack the character of Jackson's beloved wife, Rachel, whose crimes were that she had been divorced and that she smoked a pipe. Western voters backed Jackson almost solidly, and he had a strong following among eastern workingmen. He won handily. Thomas Hart Benton called it "the triumph of the democratic principle, and an assertion of the people's right to govern themselves."

His nickname, "Old Hickory," fitted Jackson exactly. He was as tough as an ax handle. In a duel, he once stood motionless while his opponent's ball hit him in the shoulder; then he carefully shot the man dead. His father had died be-

fore Jackson was born, his mother when he was fourteen. He grew up on the Tennessee frontier, fiercely independent and burdened with a furious temper. Somehow he picked up the scraps of an education. He once said that it was a poor mind that couldn't think of more than one way to spell a word. But in spite of his earthy language, his slips in grammar, his tobacco chawing, and his whisky drinking, Jackson had a keen mind, and his manners would have graced an earl. He "read law" and became good enough at it to sit on his state's supreme bench. He also became a major general, again a good one. When some of the superior Creek Indians became nasty, he fought and beat *all* of the Creek Indians. Like nearly all frontiersmen, he saw no good in any Indian. Jackson and his backwoods riflemen decisively whipped the British regulars at the Battle of New Orleans. The Treaty of Ghent had already been signed when they fought, but neither side had heard about it. Later, Jackson invaded Spanish Florida, apparently on his own initiative. All these exploits made him famous and enormously popular.

To the multitude of plain people, Old Hickory seemed to be completely one of themselves. Actu-

149

ally, he was a prosperous cotton planter who had said very little about his opinions on anything, but on the whole the people's instinct was right. Jackson was certainly not above politics: he killed the valuable Second Bank of the United States because he believed it had opposed him, and he appointed his supporters to government offices almost regardless of merit. Yet, during his administration, free public education at last got started; imprisonment for debt was finally abolished; and the first restraints were put upon business monopolies. Also, soon after Jackson became President, he persuaded England to let American ships resume trade with her West Indian islands; and he persuaded France to pay for the damage that Napoleon's navy had done to American shipping.

In the bright morning sunshine of March 4, 1829, the President-elect walked, bareheaded, up Pennsylvania Avenue to his inauguration at the United States Capitol. Hundreds followed him; thousands awaited him. They had come from the city streets, from the farms, from the "fur back," to see the first President who belonged to them. They greeted Jackson with a great roar when he appeared on the Capitol portico. They stood impressively silent while Chief Justice John Marshall, who detested all that Jackson stood for, administered the oath, and silent still while the tall lean President, his narrow leather face topped with a shock of white hair, made a speech that hardly a tenth of the crowd could hear.

Jackson put on a tall hat and rode a horse down the avenue to the inaugural reception at the White House, and much of the crowd followed him, whooping. He was in no mood for parties; in fact he assumed the Presidency without enthusiasm. His Rachel had died only six weeks before.

What followed at the White House wasn't Jackson's fault. Someone had blundered. At inaugural receptions before and since, the public has moved in line to shake the President's hand and pass on to refreshments. Guards see that the lines are orderly. This time there were no guards. Even if there had been, the crush would have overborne them; a regiment could hardly have controlled it. Mrs. Samuel Harrison Smith, who was there, wrote: "The majesty of the people had disappeared, and a rabble, a mob . . . scrambling, fighting, romping," inundated the whole building. They ruined the rugs with the mud of Pennsylvania Avenue; they broke the furniture, the china, the glassware; they carried punch and ice cream onto the lawn in buckets and tubs. Men got black eyes and bloody noses; women fainted. People escaped from the pressure inside by way of the windows. All pretense of a formal reception vanished. The President retreated until his back was against a wall. A group of stalwarts formed a cordon around him, and fought him a path to a back door. Andrew Jackson fled to his lodgings at Gadsby's Tavern.

CONCLUSION

What you have read has tried to show the changes in, and to, the United States in its first fifty-odd years; many changes are trivial; some are fundamental. The surface ones are the more obvious of course. The deeper shift, from colonial subjects to democratic citizens, has to be glimpsed from events and expressed opinions. Changes obviously continued, but probably no other period, until perhaps our own, can show more of them or more radical ones.

Many later developments began in those first fifty years. A tollgate keeper on the Lancaster turnpike would hardly recognize as roads the sprawling "thruways" that now join the cities and divide the country, but the old road could not deny its children. Nor could the president of the turnpike corporation readily comprehend *its* descendants, the huge corporate empires, which absorb the efforts of most working Americans and seem, sometimes, more important than the people they are supposed to serve.

In 1830 we were still a nation of small farmers and, talking a lot about our "rugged individualism," we continued to think we were that right up to the great depression of 1930. Actually, the United States had become industrialized by then, and farming had started to be what it is now—big business, operating on huge spreads of land. The children and grandchildren of the old dirt farmers, today's Whittles, run lathes and looms—and computers.

Index

(*Asterisks after page numbers refer to illustrations*)

academies, 130, 130*
Adam, Robert, 97, 98
Adams, Abigail, 75
Adams, John, 12, 14, 32, 52, 54, 58, 73, 89, 96, 106
Adams, John Quincy, 141, 142, 149
Africa, 91, 93, 94
Age of Reason, The (Paine), 32, 56
Alabama, 140
Albany, N.Y., 128, 143, 144, 145
Albemarle Sound, 143
Alice (brig), 81–82, 85, 86*
    launch of, 83, 84*, 100
Allegheny River, 47, 48
Allentown, Pa., 71
Alliance, Treaty of (1778), 73
Allston, Washington, 125, 126
Amelung, John Frederick, 69
American Colonization Society, 94
American Fur Company, 141
American Philosophical Society, 56
American Revolution. *See* Revolutionary War.
American Spelling Book, The (Webster), 35
amusements, 119–20, 121
Anderson, John, 135
Anglicans, 11, 32, 52
Annapolis, Md., 32, 57, 121
Appalachian Mountains, 17, 47, 63
apple orchards, 20
architecture, 97*, 97–98, 98*, 99*
    Colonial (Georgian), 38, 97
    Federal (Classic Revival), 97, 98

arks, on Ohio River, 45*, 48
Arkwright, Richard, 60
Articles of Confederation, 13, 14, 58, 60, 126, 129
Asbury, Francis, 32, 32*
Ashley River, 78
Astor, John Jacob, 140–41
Athens, architecture of, 98
Attoo, 91
Attucks, Crispus, 11
Audrick, 139, 140
Audubon, John James, 113
Austin, Moses, 140
Austin, Stephen, 140
automatic flour mill, 62*, 63

Babcock, Alpheus, 128
baking, at Whittle farmhouse, 24
baleen, 88
ball games, 119
balloon, Carnes's, 56–57
Baltimore, 15, 57, 75, 79, 85, 89, 93, 94, 96, 146
Baltimore and Ohio Rail Road, 147
banjo, 128
banjo clock, 66, 66*
"bank" barn, 17, 17*, 18
Bank of the United States, 72, 72*, 73
    Second, 150
Baptists, 32, 131
Barbary pirates, 90
barkentines, 85, 85*
barks, 85, 85*
barley, 19
Barlow, Joel, 132, 143

barn, "bank," 17, 17*, 18
barrel, coopered, 30
Bartram, John, 56
bateau, cotton planter's, 140*
bathing, neglect of, 107
"Battle of Moscow, The" (painting), 126
beans, raising, 22
bear, 25
    baiting, 121
beaver trap, setting, 140*
beef, cured, 25
Beekman coach, 118
Beethoven Society, 128
beets, raising, 21
Benjamin, Asher, 98
Benson, Jonathan, 40–41, 42
Benson Town, 23, 24, 39–42, 47, 108, 138
    Court Square of, 36*, 39
    High Street in, 37*, 39, 40, 41
    inn at, 39, 39*, 40, 42, 80
    shops in, 41–42
    trade in, 41–42
Benton, Thomas Hart, 149
Bermuda, 90
Bible, 31, 106
billiards, 119
Black Ball Line, 95
Black Hawk War, 136
"black salt," 42
blacksmith, 20, 28*, 29, 31, 41, 71
Bladensburg dueling ground, 108*, 109
Blessing of the Bay, The (ship), 81
blockhouse, in community fort, 47
blubber, 87, 88
"bluewash," 22

bonnet, Quaker, 54
bookbinding, 126
books, publication of, 126
 sold by village store, 31
Boone, Daniel, 45, 140
Boston, 12, 14, 33, 49, 52, 53, 77, 85, 90, 91, 96, 127, 128, 147
 architecture of, 97
 fires in, 51
 "Fund" at, 73
 Handel and Haydn Society in, 128
 Long Wharf at, 52
 merchants in, 89, 90, 94
 Ohio Company formed in, 43
 sea trade of, 86
 theaters in, 123
 Town Meeting in (1772), 12
Boston (frigate), 85
Boston Crown Glass Company, 69
Boston "massacre," 11
Boston Post Road, 117
Boston "tea party," 88
Bowery Theater, 118, 124
Boyer, Margaret, 135
Brackenridge, Hugh Henry, 126
Braddock, Edward, 40, 47, 79
Bradford, William, 53
Bradford's London Coffee House, 53*
brandy, 42, 83
 manufacture of, 21
Brazil, 88, 94
brick house, William Conner's, 139*, 140
bridges, covered, 77
 truss, 37, 77
brigantines, 85, 85*
brigs, 81–83, 85
Brillat-Savarin, Anthelme, 110
Brooklyn Bridge, 118
Brooks, Van Wyck, 126
Brower, A., 119
Brown, Charles Brockden, 56
Brown, Moses, 61
Brown, Sylvanus, 66
Brummell, Beau, 107
Bryant, William Cullen, 108, 127
Buchanan, Squire, 23
buckwheat, 19
Buell, Abel, 74
buffalo, 25
Buffalo, N.Y., 143, 144, 145, 147
bullbaiting, 121
Bullfinch, Charles, 97, 98
Bull's Head Tavern, 117*, 117–18
Burr, Aaron, 109, 116, 125, 127
Bush, William, 138

"butcher" furniture, 99, 99*
butter, 109

cabbage, raising, 21
cabin, in "hacking," 44*, 46
cachalot, 87, 88
Cadwalader, Williamina, 64
calico, 61
camera lucida, 124*, 125
camphine, 88
Canada, 14, 92, 93, 136
canals, 143–46
candles, spermaceti, 87–88
canned food, 111
cantaloupes, raising, 22
Canton trade, 90, 90*, 91
Cape Horn, first American ships to round, 90
capes, men's, 102
caplock musket, 65, 65*
Carey, Mathew, 56, 130
Carnes, Jonathan, 92
Carnes, Peter, 56–57
Carpenters' Company, 52
Carroll, John, 32
carrots, raising, 21
cart, two-wheeled, 20
carters, New York, 116
cartoon, first, to appear in American newspaper, 11*
Cartwright, Edmund, 61
cast iron, 68
Castle Clinton, 120*, 121
cent, copper, 73*, 74
chaises, 119
chandler, traveling, 26
Charles II, 99, 101
Charles River, 16, 77
Charleston, S.C., 53, 78, 85, 94, 97, 121, 125
Charlotte Dundas (steamboat), 142
Charlotte Temple (Rowson), 127, 127*
Charlottesville, Va., 132
Chebacco boat ("pinkie"), 87, 88*
Chesapeake (frigate), 85, 92
Chesapeake and Ohio Canal, 146, 147
Chesapeake Bay, 81, 85, 91, 93, 143, 147
Chesterfield, Lord, 105
Chestnut, Gideon, 81, 83
China trade, 81, 90*, 90–91, 92, 112
"chitterling," 102, 102*
Christmas, 120–21
church, village, 28*, 31–32

Church of England, 32, 131
Cincinnati, 129, 134*, 136, 138, 146
Clay, Henry, 92, 109, 141–42
Clermont (steamboat), 64, 118, 141*, 142, 143
Cleveland, 143, 145
Clinton, De Witt, 144
Clinton Castle, 120*, 121
clipper ships, American, 93, 94*
clocks, 66–67
 banjo, 66, 66*
 pillar-and-scroll, 66*, 67
cloth, cotton, and spinning machinery, 60–61
clothing, 26–27, 40, 54–55
 boys', 102–3
 girls', 104*, 104–5
 men's, 99–102, 100*, 101*, 102*
 revolution in, during Federal period, 99–100
 women's, 54*, 55*, 103*, 103–4, 104*
coach, 118*, 118–19
 passengers on, 106*
coachee, 118, 118*
coal, early sales of, 71
cockfights, 121
cod, handlining for, 86, 87*
"Code, The," for duels, 109
coffee, 112
coinage, 31, 73–74
Coke, Thomas, 32
Cole, Thomas, 125
Coleridge, Samuel Taylor, 125, 127
colleges, 131–33
Colonial (Georgian) architecture, 38, 97
Colossus Bridge, 77
Columbia (ship), 90, 91
Columbia, Pa., 146
Columbia River, 91
combat, personal, 108–9
commerce, 85–86
Committee of Correspondence, 12
Common Sense (Paine), 13
Compleat Gentleman, The (Peacham), 105
Compton, John, 41, 42
Concord, Mass., 13, 127
Concord, Vt., 129
Conestoga wagon, 20, 20*, 80
Confederation bonds, 72
Congregational Church, 32, 83, 131
Congress (frigate), 85

Congress, U.S., 13, 14, 43, 48, 52, 57–60 *pass.*, 66, 70, 72, 74, 79, 85, 87, 92, 94, 126, 132, 136, 140, 141, 142, 143
Connecticut, 26, 38, 93, 116
Connecticut River, 17
Conner, Elizabeth (nee Chapman), 139, 140
Conner, John, 135, 136, 137, 138, 139
Conner, Lavinia (nee Winship), 136, 137
Conner, Richard, 135
Conner, William, 135, 136, 137, 138, 139, 140, 147
Conner's Prairie, 135*, 137, 138, 139, 140
Connersville, Ind., 136, 137, 138, 139
Constellation (frigate), 85
Constitution (frigate), 85
Constitution, U.S., 59, 72, 105, 126, 129
Constitutional Convention, 57–59, 132
Continental Congress, First, 13, 52
    Second, 12, 13
Cooke, George Frederick, 123
cooper, 28*, 30
Cooper, James Fenimore, 127–28
Cooper, Peter, 117, 147
Cooper, William, 128
Cooper River, 78
Cooper Union, 117
Cope, Thomas, 95
Copley, John Singleton, 54, 124
copper cent, 73*, 74
copyright law, 126
corduroy roads, 37
corn, 19, 117
cornbread, 46
cotton cloth, and spinning machinery, 60–61
cotton gin, 64, 64*, 145
countinghouse, 88
    Wilkins's, 89*
Country Builder's Assistant, The (Benjamin), 98
covered bridges, 77
cradle, for reaper, 19, 19*, 20
Creek Indians, 149
cricket, at college, 131*, 133
Cries of New York, The, 110*, 117
Croton River, 116
crown glass, 70, 70*
cucumbers, raising, 22
Cugnot, Nicolas, 64
Cumberland, Md., 146, 147

Cumberland Road, 79, 79*
Cutler, Manasseh, 43

Daggett, Mark, 41
Dagys, Thomas Adams, 61–62, 65
dancing, popularity of, 120
dandelions, 22
Darby, Abraham, 67
Dartmouth College, 130–31, 131*
Davis, Phineas, 147
Declaration of Independence, 12, 13, 52, 56, 142
deer, 25
deism, 32, 34, 131
Delacroix, Joseph, 121
Delaware, 11, 59, 62
Delaware Indians, 43, 135, 137, 138
Delaware River, 17, 49, 53, 57, 64, 77, 78, 86, 142, 143, 146
Demming, Montgomery, 80
democracy, as personal freedom, 108
Democratic-Republicans, 142, 149
Derby, Elias Haskett, 91
Detroit, 135, 143
Dexter, Timothy, 73
dickey, 101–2
Dickinson, John, 58
dining, elegant, at home, 111–12
    public, 107*
"Directoire" dress, 103
Dismal Swamp, 143
District of Columbia. *See* Washington (District of Columbia)
divorce, 107
Doddridge, Joseph, 127
Dogue Creek, 63
Drake, Daniel, 127
Dubuque, Julien, 141
Duck Creek Iron Furnace, 42
Duckett, Peg-leg, 83
ducks, hunting, 25
duels, 108–9
    causes of, 109
    rules for, 108
Duer, William, 43
Dulany, Daniel, 12
Dunlap, William, 124, 125, 127
Durham boats, 78, 86
Durham Iron Furnace, 78

eagle ornaments, 99
East India Company, British, 90
East River, 115, 118, 121
Easton, Pa., 71
eating habits, 109–11
education, 129–33

Electors, and U.S. Constitution, 59
Elk River, 57
Ellicott's Mill, 63
embargo, Jefferson's, 92
Emerson, Ralph Waldo, 127
Empire dress, 104, 104*
Empire furniture, 98–99, 99*
Empress of China (sloop), 90
England, 14, 53, 60, 64–70 *pass.*, 73, 88, 89, 92, 93, 98, 99, 100, 106, 112, 127, 142, 147, 150
entertainments, 119–20, 121
Episcopalians, 32, 131
Erie, Lake, 143, 144, 145
Erie Canal, 144, 145, 146
    crossing Genesee River, 142*
    Lockport on, 2*
Essex (frigate), 85, 85*
Evacuation Day, 120
evangelism, 131
Evans, Oliver, 62–64, 71

Fairfax, Lord, 11
Fairmount Water Works, 63
Fallen Timbers, Battle of, 48
farmers, 12, 15 ff., 29
farmhouses, 21–23, 23*
Federal (Classic Revival) architecture, 97, 98
Federalist, The, 59
Federalists, 59, 73, 89, 93, 101, 105, 141, 149
fences, rail, 18, 18*
ferry, flatboat, 37–38, 38*
    steam, Fulton's, 118
Finch, John, 137, 138, 139, 145
finger bowl, 112
fire hazards, in towns, 51
fishing, 86–87
Fitch, John, 57, 142
Flagg, David, 145
flax, raising, 25
flintlock, 42, 65
Florida, 149
flour mill, automatic, 62*, 63
flute, 128
food, in New York City, 116–17
    preparation of, 24–25
    preservation of, 110, 111
food habits, 109–11
Forbes, John, 75
forge, Somers's, 83, 83*
fork, use of, 111–12
Forsyth, Alexander, 65
fort, community, on frontier, 47
Fort Duquesne, 75
Fort Greenville, 48
Fort Pitt, 47

153

Fourth of July, 120
France, 65, 66, 73, 78, 79, 87, 89, 92, 103, 109, 110, 142, 150
Franklin, Benjamin, 12, 24, 32, 55, 56, 58, 98, 99, 106
Fraunces, "Black Sam," tavern of, 110
Frederick, Md., 37
French Revolution, 73, 100, 105
Frenchtown, N.J., 57
Friends, Society of, 52, 94
    See also Quakers
frigates, American, 85
frontier, life on, 45–48
fruits, 109
        grown in Whittle orchard, 20
Fugio cent, 74
Fulton, Robert, 64, 118, 126, 142, 143
"Fund at Boston," 73
fur trade, 90, 91, 137, 139, 140, 141
furniture, 23, 98–99, 99*

Gainsborough hat, 54, 55*
game, wild, 25, 46
gavotte, 119*
geese, hunting, 25
General Washington Inn, 39, 40, 42, 80
Genesee River, 144
George III, 13
Georgia, 11, 38, 56, 67, 145
German settlers, 17, 18, 20, 45, 69, 106
Germantown, Pa., 56
Gerry, Elbridge, 58
Ghent, Treaty of, 137, 149
gingerbread, 117
ginseng, 90
Ginter, Philip, 71
glass cup plate, Sandwich, 71, 71*
glassware, manufacture of, 69–71, 70*, 71*
Godfrey, Thomas, 56
Goethe, Johann von, 126
grain, 19, 29
Grand Banks, fishing on, 87
Grank Turk (ship), 90
Gratz, Rebecca, 125
Gray, Robert, 91
Great Awakening (1740's), 32
Great Eastern Road, 38
Great Lakes, 93, 137
Great Migration, 137, 140
Great Philadelphia Wagon Road, 38
Great Seal of the United States, 99

Greek dress, 103*, 103–4
Greenaway, Kate, 105
Greene, Mrs. Nathaniel, 120
Grey's Ferry, 53, 77
gristmill, 28*, 29
gun factory, Whitney's, 65
gundalows (gondolas), 16*, 17
gunsmith, 42

"hacking," cabin in, 44*, 46
Haida Indians, 90
hair styles, men's, 100, 101, 102*
        women's, 103–4
Haiti, slave revolt in, 94
Hallet, Captain, 90
ham, cured, 25
Hamilton, Alexander, 21, 58, 59, 72, 74, 96, 109, 115, 119, 120
Hansel, Wilhelmina, 17, 22, 23, 23*, 26
Hanson, Nathan, 83
Hargreaves, James, 60
Harnett, Sam, 23, 25
harpsichord, 128
Harriet (sloop), 90
Harrison, William Henry, 136
Harvard College, 131, 132
hats, men's, 100, 102*
        women's, 54, 55*, 104
Hawaii, 90, 91
Hawkins, John Isaac, 128
Hawthorne, Nathaniel, 127
hay fork, 20, 20*
Hays, Moses, 33
Hazard, Erskine, 71
headgear, women's, 54, 55*
heeltapper, 86, 87*
Henry, Patrick, 12, 58, 126
Hepplewhite, George, 98
Herculaneum, architecture of, 97
Hewes, Robert, 69, 70
High Street, in towns, 37*, 38, 39
History of the Arts of Design, The (Dunlap), 124
Hoffman, Conrad, 19
hog-killing, 24–25
Holland, 89
Holland Tunnel, 118
Hollidaysburg, Pa., 146
"Home, Sweet Home," 123, 123*
hominy, 19
Hone, Philip, 108, 112, 124
Hopkinson, Thomas, 56
horse mill, 138, 138*
horse racing, 121
Horseshoe Prairie, 137, 137*, 138, 139
horseshoes, pitching, 119

housewright, 28*, 30–31
Hudson River, 17, 57, 77, 78, 113, 116, 118, 126, 143, 144, 147
Humphreys, Joshua, 85
husking bee, 19
Hussey, Christopher, 88
Hussey, Obed, 145
Hutin, Madame Francisguy, 124

ice chest, 110
ice cream, 112
ice cutter, Wyeth, 110, 111*
ice trade, 94
Illinois, 98, 135, 141, 145, 147
immigration, 15–16
Indiana, 79, 98, 135, 137, 138, 144, 145, 146, 147
Indiana Territory, 135, 136, 137
Indianapolis, 138, 139
Indians, 11, 45, 88, 92, 131, 135, 136, 138, 139
        in Battle of Fallen Timbers, 48
        in Battle of the Thames, 136
        in Battle of Tippecanoe, 136
        in Black Hawk War, 136
        Creek, 149
        Delaware, 43, 135, 137, 138
        Haida, 90
        Iroquois, 15
        Kwakiutl, 90
        Nootka, 90, 91*
        Shawnee, 43, 135, 136
        threat of attacks by, 47
        and "touching the quill," 136, 136*
        treaties with, 136
        unjust treatment of, 136
indigo, 19, 97
        export of, 86
Industrial Revolution, 60
insurance marker, cast-iron, for house wall, 1*
Iowa, 98, 141
iron, cast, 68
        pig, 67–68
        wrought, 68–69
Iron Furnace, Duck Creek, 42
ironworks, 67*, 67–68
Iroquois Indians, 15
Irving, Peter, 127
Irving, Washington, 125, 127
Ivanhoe (Scott), 125

Jackson, Andrew, 94, 141, 142, 149–50
Jackson, Rachel, 149, 150
Jacobins, 105

James II, 99
James, William T., 110
James River, 143
Jamestown settlement, 45, 69
Jarves, Deming, 70
Jay, John, 59, 65
Jefferson, Joseph, 123
Jefferson, Thomas, 12, 32, 49, 58, 65, 72, 79, 92, 94, 96, 97, 110, 132, 136, 144
Jennings, Jonathan, 138
jenny, spinning, 60
Jews, 11, 32, 33
John Adams (frigate), 85
Johnson, Samuel, 88
Johnstown, Pa., 146

Kean, Edmund, 123
keelboat, 77*, 78, 134*, 143
Kemble, Charles, 123
Kemble, Fanny, 112, 123
Kendrick, John, 90
Kentucky, 17, 45, 78, 92, 130, 138, 139
kerosene, introduction of, 88
Key, Francis Scott, 128
Knickerbocker's History of New York (Irving), 127
Kotzebue, August von, 124
Kunzelman, Emil, 23*, 25
Kwakiutl Indians, 90

Labrador, 86
Laclède, Pierre, 140
Lady Washington (sloop), 90, 91
lamb's quarters, 22
lamp, whale-oil, 87, 88*
Lancaster, Joseph, 129
Lancaster, Pa., 37, 38, 53, 57
Lancaster turnpike, 76, 77, 150
Land Ordinance of 1787, 43
language, 106
lathe, slide-rest, 66
Latrobe, Benjamin H., 98
Lavoisier, Antoine, 133
Leach, Daniel, 142
lead ore, 141
"leatherstockings," 46
Ledyard, John, 90
Lehigh Canal, 71
Lehigh River, 71
lemons, 117
Leopard (British warship), 92
letters, and postal service, 75–76, 76*
Letters of a British Spy, The (Wirt), 126
Letters to His Son (Chesterfield), 105

Leutze, Emanuel, 78
Lewis, Fielding, 143
Lewis and Clark expedition, 79
Lexington, Ky., 129
Lexington, Mass., 12, 13
Liberia, 94
Liberty Bell, 52
Lick, Jared, 41, 42
limners, 125
linen, on frontier, 47
    spinning, 25
Linnaeus, Carolus, 56
linsey-woolsey, 47, 102
literature, American, 126–28
Liverpool Line, 95
livestock, 18–19, 40
    yokes for, 18*
Livingston, Robert R., 79, 142, 143
Locke, John, 133
log houses, 17, 18, 21, 22*, 23*, 44*, 46
Long Island, 88, 113, 121
Long Island Sound, 113
loom, in farmhouse, 25
    power-driven, 61
Lopez, Aaron, 33
Louisiana, 79, 143
Louisiana Purchase, 79, 136, 140, 143
Louisville, 129, 143
Lowell, Francis Cabot, 61
lumber, export of, 86
Lutherans, 32

Macao trade, 90
machine tools, 65–66
Madison, James, 58, 59, 72
mail service, 75–76
Maine, 15, 49, 88, 140
Manhattan Island, 113, 116, 118, 135
    See also New York City
Manhattan Water Company, 116
manners, Yankee, 105–6, 107
manufactories, 61–62, 65
maple sugar, 47
Marblehead, Mass., 87
Marietta, Ohio, 48, 48*, 79
Marion, Francis, 56
marriage, 106
Marshall, John, 119, 150
Marshall, William, 137, 139
Maryland, 31, 53, 73, 79, 96
    Bladensburg dueling ground in, 108*, 109
    German settlers in, 17, 69
mass production, 65

Massachusetts, 11, 15, 33, 73, 81, 93, 94, 127
Massachusetts Agricultural Society, 90
Mauch Chunk Mountain, 71
Maudslay, Henry, 66
McAdam, John, 76
McCormick, Cyrus, 145
McGuffey, William H., 130
McIntire, Samuel, 97
Mekinges, 135, 138, 139
Melville, Herman, 88, 128
Mercantile Arithmetic (Walsh), 130
merchants, American, 88–90
Merrimac River, 16
Methodists, 32, 131, 139
Mexico, 140
Miami Canal, 145, 146
Michigan, 98, 135, 145
middle class, American, 12
Migration, Great, 137, 140
milk, poor quality of, 110
milkman, 110*
mill, 28*, 29
milling machine, Whitney's, 65–66
Mills, Patrick, 142
Milton, John, 56
Mississippi, 140
Mississippi River, 17, 78, 79, 136, 138, 140, 141, 143, 145
Missouri, 138, 140
Missouri Compromise, 140
Missouri River, 140, 141, 143
Missouri Territory, 140
Mitchill, Samuel L., 127, 133
Moby Dick (Melville), 88
Modern Chivalry (Brackenridge), 126
Mohawk Valley, 143
money, paper, 31, 73
Monongahela River, 47, 79
Monroe, James, 79, 100, 141, 142
Monticello, 97
Moody, Paul, 61
Moore, Clement Clarke, 120–21
Moore, Thomas, 110
Moravians, 139
Morris, Gouverneur, 58
Morris, Robert, 73
Morse, Samuel F. B., 126
mother-of-pearl, 91
Mount Holyoke College, 130
Mount Vernon, 59, 63
Mountain Men, 141
muff, 104, 104*
Murray, Judge, 41
music, 128
musket, caplock, 65, 65*

Muskingum River, 48
muskmelons, raising, 22
mustard, wild, 22
Mystic River, 81

nails, manufacture of, 69
Nantucket Island, 88
Napoleon Bonaparte, 73, 78, 79, 92, 102
Natchez Trace, 78
National Republicans, 149
National Road, 79, 79*, 80, 146, 147
neckerchief, 101, 102*, 103
Negro slavery, 15, 59, 65, 85, 89, 93–94, 105, 140
Negroes, music produced by, 128
New Amsterdam, 45, 69, 119
New Bedford, Mass., 88
New England, 15, 18, 21, 32, 35, 81, 86, 92, 93, 94, 107, 110, 113, 120, 121, 141
    architecture of, 98
    merchants in, 88, 92
    schooners built in, 85
    shoemaking manufactories in, 61–62
    towns in, 38
    writers in, 127
New Hampshire, 59, 69
New Haven, Conn., 65
New Jersey, 20, 23, 53, 56, 57, 69, 73, 113
New Orleans, 78–79, 95, 96–97, 140, 141, 143, 145
    Battle of, 149
New Year's morning, calls on, 121
New York (frigate), 85
New York City, 33, 43, 49, 72, 85, 90, 94, 95, 98, 105, 108, 111, 113–19, 121, 144, 145
    Battery in, 120*, 121
    Bowery in, 117, 121
    Broadway in, 115, 117, 119, 121
    Central Park in, 113–14, 116
    City Hall in, 121
    fires in, 97, 113, 115
    Fraunces' Tavern in, 110
    Greenwich Village in, 115
    merchants in, 89
    Negroes in, 120
    Park Theater in, 122*, 123, 124
    pleasure gardens in, 121
    population of (1825), 115
    preserved food sold in, 111
    school in, first, 129'
    Tea Water pump in, 113*, 116
    Wall Street in, 114*, 115, 121
    Washington inaugurated in, 59, 96
    watchmen hired by, 115*, 115–16
    water supply for, 116
    writers in, 127
New York Evening Chronicle, 127
New York Evening Post, 119
New-York Historical Society, 118
New York Philharmonic Society, 128
New York State, 15, 18, 57, 59, 142, 143, 144, 145, 146
New York State Barge Canal, 146
New York Stock Exchange, 115
Newburyport, Mass., 73, 77, 88
Newcastle, Del., 57
Newfoundland, 86
Newport, Del., 63
Newport, R.I., 32, 33, 85, 94
newspapers, 119
Newton, Isaac, 133
Noblesville, Ind., 135
Nootka Indians, 90, 91*
Norfolk, Va., 85
North Carolina, 45, 59
Northwest Territory, 43, 48, 63, 92, 140

oats, 19
Odion nail-cutting machine, 69
Ohio, 43, 47, 48, 78, 79, 92, 98, 125, 135, 136, 138, 139, 144, 145
Ohio Canal, 145
Ohio Company, 43
    land office of, at Marietta, 48, 48*
Ohio River, 17, 43, 47, 78, 79, 80, 106, 119, 136, 137, 145, 146
    arks on, 45*, 48
    steamboats on, 143
onions, 116
    raising, 21
oranges, 117
Orukter Amphibolos, 64, 64*
oxen, 19
oyster plants, raising, 22

packet boats, 94–95, 143*, 144
Paine, Tom, 13, 32, 56
painters, 124–26
Palmer, Timothy, 77
Pamlico Sound, 91
pantalettes, 104*, 105
pantaloons, 102

Parents' Assistant, The, 105
Park Theater, 122*, 123, 124
parsnips, raising, 22
passenger pigeon, 25
Patapsco River, 38, 63
Patriots vs. Tories, 11
Patterson brothers, 26
Paulding, James K., 127
Payne, John Howard, 123
peach orchards, 20
Peacham, Henry, 105
Peale, Charles Willson, 124
pear orchards, 20
peas, raising, 22
peddlers, itinerant, 26, 26*
Penn, William, 49, 52, 56, 135
Pennock, Isaac, 69
Pennsylvania, 15, 32, 45, 53, 56, 59, 63, 69, 70, 75, 76, 79, 96, 127, 138
    Bank of, 98
    German settlers in, 17, 18, 20, 45
    University of, 56
Pennsylvania canal system, 145*, 146
Pennsylvania Hospital, 56
pepper, Sumatran wild, 92, 92*
Permanent Bridge, Palmer's, 77
Peterson, William, 58
Phi Beta Kappa, 133
Philadelphia, 12, 33, 38, 41, 42, 49–57, 63, 64, 75, 77, 92, 95, 96, 105, 121, 143, 146
    architecture of, 98
    artisans in, 55–56
    Bank of North America in, 73
    Carpenter's Hall in, 52
    Chestnut Street in, 52
    clothes worn in, 54–55
    coal sold in, 71
    Constitutional Convention in, 57–59
    Filbert Street in, 49, 50
    fires in, 51
    founded by Society of Friends, 52
    High (Market) Street in, 51, 53
    Independence Square in, 52, 58*
    London Coffee House in, 53, 53*
    merchants in, 53, 53*, 54, 89
    mint in, 74
    as publishing center, 126
    as seaport, 85
    Seventh Street in, 49, 50, 51

shipbuilding in, 81
shoemakers' union in, 62
State House Row in, 52
street lamps in, 50–51
Philadelphia (frigate), 85
Philadelphia Academy, 56
Philadelphia and Lancaster Turnpike Company, 76
"Philadelphia chair," 23
Philadelphia Musical Fund Society, 128
Philadelphia Theater, 56
Philippe, Louis, 77
Phoenix (steamboat), 143
photography, 124
Phyfe, Duncan, 98–99
shop and warehouse of, 96*
piano, 128
picnic, 118*, 120
pig iron, 67–68
pigeon, passenger, 25
piggin, 30, 31*
pillar-and-scroll clock, 66*, 67
Pinckney, Charles C., 73
pineapples, 117
"pinkie" (Chebacco boat), 87, 88*
Pinkster Day, 120
pirogue, 134*, 136
pistols, for duels, 109
Pittsburgh, 48, 69, 75, 79, 126, 143,
146
plantations, 140
plow, 20, 20*
plum orchards, 20
Poe, Edgar Allan, 125, 128
Poe, Mrs. David, 123
poke bonnet, 104, 104*
pokeweed, 22
polonaise dress, 54
Pompeii, architecture of, 97
Pope, Joseph, 145
porcelain, 111
Portland, Me., 128
Portsmouth, N.H., 85, 126
Portsmouth, Ohio, 145
post-and-rail construction, 18*
post rider, 40, 40*, 75, 117
postal service, 75–76
potash ("black salt"), 42
potatoes, raising, 21
Potomac River, 72, 96, 142, 146
pottery, 28*, 30, 31*, 111
Pottsville, Pa., 71
Precaution (Cooper), 127
Presbyterians, 32, 131, 139
President (frigate), 85
press, toggle, Smith's, 126, 126*
Priestley, Joseph, 56, 133

Prince of Parthia, The (Godfrey), 56
Princeton University, 132–33
printer, in Benson Town, 40
privateers, 93, 94*
Prophet, The, 136, 139
Providence, R.I., 88
pumpkins, raising, 21
Puritans, 11, 32
Putnam, Rufus, 43, 48

quadrant, double-reflecting, invention of, 56
Quakers, 11, 52, 54, 88, 89
See also Society of Friends
"quill, touching the," 136, 136*

radishes, 115*, 117
railroads, steam, 145*, 146–47
Randall, Matt, 42
Randolph, Edmund, 58
Randolph, John, 108
Rapp, Frederick, 138
Ratification Day, 120, 121
rationalism, 33–34, 34*
readers, McGuffey, 130
reaper, McCormick, 144*, 145
Red Star Line, 95
Redstone Old Fort, 79
redware, 30
Reid, Thomas, 133
Reign of Terror, 73, 103
religion, 31–32, 129, 131
Republicans (Anti-Federalists), 73,
89, 100, 101, 105, 106, 131, 132,
142
Revolutionary War, 11, 13, 14, 16,
24, 32, 33, 55, 69, 72, 86, 89,
112, 117, 125, 131
Rhode Island, 32, 93
rice, 19, 97
export of, 86
Richardson, Samuel, 126
Richmond, Va., 144
Jefferson's capitol at, 97, 97*
rickets, 109
rifle, flintlock, 42, 46
Rittenhouse, David, 56
river traffic, 77–79
roads, and inland towns, 37–38
McAdam's system for paving,
76
See also turnpikes
Roanoke Island, 45
"roasting kitchen," 24
Robinson's glass-pressing machine,
70
Rocky Mountain Fur Company,
141

rolling-and-slitting mill, 68*, 69
Roman Catholics, 11, 31, 32, 131,
140
romanticism, 34, 34*, 125
Roosevelt, Nicholas, 143
ropewalk, Hanson's, 82*, 83
Rowson, Susanna, 127
Rumsey, James, 142
Rush, Benjamin, 56, 132
Russian fur trade, 90
Rutledge, John, 58
rye, 19
"an' injun," 110

sail loft, Tupper's, 82*, 83
sailing vessels, 85, 85*
St. Clair, Arthur, 48
St. Louis, 140, 141, 147
St. Mémin, Charles, 125
Salem, Mass., 45, 69, 81, 85, 86,
88, 89, 90, 91–92, 97, 127
Salmagundi magazine, 127
Salomon, Haym, 33
salt, in kegs, 42
saltbox house, 22
salt pork, 91, 110
Sandwich glass cup plate, 71, 71*
Santa Claus, Moore's description
of, 121
Santee Canal, 144
Santee River, 97
Savannah (packet), 95
Savannah, Ga., 145
sawmill, 28*, 29, 30*
school, public, 129–30
village, 28*, 34–35, 129
schooners, 85, 85*
Schuylkill River, 53, 77
Science Hill Academy (Kentucky),
130
Scioto Company, 43
scissors grinders, 115*, 116
Scotch-Irish settlers, 45
Scott, Walter, 125, 127
scurvy, 109
sea slug, 91
sea trade, 89–90, 91–92, 96
sealskin, 91
Second Great Awakening, 106
seeder, mechanical, 20
Seneca Chief (canal boat), 144
Seven Years War, 47, 78, 140
Shakespeare, William, 123
Shaw, Joshua, 65
Shawnee Indians, 43, 135, 136
Shearith Israel, 33
sheep, 25
Sheraton, Thomas, 98

157

Sherman, Roger, 58
shipbuilding, 81, 82, 83, 85
shipyard, Chestnut's, 81*, 81–82
shoemaker(s), 29*, 29–30, 30*,
   101, 103
   traveling, 25
   village shop of, 28*, 29
sideburns, 101
silhouette cutter, 125, 125*
Silliman, Benjamin, 133
silverware, 111
Slater, Samuel, 61, 66, 142
slavery, Negro, 15, 59, 65, 85, 89,
   93–94, 105, 140
sloops, 85, 85*
Small, Tobias, 83
Smedes, Jan, 69
Smith, Mrs. Samuel Harrison, 150
Smith, Peter, 126
snuff, 108
Society of Friends, 52, 94
   See also Quakers
Somers, Caleb, 83
South Carolina, 19, 38, 59, 64,
   117
Spain, 73, 78, 79, 87
spermaceti candles, 87–88
spinet, 128
spinning frame, Slater's, 61, 61*
spinning jenny, 60
spinning wheel, 25
sports, college, 133
Spy, The (Cooper), 128
squash, raising, 21, 22
stage wagon, 57, 57*
Stahl, Georg, 133
Stamp Act, 12
Standish village, 81, 82, 83
"Star of Bethlehem" coverlet, 41
"Star-Spangled Banner, The"
   (Key), 128
steamboats, first, 142–43
steam dredge, 64
steam engine, high-pressure,
   Evans's, 60*, 63
   Watt, 68
steam railroads, 145*, 146–47
Stevens, John, 142, 143
Stiegel, "Baron," 69
Stock Exchange, New York, 115
Stone, William L., 108
stoneware, 30
store, village, 28*, 29*, 31
stove, cook, 110
   Franklin, 24
strawberries, 109, 116*, 117
Stuart, Gilbert, 124
Stuyvesant, Peter, 117

Sully, Thomas, 125
Sumatran wild pepper, 92, 92*
sunbonnet, 104
Sunderland, Buck, 42
Sunderland Road, 39, 41
Supreme Court, U.S., 79
surveyors, 43, 43*
Susquehanna River, 17, 45, 77, 78,
   146
swans, hunting, 25
Symington, William, 142

Talleyrand, 73, 79
tannery, 28*, 29, 42
tea, 112
tea rusk, 116*, 117
Tecumseh, 136
Temple Glass House, 69
Tennessee, 78, 92, 140, 149
Terry, Eli, 66–67
Texas, 140
Thames, Battle of the, in Canada,
   136
"Thanatopsis" (Bryant), 127
theater, 122*, 123–24
Thomas, Seth, 67
Thompson, Elijah, 40
Thoreau, Henry David, 127
Three-notch Trail, 39, 40
thresher, Flagg's 144*, 145
Tilbury, Lemuel, 83
tinkers, 116
   traveling, 25–26
tinware, 26
Tippecanoe, Battle of, 136
Tisdale's Academy, 130*
tobacco, 40, 91, 108
   export of, 86
toggle press, Smith's, 126, 126*
Toledo, 145
Tom Thumb (locomotive), 147
Tontine Coffee House, 114*, 115
Tories, 11, 14
tortoiseshell, 91
Touro Synagogue, 33
towns, 37–42
   fire hazards in, 51
trade, fur, 90, 91, 137, 139, 140,
   141
   ice, 94
   sea, 89–90, 91–92, 96
   slave, 93–94
Treaty of Alliance (1778), 73
Trenton, N.J., 78
Trevithick, Richard, 63, 64
Trumbull, John, 34, 125, 126
Tudor, Frederic, 94
Tupper, Benjamin, 43

Tupper, Tom, 83
turnips, raising, 21
turnpikes, 75*, 76–77
   See also roads

Unitarian Church, 32
United States (frigate), 85

Van Buren, Martin, 109
Vancouver Island, 90
Vanderlyn, John, 125
Vauxhall Gardens, 121
vegetables, 109
   raising, 21–22
velocipede, 7*, 119
vessels, sailing, 85, 85*
villages, 28*, 29–31
Vincennes, Ind., 135
vinegar pie, 22
violin, 128
Virginia, 11, 43, 45, 59, 96
   University of, 97, 132, 133
Vitruvius Pollio, 97

Wabash and Erie Canal, 146
Wabash River, 136
wagoner, contract, 42
wagons, 20, 20*, 21*
Walk-in-the-Water (steamboat), 143
War of 1812, 70, 87, 92–93, 94,
   107, 121, 136, 137, 141
warp spinner, 61
Washington (District of Colum-
   bia), 72, 79, 96
   Pennsylvania Avenue in, 96
   population of (1800), 96
Washington (steamboat), 143
Washington, George, 21, 32, 46,
   52, 56–59 pass., 63, 73, 78, 96,
   98, 100, 106, 117, 120, 121, 124,
   132, 143
Washington, Martha, 54
waterfowl, 25
waterpower, 63, 65
Watson, Elkanah, 143, 144
Wayne, "Mad" Anthony, 48
weaving, 25
Webster, Noah, 35, 130
Wedgwood ware, 111
Weems, Parson, 56, 56*
Weiser, Dietrich, 23
Wellington, Duke of, 102, 137
Wesley, John, 32
West, Benjamin, 124, 125, 126
West Indies, 14, 81, 87, 89, 91, 93,
   94, 150
West Point, U.S. Military Acad-
   emy at, 133

western claims, and Congress, 43
whale oil, 87, 88
whaling, 87–88
wheat, 19, 91, 110, 145
    export of, 86
Wheeling, W. Va., 79, 80
wheelwright, in Benson Town, 41
"Whig Rose" coverlet, 41
Whigs, 149
whisky, 21, 42, 80, 136
"Whisky Rebellion," 21
White, Josiah, 71
White River, 135, 137, 138, 139
Whitefield, George, 32
Whitewater River, 135, 136
Whiting, Amos, 41
Whitman, Seth, 82, 83
Whitman, Walt, 128
Whitney, Eli, 64, 65, 66, 145
Whittle, Bertha, 17, 19, 21–27 *pass.*, 23*, 26*, 110
Whittle, Dan, 18, 19, 20, 22, 25, 26
Whittle, Dora, 22

Whittle, Henry, 19, 20, 22, 24*
Whittle, Jenny, 19
Whittle, Kurt, 17, 18, 21
Whittle, Nancy, 21, 26
Whittle, Sarah, 19
Whittle, Silas, 17, 18, 19, 20, 23, 24, 24*, 25, 26, 29, 30, 100
Whittle, Susan, 17, 21, 26
Whittle, Wethered, 17, 18, 20, 23, 25
Whittle place, 15*, 17, 23*
wigs, 55*, 99, 100
Wilkins, Henry, 83, 100
Wilkinson, David, 66, 142
Wilkinson, James, 109
Willard brothers, 66
William and Mary, College of, 131, 132, 133
Williams, Job, 83
Williams, Roger, 32
Williamsburg, Va., 12, 38, 121
Wilson, James, 58
Winchester, Va., 37, 77
wine, and elegant dining, 112
Winthrop, John 81

Wirt, William, 126
Wisconsin, 135, 140, 141, 145
Wissahickon Creek, 55
Wistar, Caspar, 69
Witherspoon, John, 26
wolves, 25, 137
women's rights, lack of, 106
wool, 25
wool cards, machine to make wire teeth for, 62
writers, 126–28
    foreign, 126
wrought iron, 68–69
Wyeth, Nathaniel, 110
Wythe, George, 58

Yale College, 128, 131, 133
yokes, 18, 18*
York, Duchess of, 103
York (locomotive), 146*, 147
Young, William, 101
Young Millwright and Miller's Guide (Evans), 62*

Zane's Trace, 80

About the Author

Edwin Tunis has a distinguished reputation as an artist, illustrator, and muralist. His articles have appeared in various magazines and he has exhibited at the Baltimore Museum of Art, Society of American Etchers, National Academy of Design, Victoria and Albert Museum, and many other galleries. His most ambitious art project was a mural depicting the History of Spices, which is 145 feet long and took two and a half years to paint.

The study of American history was always one of Mr. Tunis' passions, and it was natural for him to combine this interest with his art to produce the superb books of American social history for which he is famous. Among these are *Frontier Living,* which was first runner-up for the Newbery Medal; *Colonial Living,* which won the Thomas A. Edison Award; *Oars, Sails and Steam,* which was chosen by the A.I.G.A. as one of the "Fifty Books of the Year"; *Wheels,* which won the Gold Medal of the Boy's Clubs of America; and *The Young United States: 1783-1830,* which was nominated for the National Book Award in 1970.